AF559996

TEACHERS, SCHOOLS AND SOCIETY

TEACHERS, SCHOOLS AND SOCIETY

By

Dr. D.B. Rao

M.Sc., M.A., M.A., M.Ed., Ph.D. (Education)
Reader & Research Director
R.V.R. College of Education
Guntur – 52 006 (A.P.)
(India)

DISCOVERY PUBLISHING HOUSE PVT. LTD.
NEW DELHI-110002

First Published-2009

ISBN: 978-81-8356-433-5

© Author

Published by:

DISCOVERY PUBLISHING HOUSE PVT. LTD.
4831/24, Ansari Road, Prahlad Street
Darya Ganj, New Delhi-110 002 (India)
E-mail: dphtemp@indiatimes.com
dphbooks@rediffmail.com
Website: www.discoverypublishinghouse.com

Printed at:
Arora Enterprises
Laxmi Nagar, Delhi–110 092

Contents

Preface

Society consists of people, living together in an organised and ordered community. In general, it includes rich and poor, dark and fair, young and old, men and women and as well as children. There are certain rules and regulations, which are binding on everyone, without any prejudice. Its existence is a must for a man to be a man, because a man without society is but another creature in the form of man. It is in society, where a child learns and cultivates human attributes and norms of peaceful and organised life.

In this process, school is the initial place, where a child starts learning the art of living. The very first school is mother's lap. Here, a child learns how to make meaningful sounds, like *aa, baa, maa*, etc. The very first meaningful words, which a child pronounces effort-lessly, is *maa* (mother) in the Indian context, specially, because it is mother, who plays the role of the first and foremost teacher of a child. Gradually, with the passage of time, a child enters the broader and more organised form of teaching and learning. After parents, it is the Play schools, Pre-paratory schools, Primary schools and the faculty thereof, which are all responsible for moulding and shaping the personality of a child, in a proper form and direction.

The subject, being an important one, thinkers, philosophers, social reformers and educationists have written extensively about it, from time to time. Yet there was being felt a pressing need to bring out a book, which may address a wide range of issues, under one cover.

Present modest work, namely, *School, Teacher and Society*, is the fruition of meticulous efforts, made in this direction. For further enhancement, readers' enlightened comments and compliments are sought.

Teacher and Society

The Socialisation

Socialisation is a social process, and it has been variously defined. Some of these definitions are the following:

V. V. Akolkar: "The process of adoption by the individual of the conventional patterns of behaviour is described as his socialisation, because it occurs on account of his integration with others and his expression of the culture which operates through them."

E. A. Ross: "The development of we feeling in association and the growth in their capacity and will to act together."

E. S. Bogardus: Socialisation is "the process whereby persons learn to behave dependably together on behalf of human welfare and in so doing experience social self-control, social responsibility and balanced personality."

Socialisation then, is process by means of which the individual learns to behave according to the social traditions and conventions. The human child has a remarkable capacity to imitate others, and hence he develops according to the environment into which he is born. Man, being a social animal, tries to win the appreciation of the group in which he lives and hence he naturally tries to imitate the culture of that group. It is through socialisation that he is transformed from the animal into the human, and it is socialisation which gives him a balanced personality. The social aspect of the personality is no less important than the individual aspect. Socialisation teaches him to retain control over himself in the interest of others. It evolves a we feeling or community feeling in him and thereby invests him with a sense of responsibility.

School and Society

After the home, the child is exposed to the school which also influences him, for the school is nothing less than a miniature society to him. It socialises him, gives him an opportunity to manifest his qualities, instincts, drives and motives, and helps to develop his personality. For the child, the educator's personality and character provide a model which he strives to copy, thereby consciously or unconsciously moulding his personality. This is true only of those teachers who succeed in arousing in the child's mind an attachment and love for themselves. Every little action, every movement, speech, etc., impresses itself on the child's mind. On the other hand, he is often repelled by some teachers, and he wants to contradict them through every act. This repulsion may be conscious or unconscious, but it drives the child away from such a teacher. The child is attracted by the other teacher who wins his sympathy, and it is from this teacher that the child wants to win praise and appreciation.

He fears the frown of his teacher, he imitates him persistently. Apart from the teacher the child is also influenced by his colleagues, and his status and role in his school groups plays a large part in determining the status and role he is to occupy in society in later life. During the process of education, the child's personality develops under the impact of the other personalities with whom he comes into contact. It the school the child is disciplined. He is aware that disobedience brings immediate growth and may even drive him to criminal activity. On the other hand, complete absence on control may either make him liberal, free and independent or impulsive and impish. Besides, the cultural programmes of the school also help to refine his attitudes.

In this manner, the human personality is profoundly influenced both by the home and the school. Of the two, the family influence lasts for a longer time and is more comprehensive.

It is evident from the foregoing account of social development during adolescence that at this stage the individual is in real need of guidance. Many factors such as the sex drive, choice of profession, adjustment within the family and the school, etc., present such problems to the young immature mind which it cannot easily solve, and it is here that the teachers' and parents' guidance is really desirable.

Growth of Society

Education plays an important part in the child's social development at every stage, but this education is not the formal education the child derives from books and lectures. It includes the education that comes to the child from extracurricular activities, the atmosphere of the school, etc. Group camps always have a good effect on the individual's social development, for it helps to build his character and also develops many social qualities. He develops good habits, learns the elements of leadership and gets the opportunity to learn many kinds of skills. In the informal atmosphere of the camp, the members can meet more freely, and this in itself is education in social living In this manner, the teacher and the parent can cooperate with each other and create situations for the proper development of the child.

The child aspires to the social values of his own group, on the one hand, he is equally anxious to win the love and esteem of his parents as well as of his teachers, although it can sometimes happen that out of loyalty to the group he may feel compelled to neglect his parents and teachers and their entreaties. For, he is particularly anxious to win esteem in the group. Sometimes, in the group he indulges in activities that are considered specially anti-social In the case of children who indulge in such activities, fundamentally a great responsibility lies in the environment within the home and family. In families where the parents have no hesitation in giving praise and affection to their children, it will be seen that the young individuals indulge in proper and desirable activity.

On the other hand, neglect and consequently rebellious children are apt to indulge in detestable actions, and later on turn into Juvenile delinquents It is necessary that the teachers keep an eye on the development and active manifestation of such tendencies within the child groups within his domain. Groups provide opportunities for the development of the qualities of leadership, so that in their adult and more responsible years, the boys and girls can turn to leading the nation.

It should be kept in mind that all children do not evince the same liking for the group. Some children tend to avoid groups and prefer to stay with one or two children of their choice. There may be occasions of conflict between these individualistic boys and the bigger groups. An, there is not essential rule the members of the group are intelligent while these boys and girls who tend to shun the group are slow-written. It is perfectly possible for the opposite to be true. Secondly, there may be some personal reason which may actuate the individual to stay away from the group, but generally it is best to live in the group, as it benefits the individual's social development.

The child's social development is influenced in important manner, by the mutual interaction between childhood groups, competition, conflict and cooperation.

The Estimations

According to Bridges, the following Table can help to reveal the extent to which a child's social development has taken place, if at all. Positive answers indicate development, while negative ones indicate the opposites

1. Played with another child.
2. Spoken to another child.
3. Occasionally made social contact by touching or pushing a child.
4. Imitated other children's actions.
5. Imitated children's words.
6. Imitated children's laughter.
7. Often spoke to other children.
8. Originated new play activity with other child.
9. Joined group of children in play.
10. Sought another child's approval.

11. Asked another child for help.
12. Always given up toys at fair request.
13. Usually waited turn.
14. Tried to defend own right to materials or place.
15. Pointed to others' errors.
16. Tried to help others.
17. Stopped work to aid another child.
18. Comforted another child.

Further indication of desirable adjustment can be measured in terms of the extent to which a child has not rather has:

19. Turned away to avoid another child's friendly advances.
20. Usually stayed out of group marching or games.
21. Claimed others' errors.
22. Interfered with others' work.
23. Destroyed others' work.
24. Created disorder in group or led others into mischief.
25. Frequently pulled or pushed others.
26. Frequently complained of other adults for own gain.
27. Harassed new child by scoffing or shunning.
28. Hit or pinched others for fun several times.
29. Bitten or spit at other for fun several times.
30. Teased in other ways, causing irritation or discomfort.

Family and Society

The family plays a very significant part in the individual's socialisation because the child spends his early formative years in the home. He learns much by observing the people around him, by imitating them, by indulging in activities which win their approval and avoiding those which bring their disapproval and immediate punishment. It is the family environment which can create good habits in him, because the child's moral code is conditioned by the system of reward and punishment It is the family. And, it is also in the family that criminal tendencies are first generated. In their *book New Light on Delinquency and its*

Treatment, Healey and Bronner have pointed out that Juvenile delinquents are frequently found in those famines in which the fulfilment of social relationships has been hindered at one time or the other. Freud and other psychoanalysts have demonstrated that the child remains throughout life whatever he is made out to be in the family. In his *'Psychological Factors* in *Marital Happiness'*, Termann has theorised that only those individuals can enjoy marital bliss whose own parents had been happy and contented.

In the preface to *Women of the Street'*, a depth study of the prostitutes of London, it has been commented that the problem of prostitution is, in reality, a problem of the relationship between the children and parents. Children become aberrant and spoilt when the family peace is vitiated, and it is in circumstances such as these that many thieves, robbers, murderers and prostitutes are first born.

The family plays a very significant, perhaps the most significant role in the individual's development. Freud and other psychoanalysts believe that the impressions made upon the child's mind at home determine the child's personality as an adult, for in childhood, the child's mind is very flexible and susceptible to any influence. The parents' love for the child makes a deep impression on him. And, although it is true that excessive love and affection have detrimental effects, the complete absence of affection creates complexes in the child's mind, which later disbalance his personality. His personality is also influenced greatly by the behaviour of his brothers and sisters towards him. Alder, the famous psychologist, has stressed the fact that the order of the birth of children in the family distinctly and separately influences the personality of each child.

The eldest child's mental make up differs from that of the last. Besides, all great thinkers and philosophers have admitted the importance of their mother's love as far as their personality development is concerned. In India, people often gauge the personality of a young marriageable girl by observing her mother. And, as far as marriages are concerned, more attention is paid to the prospective bridegroom's parentage than to his own personality, for the family makes a lot of difference. There is little possibility of a child having a balanced personality if the personalities of his parents are not balanced. Even the social and economic status of the family has a deep impact upon the child's personality.

The family's influence does not end with the individual's entrance into adolescence, for even then the influence continues. Complete absence of control often results in moral degeneration among the young people, while excessive control manifests itself in repressed personalities and narrow minds. Only reasonable restraint and freedom can help the individual to develop a balanced personality. After marriage, the individual's personality is also exposed to the influence of his partner's personality, his or her health, mental attitudes, family background, physical beauty, attainments, etc. The ability to beget children or not is another factor which plays a significant role in the individual's personality development. In fact, considerable literature has been devoted to the subject of family's influence upon the personality by sociologists, psychologists and anthropologists.

Process of Socialisation

Individuals influence each other by imitation, suggestion and sympathy, besides which the process of socialisation is furthered by many social institutions. Man is the product of many social processes such as praise and blame, cooperation and conflict, submission and ascendency, and these forces create the individual's personality. Education is the most potent agency of socialisation available to society.

Teacher's Responsibility

The globalisation process has generated universal discontent and disenchantment. Those who applaud its arrival are fewer. Disenchantment prevails not only in the developing but also in the developed world. It needs to be analysed as to what lies at the root of such discontentment. Also, globalisation almost everywhere has given rise to a newer and sharper self-consciousness of identity. Such consciousness tends to be pervasive; it is not confined to the cultural minorities, local cultures, ethnic groups, tribes or weaker sections. The surge of identity consciousness and anxiety about preservation of cultural identity extends also in the relationships between nations.

The nation or the set of nations which plays the dominant role in controlling the financial resources or the institutional instruments of globalisation is perceived to have an unchallenged monopoly on the extension of its 'symbolic power' through marketing of its cultural products, practices, styles and symbolic forms. Amongst nations or communities which feel culturally subordinated, the sense of resentment generates forces leading to cultural nationalism or even fundamentalism. Can we treat these twin processes as contemporary pathology of globalisation? The issue needs to be examined in all its dimensions. Moreover, we notice that despite massive literature being generated on the treatment of the specific dimensions of globalisation such as its social, structural, economic, cultural and political correlates and consequences, a very substantial degree of ambiguity persists about its historicity, ideology and epistemological or conceptual status as a factor in the integrated social and economic development of the contemporary societies. This problem is global.

Globalisation is a composite process. It results from the convergence of a series of developments in society which are qualitatively new. These include: contemporary revolution in science and technology of communication, high velocity movements of finance, capital and market, increased social mobility, migration of personnel and the emergence of a global diaspora. Its associated contributory processes are: intensification of cultural interaction among diverse groups through media exposure, increased incidence of leisure-time activities, growth in tourism, infrastructures of entertainment and marketing of cultural products, personnel and styles. These developments have an evolutionary character, as they are generally irreversible despite societies going through the cycles of growth and depression in economy, polity and social system. This attribute of globalisation has social structural and political consequences which are often overlooked as most treatment of this process has focused upon a segmental rather than a holistic analysis of its nature and consequences.

In a segmental approach, analysts have studied 'financial or capital globalisation', 'telecommunication or media globalisation' and 'cultural globalisation' as separate developments, and then tried to view the impact of the one, for instance, 'financial or capital' globalisation upon other segments such as the 'media', 'communication' or 'culture'. This approach has two weaknesses: first, it fails to help us in comprehending the role of the residual social structural realities and their emergent properties and the way they interact with any one of these three aspects of globalisation, be it capital, communication or culture. Consequently, such treatment is unable to explain why some societies, communities or groups resist globalisation and reject its institutions and ideology, whereas others accept it and celebrate its arrival. It is necessary to take note of this reality since it determines the historicity of globalisation in specific societies, cultures and nationalities and takes into consideration the 'initial' historical and social-cultural realities of each society as it encounters the pressure for globalisation. Secondly, the segmental approach does not give enough weight to a holistic treatment of the process of globalisation. Particularly, it misses the point that globalisation plays a vital contributory role in the evolution of a 'new' society, variously described as an 'information society' or a 'post-modern society'. The emergence of such a society inheres a basic structural transformation of economy, polity and culture, and the potential to go beyond the systemic features of a capitalist or a post-capitalist social order. Its unfolding may eventually contribute to the birth of a new social order.

This new social order, variously described as the "information society or the post-modern society" is yet to come into being; it does not exist as yet in a systemic form in any part of the globe. We see today only a selected set of institutional, structural and cultural attributes of such a society, which is probably in the process of being born. For instance, we witness substantial growth of homogenised occupational workforce of skilled manpower, such as in the professions, technology and services; there is growing global mobility and interdependency among societies in need of such skilled workforce. It contributes to the emergence of social and cultural diaspora with huge influence upon the economy and culture both of the nation of its origin as well as that of its settlement.

The increased social mobility and cross-cultural interactions release the forces of change in each society. In the developed world, it has released intense feeling of cultural identity leading to the growth in the ideology of the 'right' on the one hand and on the dissatisfaction with that existing form of political participation in democracy on the other. Focus now is on the movement from 'representative' democracy to 'participatory' democracy; from state sponsorship of social and economic agenda of societies to its formulation and management by the civil society and voluntary associations. The new slogan is to 're-invent democracy'. The revolutionary changes brought about in the communication technology, such as telephony, internet and new mass media, make it possible to envisage the possibilities of political, social and cultural interaction within and between societies and interest groups which are truly participatory and which bring about self-governing civil society into existence.

In this process, we witness radical changes at the economic level. The basic organs of economy, such as capital, market, modes of production and trade, are getting increasingly entwined into a web of global interdependence. This interdependence is not merely geographical or of capital and market, but it increasingly draws its synergy from new technological advances in the fields of communication through satellites, internet, television, telephony, etc. These technologies are helping not only the educated and the professional sections but also the fishermen, farmers, horticulturists, floriculturists and people engaged in many other occupations. These extend the scope of their operations such as technology uses, marketing and capitalisation. Similarly, branding of commodities is increasingly transforming production processes in an idiom which is cultural, communicative. It universalises that which was once considered to be local.

To deal with its implications for a specific national society, institutional innovations within and at the international level are required. The contemporary institutions such as the World Bank, International Monetary Fund (IMF), World Trade Organisation (WTO), etc., are some of the responses, but these do not yet inspire the level of consensus and confidence that could make the acceptance of the goals of globalisation smooth. This fact, combined with the reality of the existing social inequalities among societies and its varying levels of intensity within each individual society, do not inspire confidence about the final outcome of globalisation. Many questions are posed and many challenges are faced by societies yet in the process of new transformation. The recent experiences of near-economic breakdown in Indonesia, Malaysia and Thailand, once lauded as 'little tigers' due to the flight of capital, has left memories in the developing world which evokes disenchantment rather than reassurance from the processes of globalisation.

Crisis of Identity

These developments do impinge upon the issues of identity. The social and economic developments augment the societal self-awareness within every society. The larger question of identity is related to the growth of social, economic, political and cultural self-awareness among groups and communities. Identity has its subjective root in the person, but it manifests itself objectively as a social product through the mobilisation of collective self-consciousness. This consciousness is forged by a chemistry of several factors, such as history, mythology and instrumental rationality. The sense of identity is created by one's realisation of the presence of the 'other'. For this, a historical context is necessary.

The past and present experiences of social and cultural interaction with other cultures give shape to people's consciousness of their own identity. What form the identity consciousness will take, whether it would promote adaptive, assimilative, alienative or hostile attitude towards the other culture depends upon a variety of factors. Among them are included the presence or absence of a tradition of pluralism, the nature of the civilization and its past historical experiences of cultural contacts with the outside world. For instance, exposure to colonial control and its impact upon local culture and economy play a material role in the perception of cultural globalisation in India.

Most discussions on the impact of globalisation on the cultural and social identity of people relate to questions such as: Will globalisation eventually bring about a cultural homogenisation among societies which today enjoy cultural diversity? Which culture would dominate in this process? What would be the fate of local cultures? Will they face a total loss of identity? What about the cultural minority groups, religious groups and ethnicities? Will they face extinction through homogenisation? Finally, is globalisation of culture a new incarnation of westernisation-a mark of cultural imperialism? I will like to briefly address some of these issues in the context of our own society.

India has been exposed to cultural contacts with other civilization since millennia. It has been continually making adaptive changes in its cultural styles, traits and forms as it encountered other cultures. It has a history of accommodating identities. The cultural impact of globalisation on the identity of this civilization or its impact upon the identities of local cultures, therefore, is bound to be mediated by this resilience. There are several reasons for this observation. In the first instance, the initial historical conditions of the Indian social structure have been unique. It is characterised by immense plurality of communities, languages, cultural diacritical symbols and ethnic styles. A variety of cultural traits and cultural styles have over centuries given identity to communities but not in total isolation. Cultural interaction among regions and communities has persisted in a mode of co-sharing and mutual accommodation. This commonality has existed beyond the religious and ethnic divides. A recent study by the Anthropological Survey of India illustrates this fact.

It observes that the sharing of cultural traits among communities in India, in all about 4,635 in number, shows "high correlation of traits among states within macro-regions such as those in the south, northwestern India, central and western India and so on. There is very high correlation of traits between the Scheduled Castes and the Scheduled Tribes, between Scheduled Tribes and Hindus, between Hindus and Sikhs, between Hindus and Muslims (which is very high indeed) and between Hindus and Jains. The high correlation between Hindus and Buddhists may also be explained in the same way. This fact that these communities interact across space or states is important" (Singh, 1992: 99). Thus, we notice that despite the plurality of identities, a macro-linkage of cultural bonds has existed in India throughout history. It continues to subsist even today, and constitutes the cultural unity of India despite plurality of local identities.

The cultural impact of globalisation gets enmeshed within this process of internal dynamics and resilience of the local cultures. The perception that globalisation threatens local culture is being increasingly invalidated. It is observed that in the process of globalisation local cultures are reinforced and also globalised. Ronald Robertson has called this process globalisation. It indicates how local cultures get increasingly enmeshed with the global culture through selective adaptation of symbolic forms and styles in their products through micro-marketing. Based on the Japanese experience, this process affirms how local cultures begin to occupy a global space by constructing differentiation of consumers. Its examples are witnesses in the field of tourism and the popularity of ethnic supermarkets. In India, we witness how our local cultural traditions are also making adaptive responses in the forms and styles of cultural products in tune with the inter-regional and global requirements. For instance, regional languages are being creolised across regions or even in global terms. The incidence of bilingualism has increased in our country from about 13.4 per cent in 1971 to 64.2 per cent in 1991. The culinary styles, the pattern of dress, local ethnic cultural objects, rituals, religious icons and local customs, etc., are now increasingly becoming pan-Indian and even global due to the increasing size of the Indian diaspora. The process of micro-marketing is penetrating deep into this sphere. The momentum for this is, of course, provided by the emergent forces of economic development.

It has triggered a new wave of internal and external migration, and establishes a linkage between culture and market. It also extends the space for cultural interaction as never before. No doubt, it generates a threat perception about cultural identity, but correspondingly it also reinforces the identity consciousness. This ambivalence notwithstanding, the Indian response towards the 'other' cultures has throughout remained selective and adaptive. Globalisation is, therefore, leading increasingly towards hybridisation or fusion of cultural styles and forms rather than their total displacement. This only shows the strength of cultural resilience of the Indian society.

This resilience, however, is not without tensions, both social structural and cultural. It is a global phenomenon. India, since independence, has been making conscious efforts through its democratic institutions, policies of welfare and devolution of power to the regional, ethnic and cultural minorities to establish a synergy between local identities and national development. The linguistic reorganisation of states, the policies of protective discrimination, the continual effort to bring about better and more effective federal structure of governance by improving the centre-state relationship, the policy of offering protection to the ethnic-regional and cultural entities, etc., have been continually implemented and updated to accommodate cultural, social and political identities. We have largely succeeded, but not in all cases, and not without conflict and violence. Globalisation, to the extent that it generates new inequalities or sharpens the consciousness of inequalities, does contain within it the seeds of social and cultural conflicts in society.

It makes the intensity of symbolic transmission across lands more effective and easier, and it also sharpens in people's mind the sense of social, economic and cultural deprivations. It has a regional, national and global dimension. The premise that globalisation generates conflict in societies which sometimes have disastrous consequences is based upon the possibility of extreme mismatch between globalisation and removal of poverty or deprivation of classes, communities and ethnicities.

It is true that organised violence such as terrorism and insurgency erupts in societies where people feel that they are being subordinated culturally, politically or economically, where dominant powers are perceived to be totally unresponsive to democratic protest, and where basic human rights are denied. Does globalisation increase poverty in a society or reduce it? Does it enhance the ability of some nations to structurally dominate the weaker ones? Ideological debate on these issues goes on but the result remains inconclusive. The evidence available so far suggests that globalisation reduces the absolute level of poverty but does enhance the incidence of relative inequalities among people:

If we observe the pattern of social mobility and incidence of poverty since independence in our country, we find that measures of social welfare, education and economic development have contributed to the reduction of poverty, but the relative social inequalities have increased. In absolute terms, the standard of consumption has qualitatively improved in villages and towns; the reservation policy together with focus upon education has created a 'limited' middle class among the weaker sections, minorities and ethnic groups; the quality and extent of participation in politics and power sharing by the backward classes, tribes and scheduled castes, etc. has radically changed. A substantial degree of empowerment of these groups has taken place in the political realm, but in the economic and educational fields the gap between them and the dominant classes or castes persists. In my view, globalisation does pose challenges on several fronts, foremost of which may be economic. For reasons of history, pluralistic social structure and culture and the democratic path of development that we have adopted, we enjoy tremendous resilience to meet with the challenges of globalisation. Notwithstanding this, a cautious fine-tuning and synergy in our economic policies is required. To my mind, the most strategic aspects of such a policy relate to the development of our human resource base, agriculture and infrastructure. Economic development in a balanced manner holds the key to our ability to meet with the challenges of globalisation and accommodate the upsurge of identities.

Many a Threat

Any revolutionary transformation in society brings in its wake both challenges and opportunities. This is true also for globalisation. Not that these challenges are confined only to a developing society like India. The developed world is also not immune from them; as it too faces the challenges of globalisation; only its character is different. In the developing societies, the tensions and anxieties on account of globalisation are primarily economic which spill over to the anxieties about culture and identity. In the developed world, culture seems to top over all other anxieties on account of globalisation. In Europe, we witness this in the crescendo of debate on multiculturalism and in the revival of the ideology of the 'right and the racial-cultural exclusiveness'. In India, however, the cultural and ethnic aspects of the challenges of globalisation do exist, but these are in most cases derivatives of the anticipated unpredictable consequences to the economy, polity and social structure.

In terms of social structure, India remains essentially a rural-agrarian society. Only about 30 per cent of our population is urban and the pace of urbanisation remains slow. The addition to our urban population comes mainly from the rural poor, who migrate in search of employment. They remain marginalised in the urban economy and hold the lowest position in the urban social structure. Thus, a major challenge that globalisation is likely to pose to our social structure is related to the nature of inequalities in the society. We witness these inequalities at several levels, such as between the village and town, between the middle classes and the working classes, between males and females, between marginalised ethnicities and the dominant castes or communities and between the mobile metropolitan diaspora and the illiterate masses in the villages, urban slums and at the periphery of the tribal lands. How is globalisation going to affect these sections of our society? Its pace at present is no doubt measured and slow due to choice of policies and also because of the limitations that our social structure itself imposes upon the pace of globalisation, but the challenges are likely to grow and pose serious problems in the future.

The impact of globalisation on the structural changes in the society comes generally through the changes in the economic policies. India, since independence, has been following a policy of import-substitution and inward-looking market economy. This policy handicapped the economy in global competitiveness, in the manufacturing sector and in exportable commodity production. But its focus upon higher education in science and technology and agricultural infrastructures did compensate the loss. It is evident in 'green revolution' in agriculture, in our growing strength in the sectors of information technology, the professions, the rising middle classes and in the space research which has added edge to our growth in telephony, television and mass communication. Also, the investment in the capital-intensive sectors, such as steel, petrochemicals, power, etc., have generated an economic and technological potential strong enough to cope up with the exposure to the contemporary challenges of globalisation.

The existing economic, social and cultural resilience of our society is to a large measure influenced by the rising middle class. It is estimated that by 2020 the half of the Indian population would comprise the middle classes even at the contemporary rate of the economic growth. Despite this, the challenges of globalisation felt by India in early 1990s made it inevitable to change these policies. Of course, the difference of opinion on matters related to economic liberalisation continues to persist.

The Indian economic policies on globalisation have rightly tended to be cautious. This does not rule out the need for faster movement in several areas. To some extent, our political-structural reality, our democratic path of development imposes restraints to our speed. This is inevitable, as the structural reality of our democracy is still deeply embedded in our social and economic inequalities. Besides, democracy is not merely an instrument of social and political development. It constitutes a fundamental ideal or normative principle of human development. It is an irony that globalisation of economy does not by itself translate into the growth of a democratic society. The Human Development Report (2002) recognises this fact and laments about it.

In our appraisal of the inward-looking economic policies of the past or in our overenthusiasm for the quick embrace of full economic globalisation, we should not neglect our developmental goal of growing as a strong democracy and civil society. This goal, when posited against many policy objectives of economic globalisation, calls for caution and graduated response. Our membership of the WTO and IMF, etc. has devolved upon us the responsibilities for moving towards an open market economy. It exposes our farmers, consumer good industries, small-scale sector industries and those employed in the unorganised sectors to unequal competition from strong economies, which may increase unemployment or lead to many forms of economic and social displacement.

To take these factors into account and yet to encounter the challenges of globalisation, an integrated policy is required. Increased export earnings and foreign trade on the one hand, and the need for massive foreign capital investment on the other depend upon how fast we move in this direction both at the federal and the state levels. In foreign trade and export earnings, we have a temporary advantage of low wages and human resources, but economies of scale and technological modernisation of the production process are required. Reforms in management, governance, labour legislation and fiscal and monetary policies are required. Capital investment on a massive scale is needed to develop the infrastructures in tile sectors of power, roadways, railways, airports and ports, etc.

India has lagged behind in foreign capital investment, apart from other reasons also because of our weak infrastructure. Its inadequacy hampers the growth of our trade and modernisation of agriculture. No doubt, globalisation does create a "mismatch between growth of trade, growth of output and growth of employment" (Panchamukhi in Chadha, 2001: 11), but its negative consequences can certainly be avoided if our infrastructure is modern and our policies with regard to various sectors of economy are adequately synchronised. We may need to reinforce our legal expertise, laws about the intellectual property rights, banking and insurance policies and measures to protect our economy from unfair trade policies from abroad.

Modernisation of agriculture is an urgent requirement as 70 per cent of our population depends upon it. About 90 per cent of employment in our country is offered by the unorganised sector, of which agriculture is a primary component. Studies reveal that during 1990-98 nearly 7 million Indian workers, of which about 4 million in the rural and 3 million in the urban sectors, lost their jobs. Also, the quality of workforce in the rural areas is poor; during 1993-94, 44 per cent of rural males and 80 per cent of rural females were found to be illiterate. Hence, the urgent need for the improvement of the rural human resource base of our country. This would reduce the crisis of inequalities in the social and political structure and also strengthen the pace of our economic modernisation. The farming sector in our economy has chronically suffered from underdevelopment due to lack of investment and adverse terms of trade and tariff policies. Despite this, globalisation has so far not caused any massive dislocation, may be only because of its slow pace in our country or because of our policies. But, eventually, agriculture would have to become commercial and oriented to value added production. This is slowly taking place as some studies reveal, but its scale is still minuscule due to lack of investment and poverty of infrastructure and human resources.

These challenges of economic globalisation have indeed created a social structural crisis of change in our society. The social inequalities have increased in relative terms. But to call it structural dualism may be an oversimplification. The studies on the consumption data indicate that the rural areas constitute about 80-90 per cent of the market for the factory-made consumer goods. There exists a strategic linkage between the rural economy and the industrial sector producing consumer goods. A middle class has emerged in the villages and it continues to grow in size.

In bringing about these changes the expansion of the mass media has played an important role. The incidence of telephony, access to radio and television and in some areas even the uses of the internet are linking the rural social structure and economy with the outside world as never before. It reinforces inter-regional and inter-state linkages, alters the character of the social mobility of skilled and unskilled labour and in some measures it also creates inter-regional or inter-state inequalities. These changes have the potential in the long run to influence the nature of social inequalities in our society and also the pattern of political and cultural interactions among groups and regions within and across the states.

Growth of Ideology

These operational contradictions of globalisation have generated several ideological nuances in its contemporary conceptual and substantive evaluation. A range of ideologies, such as neo-Marxism-Leninism, post-modernism, critical theories of development, particularly those related to the impact of globalisation on ecology, human rights of the weaker sections such as women, minorities, working classes and other marginalised groups, have generated a strident debate on the social, cultural and economic consequences of globalisation. The fact that globalisation has not yet resolved some of the basic contradictions in the realms of culture, economy and human relationships and in some cases it is supposed to have contributed to internal social conflicts goes only to lend credence to such ideologies. According to the contemporary Marxist-Leninist critique, globalisation is only other manifestation of cosmopolitan capitalism with its classic imperialistic orientation remaining intact. Instead of contributing to trans-nationalism, it exposes societies and nations to endemic 'disasters' such as the recent food crisis in Africa and the onset of fundamentalism and communalism, both at the global and national levels.

The acute social distresses, cultural conflicts and alienation of the weaker and marginalised communities contribute to this process. No doubt, globalisation with its emphasis on the supremacy of the market, quest for optimisation of profits by the multinational corporations, continual unemployment due to the fluctuations in economy and capitalism-friendly labour laws and control over the management or governance of globalisation by the Bretton Wood inspired institutions of the rich capitalist nations who set the agenda, policies and practices of globalisation lends credence to this critique. In fact, the Human Development Report (2002) echoes this despair and calls for reforms within the international institutions of development such as the WTO, World Bank, IMF, etc., by making them more accountable and representative.

It is said that, "nearly half the voting power in the World Bank and International Monetary Fund rests in the hands of seven countries. And though all countries have a seat and a vote in the WTO, in practice, decisions are taken in small group meetings and heavily influenced by Canada, the European Union, Japan and US. In 2000, 15 African countries did not have a single trade representative stationed at the WTO" (The *Hindu, July* 25, 2002). This political domination contributes to the acute differences in the perception as to the extent that globalisation decrease or increase the levels of economic and social inequalities within a society.

The Marxist-Leninist critique of globalisation is anchored into a theoretical paradigm which recognises the role of the historical forces, systems of political economy and social structure. Yet another ideology, the post-modernist criticism of globalisation, is essentially cultural. It derives sustenance from an epistemology which rejects the idea of a system or structure, and posits human social and cultural realities in a perpetual state of symbolic transience or flux, continually in the process of making and unmaking. "It challenges the postulate of rationality (the foundation of market economy) on which most social science categories such as, 'structure', 'system' and 'change' are anchored; it also attempts to invalidate the notions of the 'actor' or the 'subject' from the social science discourse or their moorings in the structure of social values. The French sociologist, J. Baudrillard articulates this view when he says that in matters of social discourse, "the things have never functioned socially, but symbolically, magically, irrationally". Social systems, according to the post-modern reckoning, are illusionary facades characterised by "micro-orders of domination" (Singh, 1998: 1). Thus, in the logic of its analysis, history has no role or significance. It treats the conjuncture of events and processes largely in terms of space as 'co-happenings' and not in order of temporal succession. The diversity of existence of identities is recognised but the causality of the same is rejected.

We also witness yet another ideology about globalisation which emanates from the assorted movement of the NGOs. These NGOs represent a variety of 'interest groups' and many institutionalised forms of activism. The issues of their concern are as diverse as human rights, ecology and sustainable development, rights of the minorities, women, tribes, working classes, etc., which seem to converge upon their opposition to globalisation for reasons some of which have a common basis, and others which are contradictory. Their ideology in some parts may seem eclectic with the underpinnings of Marxism, post-modernism, ecological and developmental humanism and focus on human rights, etc., which are articulated in a generalised form.

In my view, globalisation is a unique process. It is a product of such developments in the field of science and technology which are entirely new to human history. And, these offer new opportunities to humankind as also pose many challenges. It is a fact, however, that several of its features taken individually did indeed exist in the past, such as international trade by sea and land routes, capitalism and imperialism, market and capital mobility and transfer of workforce from one country to another. But, devoid as these processes in the past were of the advantages of the modern technologies, their total impact upon society and its direction of change was qualitatively different. Therefore, the nature of challenges was also different. Hence, to understand its fuller implications, a new ideological paradigm is necessary. It must be of an interdisciplinary nature, because globalisation is a multidimensional and multidirectional process.

Its implications have to be understood and analysed from a holistic perspective. The particularistic perspective, either on the basis of political economy as we find in Marxist-Leninist critique or that of culture, symbols or images as we find in the discourse on post-modernism, remain inadequate. While highlighting some of the aspects of globalisation, each one of them leaves a much larger segment of globalisation, its nature and consequences, etc., unaccounted for Sociology, to my mind, could be one such discipline which has a broad enough integrative theoretical perspective to offer a paradigm for the analysis of globalisation. It focuses upon the study of the 'specific' or local in the perspective of the 'total' and the historical. Its methodology and epistemology offer both variety and flexibility of an approach to deal with social realities that may be 'normal' or 'enigmatic' or paradoxical. Globalisation is a good candidate to merit its attention.

Role of Teacher in Modern Education

In every walk of life, aims are of unique importance. Without fixing up aims, the work that we take up remains dull and cheerless aims. In fact it makes the process lively, and they also provide satisfaction at the end. In the field of education aims are very essential. Undoubtedly, education is a purposeful and planned activity. It makes a man quite fit for the society. Therefore, we should try to fix up aims in advance and then make efforts to achieve them.

Education without an aim is quite meaningless. In the words of John Oewey, "An aim is a foreseen end that gives direction to an activity or motivates behaviour." An aim to predetermined goal which inspires the welfare activities of an individual, after careful thinking and proper planning it is achieved. In fact, an aim is that predetermined goal which stimulates human activities to achieve it.

Society and Evolution of Education

Aims of Education need careful fixation. They have to be in accordance with the needs and requirements of the individuals, the society, the nation and the situations prevailing all around.

Aims of education have been different at different times. After the independence of the country Pt. Jawahar Lal Nehru remarked, "Great changes have taken place in the country and the educational system must be keeping with them. The entire basis of education must be revolutionised." The society today is facing a number of problems. Social, political and economic conditions of the country are fast changing. It is, therefore, very important that we should assess everything carefully in the light of present situations and fix up aims of education which are suitable for the people of free India in every way. Suggested aims of education are:

1. Individual Aim of Education.
2. Social Aim of Education.
3. Vocational aim of Education.
4. Character Building Aim.
5. Spiritual Aim of Education.
6. Harmonious Development Aim.
7. Cultural Aim of Education.
8. Knowledge Aim of Education.

Targets for Individuals

Individual aim of education means that education should develop the individuals according to their interests and capabilities. It means free growth of individuality, helping every boy and girl to achieve the highest degree of individual development. Individuality is the ideal of life. An individual is the central figure in the social setup of life. All social institutions exist for the betterment and improvement of the individual. The individual is the end and these social institutions are the means. It is the fullest development of the individual. Education aims at training and development of the individual. It is only this type of individual who comes out as a good citizen.

The individual aims of education have been emphasised by various thinkers. Their view points are as under:

> The Naturalists like Rousseau believe that "The central aim of education is the autonomous development of the individual." According to him, "Everything is good

as it comes from the hands of Author of Nature, but everything degenerates at the hands of man. God makes all things good. Man meddles with them and they become evil." This group of thinkers believe that man and citizen cannot be trained simultaneously. In short, education must secure those conditions where every individual is allowed to have a free play of his personality. He is free to develop his inherent, powers the highest potentialities of self.

The biologists believe that every individual *is* unique in his own way. G. Thompson believes that "Education is for the individual. Its function being to enable the individual to survive and live out its complete life. Education is imparted to preserve the individual life. Education is given for the sake of the individual to save him from destruction. Community exists for the individual, not the individual for the community. Community being the means and individual being the end, education should not set the means over the end." Therefore, individual and not society should be the centre of all educational efforts and activities.

According to the psychologists, education is an individual process. No two children are identical in intellectual capacity. Education must be individualised. Then only they can be benefited fully.

The modern progressive thinkers also hold the view that the ultimate good of society lies in discovering the hidden value of the individual. In the words of Sir Percy Nunn, enters the human world except in end through the free activities of the individual men and women and that educational practice must be shaped to accord with the truth."

Each individual child should hold the key positions in the educative process. There is much force in the individual aim of education. However, individual aim, in its extreme form, is not desirable. The social aim has its own values and justification. This extreme and one-sided view of individual aims has teen criticised.

Professionalisation and Targets

Livelihood is important because without bread and butter, living is not possible. Education, therefore, must enable an individual to stand on his own feet and he should be able to earn for his living. Only a living person has certain needs and requirements. A dead person has no desire, no aspiration and no requirements. When we talk of a living person, we surely see to it from his all around point of view. An individual needs education in order to live. He needs education in order to live well. He needs education to do various things of life in a better way.

They are possible with the help of money only. According to Secondary Education Commission, knowledge gained is useless if an individual cannot make both ends meet. Without a vocation, the individual is a drag and parasite on others. A social parasite cannot be called a free man. He begins to feel free only when he is economically independent. Vocational education, thus, exercises a liberalising effect on man. There is no vocation without education. Every vocation has an educational value. Education with the vocational aim in the background will prepare each individual for an occupation. Vocational aim of education is also known as 'Bread and Butter aim', 'Blue Jacket Aim' and 'White Collar Aim.'

It has been rightly said that "Vocational Education is an education of most effective kind, for lack of which those who merely go to school, suffer all their lives" in the words of Gandhiji, "True education ought to be a kind of insurance against unemployment."

The Merits

Solves Economic Problems: Vocational aims make a person fit for some vocation. He becomes sound economically. In this age of material crisis, the problem of unemployment and underemployment are causing many economic problems. When education is vocation centred, it will help a lot.

Gives Social Status: Vocational aims bring vocational efficiency. With more money, a person feels satisfied in the society. It gives him good social status.

Suits the Average Learners: In every classroom, there are different types of learners. The good and brilliant are able to do well in studies. But the average types of learners find studies a big problem. Vocational education helps them, because it is suitable for them.

Helps in Moral Development: In the absence of vocation centred education, many students would become misfit for society. They will do every type of bad deeds to earn money for their living. Vocational education thus makes them morally good.

Makes a Person Active: In vocational education, the learners are able to develop their interests in the vocation. Quite a number of them are able to excel.

Makes Learning Useful: Vocational education makes learning useful. Here some vocation is of primary importance. The study of so-called traditional subjects is secondary.

A few experts pirt-forth their views as under:

> Spens Report, "Preparation for vocation is an important part of our education."

Hartshome's view, "Vocational education is an education of most effective kind, for lack of which those who merely go to school, suffer all their lives."

The Demerits

1. Only vocational aim is not sufficient for an individual. Some studies are also needed. Social and cultural aims are in no way of lesser importance.
2. It is a narrow aim of education.
3. It is too much materialistic.

It we have a professionally good doctor or a professionally good engineer, it is not sufficient. There is need of a good man in each one of them. So just vocational aim is not sufficient. All other aims which make an individual a good person, are also fleeced.

Targets for Values

Education makes a person spiritually sound. A person who is spiritually sound behaves better. He/she is able to do well while being trained for social efficiency, sound moraly and physical betterment. Spiritual aim is the pillar on which rests the edifice of total personality. Surely it is deeply linked with the character building aim. Spiritual aim gives strength to human soul and mind. The great spiritualists like Guru Nanak, Buddha, Mahavir, Swami Dayanand, Vivekanand, Shankaracharya, Aurobindo,

Gandhi, Tagore accepted the spiritual aim of education. Views of some of them on this aspect of life are given below and they are worth mentioning down:

> Aurobindo said, "Every man has in himself something divine, something his own, a chance of perfection and strength. In however small a sphere which God offers him to take or refuse. The task is to find it, develop it and use it. The chief aim of education should be to help the growing soul to draw out that in self which is best and make it perfect for a noble cause.

Finfey said, "Material progress is good thing; social and political reforms are mere valuable both to the race and the individual; their final worth lies in the aid they afford to spiritual life."

Radhakrishnan said, "The aim of education is neither national efficiency, nor world solidarity, but making the individual feel that he has within himself something deeper than intellect, call it spirit. If you like."

Merits

1. Spiritual aim of education makes a person gentle and pious.
2. It makes the students religious minded. They are able to have some values of life – and all this has its good effect on their behaviours.
3. It makes the personality of the individual strong. He/she becomes a man of character, honesty and integrity.
4. It reduces the problems of indiscipline, conflicts, quarrels to some extent corruption, greed, aggression, etc., destruction. hatred are on the increase. All these also stand checked to a considerable extent.

Demerits

1. One may think of leaving the worldly life. That is not so good for every one.
2. Spiritual aim may be achieved but one may not be so practical.

Spiritual aim of education, no doubt, is important but it cannot be given topmost priority in the aim of education. Other aims of education the vocational aim, knowledge aim, etc. will to be cared for fully. Then and then and then only it will remain practical and useful to lead a good life in the society.

Various Norms

1. They emerge out of the existing conditions.
2. They are tentative. They can be revised as per need and requirement.
3. They are well-defined.
4. They are flexible.
5. They are related to the life and aspirations of the people.

John Dewey suggested the following criteria for aims of education:

1. Good aims are related to real situations of life. They grow out of these situations and they can be achieved only under these situations.
2. Good aims are flexible. These should be flexible enough to meet the demands of changing circumstances of life.
3. A good aim represents a span of diverse activity. The real objective in pursuing an end is not the end itself but the course of the activity itself which constitutes the core of education.

The Importance

There is a great importance of aims of education. All scholars philosophers and educationists have laid great stress on the importance of aims in education. Being a systematic and planned activity, education loses much of its significance without clear-cut aims. According to Encyclopaedia of Modern Education, "Education is purposeful and ethical activity. Hence it is unthinkable without aims." In fact, without aims neither an individual nor an institution is capable of realising its potentialities."

Educational aims are important due to the following reasons:

1. Aims are necessary as they give direction to an act. Education is a planned activity. It has certain aims in view. The aim as a foreseen end as it gives direction to the education process. Without aims, the educator is like a sailor who does not

know his destination and the pupil is like a rudderless vessel which may be drifted along somewhere ashore.

2. Aims allow us to act intelligently. John Dewey has aptly remarked, "Acting with an aim is all one with acting intelligently." Thus by keeping the aim in view, one knows what one is doing and why one is doing it. It saves wastage of time and energy.
3. Aims help in assessing the outcomes of the education process. They are necessary because they help in measuring the success and failure of work done in the school.
4. Aims are necessary for efficient school administration. They help the school authorities in organising, equipping and managing the school. This refers to the selection of teachers, curriculum, planning, proper library equipment, planning of various activities, etc. Each activity is guided by educational aims.
5. Aims give direction to the work of the pupils. Once the pupils are clear about the aims, they are likely to cooperate and work with zeal for the achievement of these aims.
6. Aims are useful for parents and general public. Parents and general public can appreciate the work of the school in the light of aims. Aims put restraint on the undue criticism from the parents.
7. Aims give continuity and significance to education. Education is a continuous process. It has an intrinsic continuity. It is the aim that gives continuity and significance to the series of events and experiences that make up what we call education. So aims are potential seeds from which grows the plant of a well-defined educational policy. Aims help us in acting with meaning.

The Characteristics

Aims are the core of a workable philosophy of education. Without philosophy, an educator could not have aims and without aims he could not have a practical philosophy.

Aims are an integral part of the fabric of the educative process. They enable an individual to continue his education. As such, an aim is not an end; it is only a means to an end.

Aims are both within and without the educative process. Ward G. Reader rightly points out, "Education finds its aims both within and without the educative process. It must be kept in mind the interests and the abilities of the pupil and prepare him to share in democratic living both now and when he becomes an adult."

Practical Reasons

Many factors contribute to the determining of educational aims. These factors touch every phase of human life and also reflect socio-cultural trends. The following factors usually determine aims of education:

Philosophy of Life: Aims of education have direct relationship with the prevailing philosophy of life. Different thinkers and philosophical thoughts influence the course of education and its aims. Idealism emphasises self-realisation and divine perfection as the aims of education. According to the natural-view point, self-expression or self-gratification should be the aim of education. The pragmatic school of thought views life as the process of socialisation of an individual. Similarly, existentialism, realism and other philosophical view points recommended their own aims of education.

Human Nature: Educational aims have often been decided keeping in view the human nature. Idealists regard 'unfolding the divine man' as the aim of education. To naturalists, the aim of education is "self-expression."

Religious Factors: Though there is no state religion in India, yet different religious view points influence the aims of education. The denominational institutions run by different religious organisations have to work to realise the goals accordingly.

Political Ideology: No system of education can rise above the political ideologies of the country. In other words, political ideologies influence aims of education in a significant way. According to Brown, "Education in any country and at points reflects value of the ruling class." Under a totalitarian system, the aims of education are different from those under a democratic political system.

Under a democratic set-up, the-aims of education are flexible. The goal of education is the good man who is to be educated for life of freedom. Education aims at developing the full personality of each individual, irrespective of caste, creed, class or religion.

Under a totalitarian system, the aim of education is to propagate the state ideology. It is, in fact, indoctrination. The good of the individual lies in his working for the good of the state. Thus he dies for the state.

Socio-Economic Problems: Socio-economic problems of a country determine the aims of education. In India, we have a number of socio-economic problems. One of the objectives of education may be to establish a socialistic pattern of society which is in tune with the democratic set-up of the country. Similarly, the educational system of the country is expected to produce socially and economically independent citizens who can contribute to the betterment of the country. In the words of Secondary Education Commission Report (1952-53) : "As political, social and economic conditions change and new problems arise, it becomes necessary to re-examine and re-state clearly the objectives which education at each definite stage, should keep in view."

Cultural Factors: Socio-cultural heritage of a country largely determines the aims of education. Education has to preserve and develop the cultural heritage. The changing and developing pattern of culture directly influences the aims of education.

Exploration of Knowledge: Present age is the age of science and technology. There is almost an explosion of knowledge. Education today, has become science-oriented and technology-based. It is thus evident that exploration of knowledge is an important factor in determining the aims of education.

Education must represent these factors and be related to the realities and problems of life.

Modern Aims

Aims of Education are related to time and space. They are also changeable. The history of educational development in India stands evidence to this fact. There have been different aims of education in different periods. A brief account of aims of education in chronological sequence is given below:

Aims of Education in the Brahmanic Period: The aim of education during Brahmanic period was an all-sided development of man. Education was regarded as a means of salvation or emancipation. The chief aim of education was to unfold the spiritual and normal power of the individual. Education was thus determined by religious values.

Aims of Buddhist Education: The aim of education during Buddhist period was to create a sense of equality among all, 'Satya' and 'Ahimsa' were the directive principles of this system of education. The child was taught to control and suppress his worldly desires in accordance with the eightfold code of conduct enunciated by Lord Buddha.

Aims of Education during Muslim Rule: The aim of education during the Muslim period was to prepare an individual for the wordly life as well as for the spiritual life. It was education of Islamic culture and scriptures which regulated human behaviour accordingly.

Aims of Education during British Rule: The aims of education during British rule were different. The system of British education was implanted in this country with purely political motives. It aimed at dividing Indians spiritually and intellectually into the English-knowing class of men and non-English-knowing masses of people. It was in accordance with Macaulay's "Downward Filtration Theory."

Dimensions of Teaching

Education is never ending. It starts with the birth of an individual and then it goes on till the last day of the individual. Education makes an individual a real human being. It is an essential human virtue. Man becomes man through education. He learns something at every moment and on every day. Education equips the individual with social, moral, cultural and spiritual aspects and thus makes life progressive, cultured and civilized. About education, P.O. Bannerji said, "It is the development of the power of adaptation to an ever changing social environment."

Gone are the days when education was the right of a privileged few. Now all have the equal right to be educated as education has become *sine quo non* of civilization.

Education at School

Formal education is that which is provided in a formal way by observing all types of formalities. It is a pre-planned type of education, where specific alms are well fixed in advance, methods of teaching are decided and knowledge is given to the selected pupils by the selected teachers. This type of education is imparted in the schools, colleges and universities where the learners abide toy the rules and regulations of the agency of formal education. Formal type of education is also provided in the library. It is limited to a specified period.

It is a consciously received education for which deliberate efforts are made both by the teacher and the learner. This type of education is well-organised and so it may anywhere in the school or outside the school. There, is a well-defined and clear cut curriculum. It is not confined to the schools only. In short, we can say that any teaching where there is instruction, supervision, definite aims, etc., is called formal education. No matter whether it is given in the school or at home.

Characteristics

1. It is a well-known type of education well-cared for, well-aspired for and well-advocated.
2. Many types of formalities are observed here.
3. There is set of curriculum. Effort is there to modernise it as far as possible.
4. There are fixed goals and conscious efforts are always on to achieve the goals.
5. It is an organised type of education. Its show off is made as good as possible. It is made public to attract more and more learners.
6. It is a well-planned activity with fixed time table specially prepared for It.
7. Both the teacher and the taught make conscious efforts in the process of teaching learning.
8. The place of education and the timings are fixed here.
9. This type of education has a beginning and also the close.
10. Surely the syllabi are completed.
11. Examinations are held in a formal way and results announced keeping in view the goals fixed up.

Advantages

1. A student is able to sit in the company of other students of the same age group. That increases peer relationships, fellow feelings for one another.
2. In the formal system, many students get the opportunity of being together in different classes for a good deal of time. They have better underst‹nding with each other.

3. It makes the students learn things in a disciplined way. That gradually imbibes the quality of self-discipline in the students.
4. Here education is a continuous process and naturally it develops in the learners the habit of reading continuously.
5. "Education is in accordance with the growth and development of the different faculties of the learners. Thus it helps in having well cared for growth and development of the learners.

Disadvantages

1. Good and bad students, gifted and backward are generally made to sit together in the same class and taught by the same teachers. This shows down the ongoing rapid progress of the gifted pupils.
2. Every student has to wait for the expiry of the academic session and then only he/she gets promotion of the next class.
3. A few students may be keen to cover up more syllabus in less time. That is obstructed here in Indian system of formal education.
4. There are strains on the minds of the learners.
5. It is more or less unnatural way of teaching learning. There is artificial situations created when teaching-learning is conducted.
6. There is need of motivating the students. Sometimes student may fail to learn anything inspite of motivation by the teachers.

Role of Literacy

Education for which no formalities are observed is known as informal type of education. In this type of education, there is modification of the behaviour of the learner but no conscious efforts are made for it. Whatever is learnt here is not pre-planned. It is rather incidental. Here neither the teacher nor the lean is conscious of the process of teaching learning. For example, a person goes to the playground for physical exercise and there comes across someone who tells him very good ways of utilising leisure time. Surely in this situation one acted as a teacher and the listener was a student but none of them was conscious of the fact that the process of teaching learning occurred informally. In this way through our daily routine of life, teaching learning may take place and we are quite unaware of it. This type of education is known as informal education. It is a casual type of education which is received through daily experiences and activities.

In this type of education there are no predetermined aims, no definite curriculum, no well thought methods of teaching, no qualified and trained teachers and no definite place of education. Here education is received by the company of friends, relatives, community, etc. Whatever as education is received plays a very important and significant role in the life of the education. This type of education may result into learning something wrong or bad. That is negative education and that may create some problems.

Characteristics

1. This type of education is informal because no formalities are observed here.
2. No conscious efforts are made either by the teacher or the taught.
3. It is in no way pre-planned activity.
4. It is incidental.
5. No formal goals are fixed up.
6. No formal means are used to attain the goals.
7. There are no fixed/appointed teachers. Any and eveybody can be a teacher in an informal situation.
8. Here a situation might crop up where the student may teach a teacher something.
9. There is no prescribed curriculum and no time-table is observed.
10. There is none who organises this type of education. It is all a matter of chance that teaching in learning occurs.
11. There is no fixed place for it.
12. This type of education is never completed and there is no fixed syllabus.

13. There are no examinations of any type.
14. It is all a natural way of teaching-learning.

Definition and Ideas

Let us understand the word 'Education' etymologically :

First view is that the word 'education' is derived from the latin word 'Educatum' which means 'to bring up' or 'to nourish'.

Second view is that the word 'education' is derived from the latin word 'education' which means 'to find out', or 'to draw out'. Naturally here in the process of education, 'effort is to draw out' rather than 'to put in'.

Third view is that the word education comes from the Latin word 'Education' which means the 'act of teaching or training'.

Indian Point of View

1. According to Rig Veda, "Education is something which makes a man self-reliant and selfless.
2. According to Upanishads, "Education is that whose end product is salvation".
3. The well known Indian Economist Kautilya says, "Education means training for the country and for the nation.
4. The Indian Philosopher Shankaracharya considers education as "the realisation of the self."
5. Swami Vivekanand considered education as "the manifestation of divine perfection of existing in man."
6. According to Vedantic view point. The essence of man is spirituality. We need an education that quickens, that kindles the urge of spirituality inherent in every mind."
7. According to Mahatma Gandhi, "By education I mean an all round drawing out of the best in child and man-body, mind and spirit."
8. Guru Nanak said, "Education is self-realisation and service of the people."

9. Aurobindo Ghosh puts forth his view on education as. "Helping the growing soul to draw out that is in itself".
10. Rabindra Nath Tagore says, "Education means enabling the mind to find out that ultimate truth which emancipates us from the bondage of the dust and gives us the wealth, not of things but of inner light, not of power but of love, making this truth its own and gives expression to ."
11. In the words of Zakir Hussain, "Education is the process of the individual mind" getting to its full possible development. It is a long school which lasts a lifetime."
12. According to Swami Dayanand, "Education is a means for character formation and righteous living."
13. In the words of University Education Commission Report (1948-49): "Education to the Indian traditions, is not merely a means of earning a living; nor it is only a nursery of thought or a school for citizenship. It is initiation into the life of spirit, a training of human soul in the pursuit of truth and the practice of virtue. It is a second birth, divitiyam janma."
14. According to the Report of Indian Education Commission (1964-66), "Education ought to be related to the life, needs and aspirations of the people and thereby made powerful instrument of social, economic and cultural transformation."

Western Point of View

Concept of education as given by a few popular Western thinkers is as given below:

1. Plato's view, "Education is the capacity to feel pleasure and pain at the right moment. It develops in the body and in the soul of the pupil all the beauty and all the perfection of which he is capable of."
2. According to Aristotle, "Education is the creation of a sound mind in a sound body....It develops man's faculty, especially his mind, so that he may be able to enjoy the contemplation of supreme truth, goodness and beauty in which perfect happiness essentially consists."
3. Socrates said, "Education means the bringing out of the ideas of universal validity which are latent in the mind of every man."

4. In the words of Comenfus, "All who are born as human beings, need education because they are destined to be real men, not wild beasts, dull animals and clumps of wood."
5. Thompson said, "Education is the influence of environment on the individual with the view to producing a permanent change in his habits of behaviour, of thought and of attitude."
6. Pestalozzi remarked, "Education is natural, harmonious and progressive development of man's innate powers."
7. Adams said, "Education is a conscious and deliberate process by which one personality acts upon another in order to modify the development of the other by the communication and manipulation of knowledge."
8. Froebel's view, "Education is the unfoldment of what is already enfolded in the germ. It is the process through which the child makes internal external."
9. In the words of Milton, "I call, therefore a complete and generous education that which fits a man to perform justly, skilfully and maghanimously all the offices, both private and public, of peace and war."
10. According to T.P. Nunn, "Education is the complete development of individuality so-that he makes an original contribution to human life according to the best of his capacity."
11. John Dewey says, "Education is the process of living through a continuous reconstruction of experiences. It is the development of those capacities in the individual which will enable him to control his environment and fulfil his possibilities."
12. Herbert's view, "Education is the development of good character."
13. In the words of Redden, "Education is the deliberate and systematic influence, exerted by the mature person upon the immature, through instruction, discipline and harmonious development of physical, intellectual, aesthetic, social and spiritual powers of the human being, according to individual and social needs and directed 'towards the union of the educated with his creators as the final end."

14. Draver says, "Education is a process in which and by which knowledge, character and behaviour of the young are shaped and moulded."
15. According to Kant, "Education is the development in the individual of all the perfection of which he is capable."
16. According to Ross, " The aim of education is the development of valuable personality and spiritual individuality."

Narrower Concept: in a limited sense, education is confined to the school and the University instruction. Education starts from the day a child is admitted in a school and it ends when the child completes studies and leaves at the college or University stage. Here education is limited to class room teaching. It is formal in nature. The different examinations passed indicate his success of education. This type of education is intentional and not incidental. It is consciously received education and it is imparted by the institution through an organised way. The curriculum of studies is also of definite type. Here everything is pre-planned and education is given by the teachers in the class room controlled situations. Here education is synonymous with instruction.

Broader Concept: In the broader sense, education means the totality of experience gained by an individual from birth to death. It is not the communication of information by the teacher. It is also not just the acquisition of knowledge by the student. The fact is that it is the total development of the personality. Here learning is through any agency such as home, street, school, society, temple, playground, cinema, etc. In this regard William H. Kilpatnck said, "From the broad point of view, all life heartfully lived is education." Here the curriculum 'for studies is unlimited and also indefinite. Mark Hopkins says, "Education in its widest sense includes everything that exerts a formative influence."

Edward Thring said, "Education is the transmission of life, by the living to the living." In short we can say that education is life and life is education.

T. Raymont remarked: One is educated by one's vocation, by home life, by friendship, by marriage, by parenthood, by reaction, by travel, and so forth."

According to the Report of international Commission on the development of education - "Learning to be' ......human beings keep on learning and training themselves throughout lives, above and through the influence of the surrounding environment and through the experiences which mould their behaviour, their conceptions of life and the content of their knowledge."

Narrow and broad meanings of education have to be reconciled. Surely they are complementary to each other. The following lines by the well known educationists satisfy the whole thing:

> According to Gibbons: "Every person has two educations : one which he receives from others and one more important, which he gives to himself."

Whitehead Said: "There is only one subject matter of education and that is life in all its manifestations."

The Characteristics

1. Education is a tri-polar process where teacher taught and social environment act and react with one another.
2. Education is a never ending venture.
3. It is a process where some purpose/purposes are aimed at and efforts accordingly are made to attain them.
4. It is a life-long process.
5. Education is preparation for We through Me experience.
6. It is a process of individual development.
7. It is dynamic.
8. It is rotated to time, place and social set up life.
9. It is both theoretical and practical.
10. It is science as well as art.
11. It is an instrument which is used to attain better life.
12. It is an essential human virtue because man becomes man through it.
13. Education is essentially a process of growth and development which goes on throughout life.
14. Education is the modification of behaviour.

15. Education is getting new knowledge and a new reactions.
16. Education is adjustment with the environment.

Direction

Instruction is an integral part of education. The process of instruction generally goes on in the class room situations. Some knowledge is put into the mind of the child and he is expected to memorise it.

According to international Dictionary of Education: "instruction is often used synonymously with teaching but often specific teaching is akin to the skill of training rather than to education in a broader sense. It may be audio-visual, correspondence or individual."

It includes the activities dealing directly with the teaching of students. It is given for improving the quality of teaching.

The following are the characteristics of instruction:

1. Instruction is an integral part of education. It often goes on when a group of learners are there. It is not possible in the vacuum.
2. Instruction is not spontaneous. Rather it is pre-planned activity.
3. It helps in giving knowledge systematically.
4. Instructions are instructor oriented. The teacher is the giver and the child receives instruction passively.
5. The process of instruction goes on in a limited context only.
6. It is mostly examination oriented. The purpose of giving instruction is enabling the student to pass the examination.
7. The person who gives instruction does need language, proficiency.
8. Its main limitation is that it does not develop interest in the students. It also does not imbibe any values in the learners.

Guidance

Training is an integral part of education, we compare education with, a circle training is then a segment of circle, in training, practical activity is involved) Training helps an individual reach a set standard of behaviour. There is always a set programme to be followed. Thus in the air force, training is given to make the individual an expert pilot. Training is given for car driving, scooter driving, etc. In all these cases, some instructor is always there to give training.

Thus training is a specific programme of vocational preparation. It is a planned and systematic sequence of instruction under competent supervisor. It may include refresher and reorientation training for professionals.

Training is a time bound process. After the expiry of certain period, we say that training is over. Then the person becomes a fit person in that field.

The following are the characteristics of training:

1. Training is given in a formal way. Some agency is always working behind it.
2. In training, there are rigid rules and regulations and those have to be observed carefully.
3. Training is given by expert person of the field.
4. It is a practical activity.
5. Framing may or may not make an individual socially efficient.
6. Through training, the expert tries to formulate a set type of behaviour of the individual. Arguments or reasoning of any type are not welcome here.
7. Training is a part of education. Education aims at all round development of an individual whereas training imparts some practical skill or skills.
8. It is a time bound process.

Training

Indoctrination is an activity which helps in forming beliefs. Some ideas are infused in the minds of the learners from the beginning. Those ideas are continuously put in the mind and thus ideas become their firm beliefs. Once the ideas or beliefs are fixed in the mind then time can't easily shake off those deep rooted ideas or beliefs from them.

Broadly, indoctrination is the attempt to inculcate or fix in the individual a certain pattern of beliefs or habits. It may occur in any teaching learning situation. More strictly, it is an attempt to insinuate into the experience of the individual any doctrine whether social, political, economic or religious.

People are indoctrinated to believe certain things. In the process of indoctrination, there is almost negligible scope for reasoning.

Education brings desirable changes in beliefs, attitudes, values, etc. Naturally education is something bigger and indoctrination is a part of it.

The following characteristics of indoctrination show its nature:

1. Indoctrination shapes the beliefs and transmits knowledge.
2. There is no scope for reasoning.
3. It makes the individuals believe certain things. There may or may not be any rational thinking behind.
4. Indoctrination is a sort of strategy which may be used as per the desire of the doer or as per requirement of the situation.
5. It is a part of education.

In this fast changing arena of life, indoctrination can be used as a strategy and the results can be wonderful. To bring about desirable social change, indoctrination may be used to make the people believe certain things.

Education is an organised and imparted can be classified as under:

1. Formal Education 2. Informal Education 3. Non-formal Education.

Teachers and Students

Definition and Perception

Good's Dictionary of Education defines students, government as "the maintenance of order and the regulation of matters of conduct in school by elected representatives chosen from the students body by the students themselves."

H.C. McKown writes that students' self-government is not possible for two reasons:

1. Students lack the judgement that may accompany executive, legislative and judicial power.
2. The Principal of the school is officially charged with the responsibility for the school, its equipment and its students' welfare. The students are not so charged and cannot be.

The Council

The council should begin with concrete activities where definite success is possible. More difficult problems may be taken up as the pupils and teachers, working through the council, gain the ability to handle them.

Out of the five types of self-governments given by P.W. Terry, we shall study the possibilities of introducing any one of them.

The Informal Type: It is a temporary organisation. It is formed as occasions arise. Some senior students or other outstanding pupils are invited to cooperate with the members of the staff in helping them on certain occasions such as to receive and accommodate guests at the school function day, etc.

The Specific Service Type: Certain duties such as to mark attendance, to supervise study rooms, to maintain cleanliness, etc. are assigned to some students who are either selected by the members of the staff or elected by the students themselves.

The Simple Council Type: In this form of self-government there is a certain unit of student organisation called the students' council to deal with the different activities of the students.

The Complex Type: Under this form, there are two or more central bodies of the students. One is a small body doing executive business and the other a bigger one exercising legislative powers. The former may be compared to that of a Cabinet and the latter to a Legislative Assembly or House of Representatives.

The School City Type: The administration of the school is carried on the lines of city administration. It is an elaborate form of student government. The whole of the student population of the school is divided into wards which elect Municipal Councillors.

The Mayor, the head of the city government as president of the Municipal Council is elected by people (pupils) at large or senior class or by Municipal Councillors and so also the chief of the police. The Council is invested with legislative and judicial powers. Standing Committees are also constituted for finance, athletics, social welfare, safety, traffic and publicity, etc.

Necessary Elements

Change in Teacher Attitude: For the successful working of this programme it is very essential that the teachers must confide more in their students. The sense of responsibility can only grow and flower in an atmosphere of trust and freedom. The responsibility should be really handed over to the students and there be no pretext about it. "It is useless to institute self-government in name only, i.e. to call self-government system where the Head-teacher impresses his or her views upon the prefects and they accept them and impress them on the pupils. Nor is it of any value to have a system of self-government with a master or mistress always just round the corner to exercise authority," writes H.G. Stead.

G.R. Dustin is of the opinion, "A successful scheme requires a demonstrative organisation of the teaching staff of the school. The principal must first realise the meaning of democratised education. Teachers must also democratise their teaching and classroom management. Autocracy will never cooperate to make a democratic form of government a success."

Gradual Development of the Programme: Heavy responsibilities on the shoulders of children should be placed gradually. We should not demand too much from children who are immature in their judgement. It is wrong to think that a teacher's work is reduced by the introduction of self-government or a students' participation programme. Students need constant help and guidance from the teachers. The students must be told that the efficiency of an organisation depends upon the personnel of committee for the selection of which sober judgement is required. The teachers would do well if they acquaint the students with the general principles which govern the selection of suitable representatives. This will help the students in selecting their representatives.

Constant and Intelligent Supervision: In connection with the supervision work of these activities, W.R. Smith writes, "A school, city state, students' council or any other form of student management, requires a constant and intelligent supervision in which neither dictation nor aloofness is conspicuous."

Strict supervision should be made of the financial policy of the Sabha or the Council.

Very Few Restrictions on Students: Every good system of self-government should provide opportunities for as many pupils as possible to participate in its programmes. No restrictions on council membership should be imposed as far as possible.

Regular Meetings: The meetings of the various Boards should be held regularly. Each Board, committee or subgroup should be given specific responsibility and held accountable for it.

Due Publicity: The activities of the Sabha should be continuously publicised.

Non-involvement of Students: Care should be taken to see that the Sabha does not become a tool in the hand of the politicians to grind their own axe.

Constant Evaluation: The work of the council should be continuously evaluated.

Advantages:

- The students develop love for the school.
- They realise the necessity of having rules and regulations for the efficient and successful working of an institution.
- They learn to respect authority.
- They learn to tolerate difference of opinion and develop tolerance.
- They learn the principle of 'give' and 'take'.
- They learn to rise above casteism and communalism.
- They get opportunities to make decisive choices.
- They learn to lead others and develop qualities of leadership.
- They learn to handle public money.
- They learn to prepare themselves for future life as enlightened citizens of a democratic country.
- They get an idea of the actual working of the Assembly and Parliament.
- They learn to discipline themselves.
- They realise their rights and responsibilities as citizens.
- They learn the mechanics and devices of government and develop true spirit of citizenship.

Historical Aspects

The concept of self-government is nearly as old as education. Flato's "Academy" was partially governed by elected student "Scholarchs". Aristotle extended the field of student self-government in his "Lyceum".

The student monitor system and the school court grew out of the educational experiments of TROTZEN-DORFF in Renaissance

Germany, and of Lancaster, Bell, and Hill in England and India. Rousseau, Froebel and Pestalozzi contributed much to the self-government movement through their teaching and writing.

In America, a self-government plan was established before 1800 in the Willian Pen Charter School in which the school "Assembly" was elected monthly and charged with law-making powers.

In 1941, two surveys of student participation revealed that 81 to 92 per cent of American High Schools had some organised form of student participation. The phrase, 'student participation in school government' replaced the older phrase, 'Student government'.

Need for Student Self-government: School life is not divorced from social life. An ideal school in a democracy must present a segment of real life. Its activities must be geared to the needs of social life around and it must present an idealised epitome of the social life. Just as we cannot learn speaking or writing a language without practice, in the same way our children cannot learn how to govern themselves and to get training in the democratic way of life unless they are provided opportunities for practical training in the democratic way of life.

Therefore we must make the children themselves responsible for most of the activities concerning school management. When the students plan, execute and assess various activities and projects, they learn and practise democratic ideals and practices and their sense of social and civic responsibility is awakened. It has been stated by E.B. Castle, "Edicts from above do not conduce to the best human relationships; no one man or small group of adults working in a hierarchical formation can produce the pleasantness of tone that usually results from common purposes commonly achieved. Where a hierarchy of status exists and orders are received from above, those in the lower ranks of the hierarchy are almost certain to impose good behaviour instead of attempting to evoke good feelings."

The educators and others experienced in social relations feel that the greatest unity of spirit and self-discipline results when members of the group have a voice in making decisions which affect them.

Not Being an Alumni

Complete government by the pupils is not possible even in well-established progressive schools in our country. Nevertheless, there are practical undertakings in the schools which provide opportunities to the students to get training for future citizenship. The simple council type of self-government seems to be the best.

To start with a school may have a school Sabha. Each class or Section should elect one representative to it. Some talented students may be nominated by the head of the school in consultation with the staff adviser. The Sabha may have six Boards under it and the members may be elected from among the elected representatives. One staff-member may act as an adviser to each Board. The following activities may be undertaken by these Boards:

1. Games and sports.
2. Health and sanitation.
3. Activities like debates, dramas, magazines, etc.
4. Disciplinary.
5. Social service activities like adult literacy campaigns, flood relief, etc.
6. School cooperative store.

Actions of Sabha

No rigid rules can be laid down for the range of activities to be undertaken by the Sabha. Every type of activity which has some educational significance may come under its purview.

H.C. McKown has given a list of 147 activities which can be undertaken by the Sabha or the Council. Some of these activities are given here:

- To welcome new students.
- To supervise and help in the maintenance of good sanitary conditions in the school.
- To decorate the classrooms and the school premises.
- To visit sick students.
- To meet and welcome the visiting teams.
- To provide assistance to the weak and handicapped students.

- To plan campaigns courtesy, safety, punctuality, etc.
- To organise contests and competitions.
- To publish school magazine.
- To organise and manage a lost and found department.
- To promote better lunch-room and cafeteria manners.
- To promote good manners at athletic contests.
- To appoint library and reading-room monitors.
- To promote good behaviour at assembly, public events, before, in and after school.
- To arrange lectures.
- To organise exhibitions.
- To organise the school store.
- To organise the school-bank.
- To introduce students to new movements in education.
- To promote and arrange inter-school visits.
- To arrange inter-school sports tournaments.
- To promote inter-home room programme exchanges.
- To hold academic contests.
- To organise excursions and trips.
- To provide for publicity of commendable school work.
- To promote good dress and neat appearance.
- To look after school bulletins.
- To collect material for school museum.
- To supervise ventilation.
- To discourage smoking.
- To discourage seeing bad pictures.
- To look after the school garden.
- To promote good habits.
- To arrange medical aid for the needy.
- To assist health and police authorities.
- To organise health social service at various occasions.
- To assist in community-fund drives.

- To organise school functions.
- To organise literacy campaigns.
- To budget its finances.
- To conduct campaigns to improve school spirit.
- To plan and promote a "better manners campaign".
- To visit other schools to gain new ideas.
- To take school government for a day.
- To design student awards and emblems.
- To run campaigns for new cheers, songs for school.
- To act as coaches.
- To act as tutors.

The Importance

The Secondary Education Commission observes, "Nothing is more calculated to develop a proper sense of self-discipline, and proper behaviour than their enforcement not by any outside authority with any symbol of punishment but by the students themselves. They should choose their own representatives to see it that proper codes of conduct are observed, both for the sake of the individuals and for the good name of the school. It is from this point of view that we commend what is known as the house system in schools, with prefects or monitors or Student Councils, whose responsibility will be to draw up a code of conduct and to enforce its observance in the school."

The Report of the "Workshoppers' seminar" held at Delhi in 1955 observes : "Student participation in the government of the school is an effective method of citizenship training and is a means of keeping the energies of the pupils canalised for useful purposes in the development of a wholesome personality through a definite, constructive, well-planned programme". The Report of the Secondary Education Workshop held at Hyderabad in April-May 1955 states that the student government gives, "opportunities to pupils to learn the skill in electing leaders and of conducting their deliberations on democratic lines, thereby giving ample scope for self-expression, evaluation and judgement."

Principles Underlying Student Council Organisation: H.C. McKnown has given the following principles:

1. The school must feel a continuous need for the council.
2. Participation should be introduced gradually.
3. A study of objectives should precede any attempt at definite organisation.
4. The council should represent the school as a whole.
5. The average student should feel that he is represented.
6. Both student body and faculty should be fairly represented.
7. The council should not be too large.
8. The council should have definite powers and duties.
9. The council should not be considered a dumping ground.
10. The head of the school should retain veto power.
11. The work of the council should be continuously evaluated.
12. Each member of the council should assume some specific responsibility.
13. Each committee should be held strictly accountable for its particular responsibility.
14. Officers and committee chairman should receive specialised training.
15. The cooperative aspects of participation should continuously be emphasised.
16. Council meetings should be held regularly and on school time.
17. The council should give continuous publicity to its ideals, activities and problems.

The Problems

1. The members of the staff and the head are hesitant to part with power. They think that their prestige is in danger when students share powers with them.
2. The students are immature and lack power of independent and critical thinking.
3. Good students sometimes are reluctant to hold office as they think that this will have an adverse effect on their studies.

4. Many a time it is seen that the students fail to elect their representatives who can handle various offices satisfactorily. This leads to constant troubles between the students and the educational authorities and the standard of education deteriorates.
5. The politicians try to use students' council as a tool to further their ends and this discourages the educational authorities to allow the formation of students' unions in educational institutions.
6. The elections of the students' council create bad blood among the students themselves. Not unfrequently they come to blows.
7. The students' council can function effectively under ideal conditions. At a time when most of our schools are ill-equipped and under-staffed it will not be advisable to introduce such councils.

Teaching at Home

In National Education Policy 1986, it is stated – 'life long education is a cherished goal of the educational process. This presupposes universal literacy, opportunities will be provided to youth, housewives, agricultural and industrial workers and professionals to continue the education of their choice, at the pace suited to them. The future thrust will be in the direction of open and distance learning.' This statement reflects over the new thinking regarding the universalisation of education. Life long education and its conceptual framework is now old enough.

The system of education in India has a great historical and cultural heritage. It has been changed from time to time because of the socio-economic and cultural pressures. Many branches of knowledge and culture were the contribution of lust for it, but the concept and need of mass education and democratisation of education have a recent origin. These changes are effected by historical necessity.

Since the age of Vedas, there was learner motivation. Those who were interested to learn, approached the Guru and stayed with him in his Gurukul for few years. There actual instructions were given and the skills were developed. This type of learner-motivation was also found in Buddha Period. During this period, education was institutionalised. Nalanda, Taxshila, Vikramshila and so many others were the universities where the learners from all walks of life used to come for study.

During Muslim period, there were Pathshalas for Hindus and Madrasas for Muslims. In Madrasas Hindus, who were desirous to serve the Emperors and nawabs, also secured their education. The system, recognised by the state was Perso-Arabic. Upward mobility was the aim of this system.

During British period, English system of Education was introduced. Learners from families with some educational background thronged the schools which were situated in towns. The purpose of education in British period was to prepare persons who might be helpful to run the administration.

Dr. Radhakrishnan Commission says in its report that education must be universalised and equal opportunities for all be given. Each and every citizen be given education irrespective of his caste or creed, social or economic status, motivation or aptitude.

Development and Growth

Distance education is a world wide phenomenon. In Africa, Distance education was spread over to train teachers and to educate the masses. Countries like Nigeria, Kenya, Tanzania, Guyana, Ethiopia and Ghana offer distance education courses. Print and electronic media and personal contact programmes are the primary means used to impart knowledge and skills.

In North, South and Central America, the following forms are found: i) application and professionally oriented courses are being offered, and ii) print and electronic media play an important role in disseminating information, knowledge and skills.

In Asia, countries like India, Pakistan, Thailand, Sri Lanka, Philippines, China, South Korea, Indonesia and Japan adopted Distance education system and courses are based mainly on print materials which are supplemented by electronic media and contact programme.

In Australia, the university level courses are based on an integrated model-New Zealand, Papua New Guinea and Pacific Islands promote distance education in a big way.

Actual Situation

About 25 years ago, correspondence education in India was started as a pilot project in the University of Delhi. The success of this experiment encouraged other universities to take up instructions through the distance education. By 1985, 31 universities adopted this scheme. About 40,000 students at various levels were enrolled by the universities under this scheme. Though the universities are providing education through this media, but there was a great demand for an open university. As a result in 1985, the Govt. of India decided to set up Indira Gandhi National Open University. The focal points of this university are as under:

1. To promote open university and distance education system.
2. To determine the standards of teaching evaluation and research in such system.
3. To allocate and disburse grants to colleges, whether admitted to its privileges or not, or to any other university or institution of higher learning as may be specified by the Statutes.

Indira Gandhi National Open University is providing Degrees in B.A., B.Sc. and B. Com., Diploma Courses in Distance education, Creative writing, Nutrition, Management, Local Self Government, Library Science, Banking, etc.

Separate Radio and TV channels have been started to broadcast and telecast the educational programmes.

As a measure for implementation, the programme of action has also favoured and recommended Open Universities System to provide higher education through non-formal channel. The main suggestions and recommendation of this Action Programme are given as under:

1. Action Programme suggested the Open University System. This should be cost-effective, flexible and innovative.
2. Indira Gandhi National Open University has been established and is running effectively.
3. Non-formal education system should be structured on modular pattern.
4. Minimum level of learning should be objectively assessed.

5. Separate Radio and Television channels be used for the use of distance education.
6. Network of course be framed.
7. Quality of programmes be ensured.
8. Financial Assistance will be ensured very carefully.

Advantages: Distance Education is a very continuing education. Rather to say it is an effective media of life long education. National Education Policy of Education (1986) has rightly explained the life-long education. It is a cherished goal of educational process. This presupposes universal literacy. Opportunities will be provided to the youth, housewives, agricultural and industrial workers and professionals to continue the education of their choice, at the pace suited to them. The future thrust will be in the direction of open and distance learning.'

National Education Policy 1986 has rightly stressed that distance education will provide many opportunities for education and will lessen the burden of formal education.. The advantages of Distance Education are as under-

Reliable: Distance education is reliable. It has the cost-effective alternative and new means of communication.

Education at Learners, Door: Distance education is the only way which provides the education to the learner at his door. It provides equal educational opportunities even to those who used to live in remote areas.

Beneficial to Adults: Distance education provides many benefits to adults. They may update themselves for the development of skills and-knowledge.

Variety of Programme: Distance education provides variety programmes according to the needs of the learners.

Coordination: Distance education is the coordination of various educational factors, i.e., general, basic, professional, technical, life-long, in service and expansion.

Minimising Pressures: Distance education minimises the educational pressures caused by the explosion of population.

Educational Needs: Distance education fulfils the need of society through variety of educational programmes.

Learner Centred: Distance education is learner-centred, therefore, there is no doubt in its success.

Freedom: This system provides freedom to learner. A learner, learns according to his needs, conditions and facility.

Lust for Knowledge: Distance education provides the opportunities to gain knowledge to those who are really thirsty for it.

Distance education is still in an experimental stage. Even then nobody will disagree that this system will be helpful to solve our educational problems and minimise the pressure of population over the traditional system of education.

Education from Distance

Peter says, 'Distance education is a method of indirect instruction, implying geographical and emotional separation of teacher and taught whereas, in mainstream education, the relationship between a teacher and student in class room is based upon social norms, in distance education, it is based upon technological rules.' Jack Foks stated about Distance education: 'Distance education is a mode of learning with certain characteristics which distinguish it from the campus based mode of learning.'

These definitions explain the system of education through which one gets education but he maintains a distance; what is that distance? Regarding this some studies have been done. We are mentioning them.

Autonomy of Learner: Wedemeyer expresses Distance education as an independent study, open learning and distance education. The three terms expressed the following meanings:-

Independent Study → Correspondence Courses.

Open Education → Open University.

Distance Education → Correspondence Education.

Wedemeyer has outlined this idea about 'Independent study' and its purpose.

1. It consists of teaching/learning arrangements, and these arrangements have various forms. The special feature of

these arrangements, is that, the teachers and learners stay away from each other and didatic communication takes place in various ways.

2. Its purpose are to facilitate learning activities of both the on campus and the off campus students.

Distance between Learner and the Teacher: The learner has to learn apart from the teacher. There is a vast difference between traditional classroom learning and learning with distance. The innovations in education and technology have given a different way of learning as well as teaching. Writing made possible to record communication and transfer them over space and time. Printing broke down the monopoly of a single copy writing, telecommunication collapsed the dimensions of space and time, democratic philosophy broke down the monopoly of elites. Correspondence education was the result of needs and pressures. The development of programmed learning and teaching machines pointed to the possibility of self instruction and learner based education.

Structural System: The structural system is based on the institutional philosophy of the society. In one, society, there are many socio-economic and cultural changes which effect the structure and motivate the aspirations of the people. Therefore non-contiguous educational communication is suggested. It means that main characteristic of distance study means that the learner is phycically at a long distance from the teacher for much, most or even all of the time during the teaching learning process.

Moore's Motion or Independent Study: Michael Moore expressed his views in his work 'Teaching at a Distance' about Distance Education. Distance and Autonomy are the two variables of this programme. There are three phenomenon of it: i) Dialogues, ii) Individualisation, and iii) Structure. Dialogue means the face to face communication. Individualisation refers to curricular components — objective, methods, material, and evaluation. Structure means that the process of instruction be maintained.

Function of Dialogue and Individualisation: In Distance education these are as follows:-

1. Programmes with no dialogue but with structure, i.e., radio, television and audio, audio-video programmes.

2. Programmes with no dialogue and no structure, i.e., independent reading or self directed study.
3. Programmes with dialogues and structure, i.e., correspondence method.
4. Programmes with dialogue and no structure-a tutorial programme.

Learner Autonomy: The concept has an autonomy in learning and teaching. In an educational programme there must be the autonomy of objectives, methods, materials and evaluation, and these must be decided by the institute and the teacher.

Basic Rules

Philosophy of Distance Education generates the idea that each individual has the right to gain education and to crop with the development of knowledge and skill. Distance education has the idea of life long education. The age, time and place has no significant value for this programme. This is meant for adults who have left schools or traditional system of education and are busy for their livelihood. Therefore, the process of communication is more important. Use of the means of communication for educating the individual sitting on a long distance, i.e., another city, District or province, Print media, Programmed instruction and Postal Service are the basis of the Distance education. Distance education accommodates the term correspondence education.

Teacher and Morality

An important feature of value-education is the ability of the educator and the education skill to discriminate between right and wrong. What may be nectar for one may be poison for another. We may be clearing forests to build human habitats, which is a laudable objective, but in the process we may be depriving animals of their natural shelter and food and humanity of many environmental benefits.

In many Indian communities, a wedlock between a girl and a boy may not be permissible unless the two are removed from each other by a gap of some generations; whereas among some, marriage between cousins may be auspicious. A debate on the subject can go ad infinitum without coming to any precise conclusion; but as pointed out earlier every community has its own written as well as unwritten behavioural norms which it expects its members to observe.

In order to decide if the educational institutions should play some part in the dissemination of these accepted norms, the following statement was included in the questionnaire for students:

> "Value-education, i.e., education regarding discrimination between what is right or wrong, should be impacted in schools and colleges." (S-1)

The reaction of the five categories of students, constituting the total student-population of 267 was as follows:

Value-Education

a S. No.	*b* Category. Agreeing.	*c* Number Undecided.	*d* Number Disagreed.	*e* Number persons who expressed no opinion
(1)	Total no. of student respondents (267)	254 (95.2)	6 (2.2)	61 (2.2)
(2)	School students (Male) (70)	68 (97.2)	1 (1.4)	1 (1.4)
(3)	School Students (Female) (86)	(97.6)	84 (1.2)	I (1.2)
(4)	College Students (M)* (34)	27 (79.6)	4 (11.8)	3 (8.8)
(5)	African College students (M)* studying in the Delhi Colleges. (7)	7 (100)	3 –	4 –
(6)	Indian College students (F)* (70)	68 (97.2)	– –	11 (1.4)

(i) Abbreviations M and F stand for Male and Female respectively throughout this work.

(ii) The following norms has been adopted in this study for categorisation of scores:

Below 26% Poor 50% Average 51-74% Above Average
26-49% Below Average Above 74% High

It is thus observed that every category of students expressed high degree of agreement for making a provision of value education in the educational institutions. Speaking in comparative terms, more of college students (males) expressed their disagreement with the statement or were undecided in this regard.

Therefore, if one were to work for a programme of moral or value-education in our educational institutions, one is likely to come across a receptive rather than an indifferent audience, provided the programme is give. ue importance in the curricula and the teacher imparting value-education is capable of doing justice to the job.

The following news-item appearing in one of the national dailies in India shows that there is a worldwide demand for imparting moral education to the students.

"The (UK) Government is to direct its latest attack on violence, disorder and crime at children as young as seven". In a Cabinet meeting it was felt that 'the roots of criminality' must be tackled early and that "moral dimension will be added to the new national curriculum".

Sometime earlier to it in the economic summit in Toronto (Canada), Mrs. Thatcher, the British Prime Minister had raised her concern on the behavioural problems of the young people. She said that although western nations had gone a long way to bring about a technological change, they had to do much in terms of training people to have respect for the law. The Government (of UK) had proposed preparing experimental lessons for the youth with this objective in view.

For example, in such lessons the school going youth may be told about a young man who drinks, steals a car, becomes a hit-and-run driver and ultimately one day lands in the custody of the police. The lesson may depict the consequence (jail, etc.) to be faced by the delinquent youth, misery of the family whose members had been hit by this criminal and also the misery of the criminal's own family because of his unlawful act. For this purpose parents, teachers and media have to unite. Teachers cannot provide lessons which are the responsibility of the parents.

Resembling the above statement (S-1) in the questionnaire for students, there was a statement (G-13) in the questionnaire for the general public. The statement was as follows:

Moral education, i.e., education regarding what is right or wrong should be imparted:

1. In schools,
2. In colleges, and
3. Through mass media such as radio, TV, newspapers, etc. (G-13).

Number of persons who agreed, disagreed with the above, three parts of the statement or were Undecided in this regard was as follows:

Moral Education

a S.No.	*b* Category	*c* No. Agreeing	*d* No. Undecided.	*e* No. Disagreeing.	*f* No. of persons who expressed no opinion
(a) In schools	Total no. of respondents (881)	717 (81.6)	136 (15.5)	16 (1.8)	10 (1.1)
(b) In colleges	Total no. of respondents (881)	510 (57.9)	315 (35.8)	43 (4.9)	13 (1.4)
(c) Through mass media	-do-	655 (74.4)	194 (22)	16 (18)	16 (1.8)

The above statistics show that the elements of disagreement and indecision are comparatively higher in the case of part (b) of the statement. Also the largest number of the respondents appeared to be of the opinion that moral education should be imparted in schools.

Parts (a), (b) and (c) of the statement were further analysed with reference to age, educational qualifications and income of the respondents. Some of the results obtained were as follows:

Analysis with Reference to Ages of the Respondents

a S.No.	*b* Category of Respondents	*c* No. Agreeing	*d* No. Undecided	*e* No. Disagreeing	*f* No. of Persons who expressed no opinion.
1.	Below 18 years (11)	9 (81.9)	2 (18.2)	–	–
2.	18-25 years (52)	37 (71.2)	15 (28.8)	– –	– –
3.	25-40 years (234)	191 (81.6)	38 (16.2)	2 (0.9)	3 (1.3)
4.	Above 40 years (574)	474 (82.6)	79 (13.8)	14 (2.4)	7 (1.2)
5.	Those who did not indicate their ages (10)	8 (80)	2 (20)	–	–

Analysis with Reference to Educational Qualifications of the Respondents

S.No.	*Category of Respondents*	*Number Agreeing.*	*Number Undecided*	*Number Disagreeing*	*Number of persons who expressed no opinion.*
a	*b*	*c*	*d*	*e*	*f*
(1)	Below High school (15)	6 (40)	7 (46.7)	2 (13.3)	– –
(2)	High school or equivalent (123)	66 (53.7)	50 (40.6)	5 (4.1)	2 (1.6)
(3)	B.A. or equivalent (267)	157 (58.8)	96 (35.9)	13 (4.9)	1 (0.4)
(4)	M.A. or above or equivalent (464)	274 (59.0)	157 (33.8)	23 (5)	10 (2.2)
(5)	Those who did not indicate their educational qualifications (12)	7 (58.3)	5 (41.7)	– –	–

Analysis with Reference to Monthly Income of the Respondents

a	*b*	*c*	*d*	*e*	*f*
(1)	Below Rs 1000 (28)	16 (57.1)	11 (39.3)	- -	1 (3.6)
(2)	Rs.1000-1999 (98)	68 (69.4)	27 (27.5)	1 (1)	2 (2)
(3)	Rs. 2000-3999 (334)	246 (73.6)	75 (22.5)	10 (3)	3 (0.9)
(4)	Rs. 4000 or above (407)	318 (78.1)	74 (18.2)	5 (1.2)	10 (2.5)
(5)	Those who did not indicate their income (14)	7 7 (50)	7 7 (50)	– –	– –

The analysis in the case of the statement 13(a) indicates that in comparison to the remaining age-groups of the respondents, those between 18-25 years of age expressed lesser degree of agreement (of 71.2%) with this statement. The remaining 28.8 per cent of the respondents in this group were undecided.

Analysis of the reactions of the respondents on the basis of their educational qualifications revealed that quite a large number of respondents in every group, subgroup seemed to be undecided on the issue whether moral education programme should be introduced at the college stage. The reasons for this must be as follows:

1. Higher education is a stage of specialisation in one or the other discipline, therefore general education in morals was not supported by any subgroup as was done in the case of the school stage.
2. The college students are mature enough to decide for themselves as to what is right and what is wrong.

It would be interesting here to study the attitude of male and female college teachers to the same statement, *i.e.* 13(b).

a S.No.	*b* Category of college teachers	*c* Number Agreeing	*d* Number Undecided	*e* Number Disagreed.	*f* Number of persons who did not express any opinion.
1.	Female (39)	25 (64,1)	11 (28.2)	2 (5.1)	1 (2.6)
2.	Male (50)	37 (74)	10 (20)	1 (2)	2 (4)

The degree of support expressed in case of statement that moral education should be imparted in colleges is considerably more both by female and male college-teachers than the overall support given by the general group. College students themselves (of both sexes) also expressed considerable support to the idea of providing moral education in our educational institutions while reacting to statement S-1.

In the case of statement 13(c), maximum agreement was expressed by the income-group having a monthly income of Rs 4000 and above. Starting with this, as we come to the sub-groups with lower monthly incomes, the degree of agreement to this statement successively decreases. May be that the people with higher incomes have a better appreciation of the role of mass-media on account of their greater exposure to these media.

It would be desirable to briefly mention here some basic factors which influence our thought and behaviour pattern.

1. *Samskaras or Natural Tendencies:* Every person is born with certain propensities, likes and dislikes, potentialities – inherited or otherwise. The ancient thinkers of India called them samskaras or impressions accumulated by an individual spirit in its previous births. All this is called individual's inherent nature which differs from person to person. The nature of an individual plays an important role in determining his or her behaviour.
2. *Education and Environment:* It may be difficult to say if an individual's nature or his nurture plays a greater role in shaping the individual's conduct; but it goes without saying that nurture in the form of education and environmental influences have a significant impact in shaping the character of a person.
3. *Free Will:* Every individual is endowed with a 'free-will'. By exercising his free-will an individual becomes the architect of his own destiny.

Every individual, when he enters this world, brings with him a set of samskaras – impressions, tendencies, and attitudes. As he goes through his life, by the process of education and interaction with various situations in the social milieu, he acquires new samskaras and his old samaskaras get modified. With the judicious application of one's free-will, every individual raises the behavioural edifice of one's life and becomes the architect of his own future.

History of education reveals that in ancient times, say upto the 6th century AD, many countries laid considerable emphasis on character-training of the young children. In India, religion emphasised ethical conduct, art, literature, jurisprudence, etc. In Rome, cultivating respect for traditions, austerity and frugality was an important function of education. Character-training was a salient feature of the Mauryan education. Chinese regarded moulding of character a prime concern of education. Zoroastrians, in ancient Persia, attached considerable importance to training the young in practices of good thoughts, good words and good actions. Byzantine system of education went even to the extent of mostly confining itself to religious instruction to students and encouraging among them ascetic practices and thus developing in them an attitude of indifference towards secular subjects.

Athens, the cultural centre of ancient Greece, was known for the stress it laid on moral training of the youth and cultivating good conduct and grace in them. Sparta in Greece, besides training the youth (from the age of seven) in physical culture, taught them the art of lying and theft, etc., as these were some of the values with the Spartans. Spartan morality, however, demanded that this kind of Machiavallianism was to be practised only while dealing with the foreigners.

During the medieval India, when there was Islamic rule in the country, maktabs, i.e. institutions of early education taught the students to say their daily prayers as indicated in the Holy Quran. In the institutions of higher learning, i.e. madrasas, Hadith was taught. A number of denominational schools in India still teach students religious practices of their respective faiths. Bible discourse is still compulsory in the schools of England. In Russia after the great Revolution character was attempted to be moulded through the teachings of communism:

Educational Institutions: Educational institutions constitute the biggest organised sector for imparting various kinds of training, including moral training, to the growing youths. As regards the stage at which moral education programme should begin in the educational institutions, Meriel Downey says:

> "It (moral development) is an area to which no pupil owes 'cold', since moral learning, the development of values and attitudes begins at birth and is fed from many sources. For this reason, it is not something that

can be delayed, like, say, the learning of Latin, until we feel that pupils have readied an appropriate stage of mental development to cope with the demands which it will make upon their intellectual abilities".

A number of people are of the view that moral education, in the school system, should begin from the pre-primary stage so that students develop proper samskaras and attitudes from the early years of their lives.

Official Documents: It would be relevant to study the views of various commissions and committees on the subject of moral education

(a) Pre-independence Period

(i) The Education Commission of 1882 had recommended that, based upon the fundamental principles of natural religion, an attempt be made to prepare a text book on moral education. This book should be taught in all Government and non-Government colleges. The principal or one of the professors in each Government and aided colleges should deliver a series of lectures to all the classes on the duties of a man and a citizen.

The Government, however, rejected the proposal by its Resolution No.10/309 of October 2, 1884.

(ii) Thereafter a significant recommendation in this regard was made in the Memorandum of the Post-War Educational Development (1944). The recommendation runs as follows: "Religion in the widest sense, should inspire all education and that a curriculum devoid of an ethical basis will prove barren in the end".

(iii) The Religious Education Committee of the Central Advisory Board of Education (CABE) recommended in 1945, "Spiritual and moral teachings common to all religions should be an integral part of the curriculum and provision/facilities for instructions therein should be the responsibility of the State."

(b) Post-independence Period

(i) The 42nd Constitutional Amendment of 1976, inserted as Article 51A in Part IVA of the Indian Constitution lays down ten Fundamental Duties (or values) for each citizen. This amendment was inspired by the idea of arresting the falling moral standards in the country and that of ensuring higher level of moral conduct from the citizens.

(ii) The University Education Commission (1948-49) recommended that: "unless morality is taken in a larger sense, it is not enough. If we exclude spiritual training in our institutions we would be untrue to our whole historical development".

(iii) The Secondary Education Commission (1952-53) asserted that 'religious and moral instruction played an important role in the growth of individual's character.

(iv) Sri Prakasa Committee on Religious and Moral Instruction (1959) held the view that:

"Many ills that our world of education and our society as a whole is suffering from, resulting in widespread disturbance and dislocation of life, are mainly due to gradual disappearance of the hold of basic principles of religion on the hearts of the people — The only cure, it seems to us, is in deliberate inculcation of moral and spiritual values from the earliest years of our lives."

(v) The subject was also dealt with by the Indian Education Commission (1964-66), which recommended that:

"Conscious and organised attempts be made for imparting education in social, moral and spiritual values with the help, wherever possible, of ethical teachings of great religions".

(vi) Challenge of Education (1985), published by the Union Ministry of Education, summed up the position in this regard as follows:

"Thoughtful people in all walks of life are greatly disturbed by a progressive erosion of values and the resultant pollution of public life. The fact that this crisis of values is as pervasive in schools, colleges and universities, amongst teachers as well as students as in other walks of life, is seen as a highly dangerous development. It is, therefore, being urged that the process of education should be reoriented and young people should be made to realise that exploitation, insecurity and violence cannot be contained nor can an organised society be sustained without adhering to and enforcing some norms of social, political and economic behaviour. Learning from past experience, it is expected that a coherent and an operationally viable value-system would be inculcated through educational process, based upon rational and scientific and moral approach to life".

(vii) The Document on Approach to the Seventh Five Year Plan (1985-90) published in July 1984, states, " Value-orientation in education should constitute a special thrust in the Seventh Plan, teacher-education in particular-being reoriented for this purpose".

Various Approaches

1. At the boyhood stage, individual's physical propensities have a full play; during manhood and old-age intellectual and spiritual values start dominating the corporeal values. Therefore, while imparting moral education, educators must keep this fact in view and no attempt be made to burden the students with intellectual exercises in moral education during early years of their lives.

2. Value-perspective may be two-dimensional or three dimensional. A two-dimensional view is caring for oneself as well as for the other because both need each other and any transgression of values may harm both sides. USA and USSR had been very unfriendly till the eighties of this century; but both have respected each other's sovereignty because either of these countries could destroy the other with the pile of destructive weapons it possessed. This kind of need and reciprocity-based value-system would be followed by many people. When the value system is ideal-based as well, it becomes a three-dimensional value system. The three dimensional value-system can be followed over a long period of time by a few persons only.

3. The Education Commission (1964-66) suggested that social, moral and spiritual values should be imparted both through indirect and direct methods. The Commission remarked, "We attach great importance to the role of indirect influence

in building up good character. The school atmosphere, the personality and behaviour of the teachers, the facilities provided in the school, will have a large say in developing a sense of values. We would like to emphasise that the consciousness of values must permeate the whole curriculum and programme of activities in the school. It is not only the teachers incharge of moral instruction who are responsible for building character. Every teacher, whatever be the subject he teaches, must necessarily accept this responsibility. The school assembly, the curricular and co-curricular activities, the celebration of religious festivals of all religions, work-experience, team games and sports,, subject clubs, social service programmes — all these can help in inculcating the values of cooperation and mutual regard, honesty and integrity, discipline and social responsibility. These values have a special significance in Indian society today, when young men and women are passing through a crisis of character,"

In regard to direct moral instruction, agreeing with the recommendations of the Sri Prakasa Committee, the Commission stated that " one or two periods a week should be set aside in the school time-table for instruction in moral and spiritual values".

At the early school-stages, moral instruction can be imparted through parables or stones which have an appeal to the emotions of the children. At the secondary stage, there can be discussions between the teacher and the taught on the values to be imparted, thus resorting to an intellectual approach to the subject. According to V.K.R.V. Rao, one time Union Education Minister, "Ethics should be taught only through parables, stories, religion, and sayings of great people and their lives. Right from the start, children should be taught about the founders of great religions of India. Films should be shown to them depicting temples, mosques, gurudwaras, etc."

4. In ancient times, some states imparted moral education through edicts or some other forms of permanent writings. For example, the Romans expected the children to learn by

heart the Twelve Tables of laws. The Japanese employed the imperial edicts for this purpose. One example of the edict is given below.

Knowledge of the Subject

"Our imperial ancestors have founded our Empire on a basis broad and everlasting and have deeply and firmly implanted virtue; our subjects, ever united in loyalty and filial piety, have from generation to generation illustrated the beauty thereof. This is the glory and the fundamental character of our Empire, and herein also lies the source of our education. Ye, our subjects, be filial to your parents, affectionate to your brothers and sisters; as husbands and wives be harmonious; as friends true; bear yourselves in modesty and moderation; extend your benevolence to all; pursue learning and cultivate arts, and thereby develop intellectual faculties and perfect moral powers; furthermore, advance public good and promote common interests; always respect the Constitution and observe the laws; should emergency arise, offer yourselves courageously to the state; and thus guard and maintain the prosperity of our imperial throne. So shall ye not only be our good and faithful subjects, but render illustrious the best traditions of your forefathers."

5. In the teaching of moral practices, both theory and practice are of equal significance, because cognition, feelings and action are interdependent. The quality and depth of information and its sources - all play an important role in influencing our attitudes. Without a proper conceptual background, all action may be reduced to a blind ritual only. However, translation of information into proper action is of great importance, because simple parroting of Ten Commandments cannot make a Moses of an individual. Emphasising the superiority of example over precept, N.K. Dutt says:

"Albert Camus once experimented with inculcation of moral values through teaching. He encouraged students to write an essay on 'Truthfulness'. The best essay was written by the biggest liar of the class. He further said that if the purpose of education is merely to impart information and skills, then thanks to the present day teaching technology, perhaps an idiot can teach another idiot calculus."

The same remarks apply to speech-making also. A person may play a big hoax on the people by play of words and thus claim to be a big preacher of values whereas his own actions may be just the opposite of what he might say.

N.K. Dutt adds that according to Mao-Tse-Tung, "The thoughts of intellectuals are like arrows in a quiver which scratch the back but never fly".

6. Value orientation is a continuous process. As man evolves intellectually and otherwise, his expectations also get modified. This is true in regard to values also. Society's expectations rise in respect of moral values also, therefore imparting of value-education and adjustment to values should be a continuous process.

Role of Mass-Media: Apart from the educational institutions mass media, i.e. media which has the potential to transmit messages to the masses at large, can play a far-reaching role in any scheme of imparting value education - formal, non-formal or informal. Some of these media are privately owned and independent of the government whereas others are directly under the government machinery. Although some government departments bring out various kinds of journals, etc., but by and large press and publications in India are free of government control. Some of the mass media under the Union Government are television, radio, Department of Field Publicity, Publication Division, Department of Advertising and Visual Publicity and Song and Drama Division. Though there is a Films Division under the Union Ministry of Information and Broadcasting, it produces documentaries only. Feature-films production is totally in the private sector and this medium is very powerful in influencing the attitudes of the people.

One may, of course, argue that in India mass-media has not been the mass media in the real sense – some of the reasons for this being as follows:

According to 1981 census, India had nearly 140 million families and only 25 million radios and one million TV sets. If TV sets are possessed by the same 25 million who own the radio sets, the reach of these two media is only to 17.9 per cent population and if the TV sets are considered to have been owned by some who own the radio sets and some who do not own the radio set, even then the reach of these two media is to a maximum population of 18.6 per cent of the country's population. The total circulation of newspapers and journals in India is around ten million which comes to less than 1.5 for every hundred people.

As nearly half the population in the country is still illiterate, the newspapers and journals have a limited impact on the education of the masses. One may agree that the mass media are not able to reach the vast masses of India inhabiting the length and breadth of the country, yet they have, admittedly a great potential of wielding a considerable influence on human minds, therefore these media can be gainfully employed in the moral education programme.

It is, thus, observed that there is a general consensus that moral education should be imparted in our educational institutions as well as through the mass-media. Various commissions and committees on education have been stressing the need for social, moral and spiritual education programme being introduced in our educational institutions. Any programme of value-education must take into account the age and other factors of the target population. The programme, in order to be useful, should lay equal emphasis on precept and practice.

The character of the teacher or any other person imparting moral education is of greater significance than his precepts as actions always speak louder than the words and the totality of the educator's personality is far more important than his utterances, howsoever loud and pious these might be. Mass media, which have a deep and powerful influence on human minds, should also devise a well-planned programme in respect of moral education and thus contribute to resolving the present crisis of character in the society.

System of Values

Article 51A of the Constitution (Fortysecond Amendment) Act, 1976, lays down the following Fundamental Duties. These may be termed as a value-system which the government expects every citizen of India to observe faithfully.

"Article 51A: It shall be the duty of every citizen of India –

1. To abide by the Constitution and respect its ideals and institutions, the National Flag and the National Anthem;
2. To cherish and follow the noble ideals which inspired our national struggle for freedom;
3. To uphold and protect the sovereignty, unity and integrity of India;
4. To defend the country and render national service when called upon to do so;
5. To promote the spirit of common brotherhood amongst all the people of India transcending religious, linguistic and regional or sectional diversities; to renounce practices derogatory to the dignity of women;
6. To value and preserve the rich heritage of our composite culture;
7. To protect and improve the natural environment including forests, lakes, rivers and wild life, and to have compassion for living creatures;
8. To develop the scientific temper, humanism, and the spirit of enquiry and reform;
9. To safeguard public property and to abjure violence;
10. To strive towards excellence in all spheres of individual and collective activity so that the nation constantly rises to higher levels of endeavour and achievement.

Based on the study of the Gandhian literature and reports given by committees and commissions on social, moral and spiritual values in education, the National Council of Educational Research and Training, New Delhi compiled an exhaustive list of 84 values given in the Appendix to the questionnaire.

It is difficult to make comparison of the moral standards between societies. Laws, rules, customs, opinions vary from society to society, from individual to individual and from time to time. Moral relativism is an eternal phenomenon.

Relative Factors: According to ardent Indian scriptures, there are seven seminal concepts of values. These are rta (cosmic order); Verna (class); ashrama dharma (duties for different stages of life); law of karma (moral causation); samsara (transmigration); shames (harmlessness); and moksha (liberation).

Indians have the unique distinction of producing and practising philosophical and ethical thought from very early days. "Unlike ethical teachings of ancient Egypt and Babylon, Indian ethics was philosophical in the start. In the oldest Indian writings, the Vedas, ethics is an integral part of philosophical and religious speculation about the nature of reality. These writings date from about 1500 BC. They have been described as the oldest philosophical literature in the world, and what they say about how people ought to live may therefore be the first philosophical ethics." Ancient Chinese regarded filial piety, reverence for the superiors, love of the past and exercising moderation as cardinal virtues.

The ethical ideals of ardent Greeks were not influenced by theological considerations. They were more concerned with the duties of an individual as a member of the city-state. Christian-values like humility, meekness, gentleness, compassion and renunciation of the world were held in dewesteem by the Greeks as well as the Romans who were more inclined towards materialistic ideals.

Moral Standards: Anthromorphic man today presents a picture of a mechanomorphic man. There is a general feeling that the industrial man has gone far ahead of the moral man, hence, the present crisis in all our walks of, life. On the contrary, people like Myers hold. In no domain has progress been greater, the gains larger or more precious, than in the moral domain. From clan morality, based on physical kinship, mankind has advanced or is advancing to world morality, based on ethical kinship of man. There appears not only a new physical but also a new moral man. 88 per cent of the respondents to statement G-1 of the questionnaire felt that moral values among Indians have declined over the past 5-10 years. To a similar statement (S-4) that "Majority of Indians are selfish and lack dedication of ideals", students reacted as follows:

Significance of Ideals

Sl.No.	*Category of Respondents*	*Number Agreeing*	*No. Undecided*	*Number Disagreed*
1.	Total Population of students (267)	140 (52.5)	42 (15.7)	85 (31,8)
2.	School students (M) (7)	38 (54.3)	13 (18.6)	19 (27.1)
3.	School students (F) (86)	51 (59.3)	15 (17.4)	20 (23.3)
4.	College students (M) (34)	16 (47.1)	5 (14.7)	13 (38.2)
5.	African College students (M) (7)	3 (42.9)	1 (14.2)	3 (42.9)
6.	College students (F) (70)	32 (45.7)	8 (11.4)	30 (42.9)

Diversity of views on the subject notwithstanding, the nation, in general, feels that there is urgent need for elevation of moral standards in the country.

Significance of Behaviour: For planning any programme of moral uplift, it is necessary to delineate the factors which influence human behaviour. Broadly speaking, some of the important determinants of man's behaviour are as follows:

(i) *Religion and Science:* According to religious people, most of our ills arise from inside ourselves; from desire, pride, lust, etc. For others, the ills come from external agents like poverty and natural disasters, etc., and that we can overcome these external forces through technology and industrialisation. There is no denying the fact that both mora health and material-progress are necessary for mankind's balanced progress.

Science seemed to hold that religion was irrelevant and it was a creation of man's childish ignorance. Having achieved considerable success in science and technology, Europe, today, seems to be turning to East for discovering its spirit. And, surprisingly, Orient is getting lured by material progress of the west!

(ii) *Nature, Nurture and Free Will·* In cold regions, where struggle for existence is hard, life is lived n... ... he physical plane. That is why cultural growth is comparatively slower there and faster in warm, temperate and fertile regions. This also explains why the story of all conquests is the story of more civilised nations getting conquered by less civilised nations and thereafter the victorious being absorbed by their victims .

The biological or the social environment is also important. Man has considerable influence on another man. The cultural influence of India over East and South East-Asia and that of Egypt on the West are testimony to this fact. The art of coining money and building temples in India is considered to have Greek influence. Conversely, Buddhism influenced the Gnostic Greek sects. "Numerous drugs of Indian origin are noticed by the Greeks – A variety of treatises on medical science were translated from Sanskrit into Arabic and Persian – The Saracens introduced the Indian method of Arithmetic and the Indian Algebra and Geometry into Europe."

It does not carry conviction that human beings perform their role in this world only at the bidding of fate or some providential force. The inherited genes, and according to Hinduism, the Samaskaras of previous life-cycle, no doubt influence our behaviour pattern, but the claim of nurture in human development cannot be undermined. The environmentalist, J.B. Watson, said in 1920, "Give me a dozen healthy infants, well formed, and my own specified world to bring them up in, and I will guarantee to take any one at random and train him to become any kind of specialist. I might select doctor, lawyer, artist, merchant; and, yes, even beggarman and thief -regardless of talent, penchant, tendencies, abilities, location, and race of his ancestors."

According to Toynbee heredity and environment alone can not explain all behaviour patterns. He says, "I part company with the behaviourists over their belief that behaviour is wholly and exclusively determined by heredity and environment. According to him, self-determination (or free-will as the Hindu scripture Gita puts it), has a good claim to be considered as one of the important determinants of human behaviour.

(iii) *Materialism:* Economic pulls, today, seem to be exercising a great influence on human kind. We seem to be drifting towards Machiavellian philosophy that the end of human existence is profit alone. When a man is dedicated to economics to the exclusion of laws of life, virtue no longer remains his prime concern.

Man's behaviour can be modified in two ways:

(a) By use of behavioural science and technology.

(b) Through the process of education.

Role of Science and Technology: Scientists have been doing considerable research on the modification of human behaviour in order to find ways and means to remove behavioural pollution.

1. *Drugs:* It is learnt that leading nations are secretly engaged in what is known as chemical factors or behavioural drugs; for example drugs which can be sprayed over large population centres and which can make them docile in a manner so as to make the work of the invading armies easier.
2. *Foods:* It may be possible to achieve similar results (as by drugs) by proper kinds of foods. The type of food, its quantity as well as quality – all influence the physiology and psychology of living organisms. Therefore, by appropriate kinds of foods it may be possible to shape the desired type of individuals.
3. *Electronics:* Electronics provide another measure of behaviour control. Electrodes are implanted in the human brain so as to stimulate certain behaviour centres. The stimulation can be achieved by remote control also.
4. *Genetic Engineering:* This has made it possible to remove congenital defects and, in course of time, to engineer a human being of one's choice (good as well as bad).
5. *Reinforcement and Aversive Stimuli:* Reinforcement is negative as well as positive – i.e., removing certain things from the environment or adding certain things to it. One can escape from the consequence of fire either by fleeing it or removing the fire from the environment.

   Punishment for undesirable behaviour is an aversive stimulus. It may have side effects also. For example, a prisoner may become more intrepid in the jail in the company of other prisoners and pick up more techniques of committing crimes. Motivating a person to do something by offering awards is a positive reinforcement. It has fewer side effects.

6. *Experimental psychology:* Considerable theoretical and experimental work has been done in the field of psychology – a science which deals with the functioning of human mind. This is becoming available to modern man for modifying individual's behaviour.

Some of the technologies described above are still a distant possibility and may not be available to mankind at least for immediate and large-scale application. Therefore one has, at the present juncture, to rely more on the educational process.

Educational process:

1. *Role*: Education is a major instrument in modifying human behaviour. In addition to the family, educational institutions have considerable influence on how individuals behave and function. It is, therefore, important that education – defined both in narrow and broader sense- concerned itself with educating the future generation in desirable values. Comenius and Locke described value-education as the hub of educational activity. "Indeed the term 'Humanities', as used to designate a very large section of the curriculum (for a long time, in fact, the whole of the curriculum) indicates by its derivation that relations between man and man were seen as the central, or even the only, concern of education in the full sense. Moral upbringing, or character training, therefore, was far long the central feature of what education itself was understood to be by the great theorists and, indeed, by great practitioners. -It was probably with the development of education for all and the concomitant introduction of a vocational component into the curriculum that moral education lost, in part, this central role."

   Moral education programme can be accomplished through educational institutions, religious institutions and the mass media. Whereas schools and colleges will impart moral education to students, religious institutions can be more usefully employed for inspiring the general public and mass media for both these groups to develop in the individuals propensity for higher standards of conduct.

2. *Personal Example:* Formal teaching can promote moral values only when children see that teachers themselves practise the

code of conduct which they want their students to follow. In the case of moral education, it is necessary to have the marriage of thought and action. Action without thought is blind and is likely to degenerate into superstition; whereas thought without action is of no consequence. Teachers' training-programme should educate the individuals, both, in content and methodology of moral education.

3. *Proper Syllabus:* National Council of Educational Research and Training, New Delhi has worked out a syllabus on moral education. Some broad outlines in regard to syllabi on social justice, sex-education, smoking, drinking and protection of environment have been given. Certain schools in the country have made some *ad hoc* provisions for imparting moral education to their students.

4. *Inter-disciplirtary Approach:* Values concern all life-forms, birds, plants and even non-life such as use of natural resources, etc. Therefore value-education calls for an inter-disciplinary approach. The following episode would explain the usefulness of such an approach.

   Once the residents of a housing complex complained to the owner of the housing complex that they had to wait for a long time for the lift. The owner called engineers to find a solution to the situation. One suggested fixing of an additional lift; the second replacement of the old lift by a new one; but the owner turned down these suggestions as costly. A psychologist happened to pass that way. He advised fixing of two mirrors in the waiting lounge, hoping that ladies would keep looking into the mirrors and arranging their hair, etc., and men would keep looking at the ladies in these mirrors and thus waiting will become easy. The suggestion worked wonderfully well with a nominal expense.

5. *Production of Literature:* Another important work to be done in this area is the writing of suitable books suiting various age-groups of students. These books as text books or supplementary readers should emphasise the proud record of India's cultural heritage and lives of those who dedicated themselves to the service of mankind. A good deal of published material exists already also and can be used

judiciously for this purpose. Besides, import of foreign literature beaming with sex, violence and other unhealthy trends should be stopped. Educational institutions and mass media have, no doubt, an important part to play in restructuring the moral fibre of the society, but it should be remembered that they are surrounded by a system which negates the promotion of moral values and makes their work difficult. Unless their difficulties are resolved, success would remain a distant goal. Further, it should be ensured that no dominant religious, caste, political or any other pressure group is allowed to promote values which serve its particular vested interests. The work is obviously not easy. The example of Vidur, the moral teacher in the *Mahabharata* Epic, is a proof of this statement. However, if adequate steps are not taken to implement the programme of value-education in right earnest, mankind may have to face serious consequences. In the end, it may be added that in India — there is no dearth of ideas and philosophical thought, but unfortunately, most of the reports of research studies, workshops and committees or commissions find their place on the shelves of cold storage only. Preparation of such reports can, in a way be likened to marriages of elephants where everything takes place at high level; there is lot of trumpeting but nothing happens for (two) years. We need to be more realistic as well as practical. The world is moving fast. Our survival depends on our capacity to keep pace with the changing times.

Culture and Religion

Culture is the level of sophistication achieved by a community in various fields of human activity, including politics, economics, religion, arts, sciences, literature, etc. There is a fine distinction between civilization and culture. All that we possess in concrete shape is our civilization but the abstract permeating the concrete is our culture. The houses that we have, the dress that we wear are parts of our civilization; but the design and the abstract planning behind them signify our culture. Similarly, the values that we observe in our speech and conduct are the constituents of our culture. All our cultural- possession is either a result of our own efforts or it has been passed on to us by our ancestors.

Cultural Legacy

As culture is the sum total of the rich experience stretched over centuries of our human existence, there is no reason for us to remain indifferent to it. The Constitution of India, in Article 29 (1), gives every section of the citizens the light to conserve its own culture. Article 51 A assigns to every citizen, as one of the Fundamental Duties, 'to value and preserve the rich heritage of our composite culture'. The Union Ministry of Human Resource Development has a full-fledged department as well as a Cultural Heritage Division for the promotion of arts and culture.

Cultural Education: A statement was included in the questionnaire for the general category of respondents to know the public opinion in regard to one of the aspects of the Indian culture. The statement was as follows:

"Indians need to be made better aware of their cultural heritage." (G-6)

The general pattern of responses to the statement is given in the following table:

a S.No.	*b* Category of Respondents	*c* No. Agreeing	*d* No. Undecided	*e* No. Disagreeing
(1)	Total population (881)	833 (94.6)	24 (2.7)	24 (2.7)
(2)	Age-group 18-25 years (52)	49 (94.3)	1 (1.9)	2 (3.8)
(3)	Above 40 years (573)	54 (94.4)	17 (3)	15 (2.6)
(4)	High School & equivalent (123)	435 (96)	12 (1.6)	16 (2.4)
(5)	M.A or above & equivalent (463)	435 (94)	12 (2.6)	16 (3.4)
(6)	With income from Rs. 1000-1999 pm 92 (98)	5 (93.9)	1 (5.0)	(1.0)

Contd...

a S.No.	*b* Category of Respondents	*c* No. Agreeing	*d* No. Undecided	*e* No. Disagreeing
(7)	With income of Rs 4000 pm and above. (406)	380 93.6)	14 (3.4)	12 (3)

More than 90 per cent of respondents in each category have expressed agreement with the statement.

It would be interesting to also study the responses of the student-community giving identical statement which is reproduced below:

"Students should be made aware of Indian culture through history, literature and other books".

The following table sums up the responses of the students:

Dissemination with Books

a S.No.	*b* Category of Respondents	*c* No. Agreeing	*d* No. Undecided	*e* No. Disagreeing
1.	Total population (267)	256 (96)	6 (2.2)	5 (1.8)
2.	School students (M) (70)	64 (91.4)	3 (4.3)	3 (4.3)
3.	School students (F) (86)	84 (97.7)	0 (0)	2 (2.3)
4.	College students (M)	33	1	0
5.	College students (F) (70)	69 (98.6)	1 (1.4)	0 (0)
6.	African students in Indian colleges (M) (7)	6 (85.7)	1 (14.3)	0 (0)

The pattern of students' reaction to this statement is, more or less, similar to the one indicated by the general population to statement G6, which has been analysed earlier. There are, however, differences in the responses of school-students when compared to those of college-students. Fewer male school students agree with the statement.

Official Schemes: The Education Commission (1964-66) had urged Indian Universities to ensure "that every student who passes out of an Indian university takes with him some understanding of India's cultural heritage, its past achievements and triumphs in the field of art, philosophy, science and so on. He should, in other words, know what he is heir to. This could perhaps, best be done at the first degree stage where such a study could form a part of a programme of liberal education. It is noteworthy, in this connection, that all university students in America have to take a course in Western civilization".

The Programme of Action published by the Government of India for implementing the National Policy on Education 1986, elaborates this point at some length in the chapter on 'The Cultural Perspective'. It speaks of several strategies intended for creating better awareness among students of the country's cultural heritage. A few strategies are summed up below:

1. A suitable hand book should be prepared for the guidance of teachers of each stage of education. Reorientation programmes should be organised for them and audio-visual and other material such as musical instruments, pictures, posters etc., should be prepared for students. A separate room in the school, could be earmarked for cultural exhibits, wherever it is possible;
2. One teacher for culture should be provided in each institution.
3. Distortions in curriculum, particularly in social studies and history should be corrected. Value-orientation should be given to lessons by drawing material from Indian heritage and great classics.
4. Exhibitions of the work of local artists should be organised.
5. Students should be encouraged to undertake the conservation of local historical monuments.
6. Inter-school cultural meets should be arranged so as to bring out India's rich cultural diversity.

The programme of action makes the following suggestions in this regard for university stage:

1. Broad-basing and diversifying cultural courses as of fine arts, music, dance, etc.

2. Correction of existing historical and cultural distortion in the courses of study such as of social sciences, humanities and languages, etc. In this regard a *tour d' force* would have to be attempted but this is necessary in order to rectify the faulty perspectives;
3. Developing special courses in technical and professional institutions for conservation of monuments which are of immense importance as country's valuable ancient heritage;
4. forming clubs and societies devoted to the promotion of various cultural aspects;
5. earmarking incentives, fellowships, scholarships, etc., for creative work and research in the field of culture.

Dimensions in Curriculum: The dissemination of India's cultural heritage should aim at acquainting students with:

1. Customs, traditions and festivals, etc., of various ethnic, religious and linguistic groups inhabiting the country.
2. Works of ancient rishis, sufis, saints, insight into all-time epics, and other great classics.
3. Contributions of great men in various fields of the country's national life.
4. Cultural wealth contained in our works of religion.

   Religion is an important part of the cultural heritage, and more so in the case of India where fine and performing arts and literature have a strong spiritual/religious basis. However, while debating cultural themes related to religion, theocratic education should be excluded.
5. Intelligent interpretation of myths and poetic fantasies.

Myths form an important part of India's, or for that matter, any culture. Some of the writings described as myths have proved to be meaningful today, whereas others are meant to convey some message to mankind. Pushpak Viman was a myth a century ago; but today one can perceive it as it 'might have been a reality' also. In the great work of the Sufi poet Malik Mohammed Jayasi, the heroine Padmavat is found talking to a parrot and the bird is talking to her. This might have been a total myth; but it points towards the level of sensitivity of the people towards birds in those times. In Kalidasa's famous work *Meghdoot*, the clouds are taking the message of a lover to his beloved. It is unbelievable and cannot be taken as truth; but it shows how a poet could conceive nature as part of man and man as part of nature.

The stories in the Puranas may have more or less as much element of imagination as of truth; but such writings have a great cultural significance.

They have been called by Socrates as noble lies and have their place in the cultural heritage of man and deserve attention by framers of the educational curricula.

In this context, we may keep in mind a couple of other things also in mind. Firstly, the study of Buddhism in India can be very must a part of the cultural heritage of India; but study of the Chinese or the Japanese version of Buddhism does not constitute a part and parcel of the Indian cultural heritage, though the merit of these studies otherwise cannot be denied. Secondly, there might be certain aspects of the cultural heritage which must have had their value and importance in the past, but stand invalidated today. For example, the practice of 'devadasis' in some Indian temples had the merit of promoting vestal virgins and dance as a part of worship; but it has degenerated and has become an anachronism today. Similarly, caste which was evolved as a measure to promote professional excellence stands condemned today on account of the infiltration of many evils into it. Any debate on cultural heritage must discuss all such issues objectively and rationally and ought not to unduly support degenerated practices.

One of the important functions of the Indian missions in other countries is to project India's image abroad. It is sad to note that our Embassies, High Commissions and Consulates are totally ill equipped for dissemination of India's rich cultural heritage in the countries to which they are accredited. These Missions neither have suitable personnel nor adequate material which could provide information on India's diverse and rich cultural heritage. India needs to follow the example of other countries in this respect and establish richly equipped and properly-functioning cultural centres in all foreign countries. In the present-day world rendered smaller by communication facilities, there is scope for greater interaction between peoples of the world. Widening of the scope of cultural interaction through our embassies is bound to enhance India's prestige.

The popularity and esteem of India's culture in other lands is likely to influence, to a certain degree, the attitude of her own people to their own cultural heritage. Thus the investment in projecting India's culture abroad would serve several purposes, some of which are —

1. A boost in India's prestige, as her cultural achievements excel most, rather all countries of the world;
2. Infusion of a sense of self-esteem among the people of India and thus also lead to greater enthusiasm among the Indians for imbibing their own cultural values;
3. Dissemination of India's cultural message for the benefit of mankind as was done by her predecessors in South East Asia, China, Japan, Mexico and elsewhere.

Culture is the totality of thoughts, symbols, beliefs, sentiments, etc., which a group has developed and refined over a period of time and with which it has enriched its material life. Indian culture, broadly speaking, has material, spiritual and intellectual aspects. The historical remains and ancient writings testify to India's material progress since time immemorial. The Vedas, and the Upanishadas which are the oldest philosophical works in possessions of mankind today indicate the occupation of the Indian mind with the intellectual and spiritual aspects of culture. Hegal says, "A civilization without a philosophy is like a temple without the holy of the holies". The speculative aspect of Indian culture first dived into the mysteries of nature, as in the Vedas, and thereafter it tried to unravel the mystery of man, universe, matter and energy through the Vedanta. In this connection, Max Muller writes in his work Six Systems of Indian Philosophy (p.182):

"It is surely astounding that such a system as the Vendanta should have been slowly elaborated by the indefatigable and intrepid thinkers of India thousands of years ago, a system that even now makes us feel giddy, as in mounting the last steps of the swaying spire of an ancient Gothic Cathedral. None of our philosophers, not excepting Heraclitus, Plato, Kant, or Hegel has ventured to erect such a spire, never frightened by storms or lightnings. Stone follows on stone after regular succession after once the first step has been made, after once it has been clearly seen that in the beginning there can have been but one, as there will be but one in the end, whether we call it Atman or Brahman,"

On the glory of the Upanishadas, Schopenhauer says, "In the whole world, there is no study so beneficial and so elevating as that of the Upanishadas. They are destined sooner or later to become the faith of the people."

According to Deussen, "The Upanishadas formulate philosophical conceptions unequalled in India or perhaps anywhere else in the world."

Thus, the Indian culture is very rich. It is, therefore, surprising that Indians themselves should not be able to fully appreciate the worth of their own achievements. This can be, to an extent, attributed to centuries of foreign rule which tried to demolish the vestiges of India's culture. The absence of a culture base in education, which unfortunately continues even now, could be the other reason. Afterall, Macaulay, on whose Minute, the foundation of India's modern system of education was laid, believed that a few shelves of English literature were sufficient to contain the totality of India's literature. Whereas a section of the population under the influence of foreign education moved away from its rich cultural values, the village folks and the women, who were somehow left out from the western and other foreign influences, adhered to the old cultural values and preserved them. Unfortunately, these people having been relegated to a subservient position, were preoccupied with the struggle for existence and did not have much power to contribute to cultural regeneration of the country. Through folklore and religious practices, however, they contributed to the preservation of culture and the values which are so characteristic of the Indian psyche.

Today, India's cultural heritage is mostly treasured in our ancient books, subsequent commentaries of scholars on this literature and with the village and the women folk. The government, has, in recent times, initiated steps to preserve the contributions that were made in the past. These include preservation of monuments, support of performing and plastic arts, etc. A number of organisations are also now engaged in the work of dissemination of India's past cultural heritage as well as of its present achievement. It is for the educational institutions to carry forward this work with speed and in a big way.

Religious Force

The *Concise Oxford Dictionary* defines religion as a "particular system of faith and worship – human recognition of superhuman controlling power and especially of a personal God or Gods entitled to obedience and worship". The main components of any religion are theology, rituals and code of conduct.

It is believed that in India, the conception of Supreme Being, the first cause of the universe, i.e., the Brahma, had a great impact on the moral code of the Aryans. Starting from the worship of various elements of nature such as the sky, the earth and various forces of nature, there was a trend towards finding unity in them. Polytheism was correlated to monotheism just as forces of nature namely, heat, light, electricity to one single thing 'energy'. This Single Cause of the universe, was impersonal, absolute, passionless and beyond consciousness, just like energy in this material world, is the primal cause of the universe. This chain of thought led our ancestors to one of the greatest philosophical conceptions – that the whole world was one.

The concept of religion is bound to vary from person to person and from society to society. For example, in Hinduism, the equivalent of religion is 'dharma', which is far more a comprehensive word than the word religion. The word 'dharma' is from the root 'dhara', which means something which holds the society and this universe together. As such, 'dhama' lays greater stress on one's goals, functions, obligations and duties. It is, difficult to say which conception of religion (which) the respondents had in mind when reacting to the following statement:

It would be appropriate to impart moral education,

1. Without reference to religious teachings;

   or

2. With reference to teachings in various religions. (G-2)

Moral Teaching

Option	*No. of Persons Agreeing.*	*No. of Persons Disagreeing*	*No. Undecided*
(a)	382 (43.3)	7 (0.8)	
or			19 (2.2)
(b)	469 (53.2)	4 (0.5)	

Positive Role of Religion: Thus more than 50 per cent of the respondents favoured moral education with reference to religious teachings. There could be several reasons for it, some of which may be as follows:

1. Religion plays a positive role in the moral uplift of man. It may, at times, be the fear of gods which may be the motive factor for individual's right conduct. William Newton Clarke considered the role of religion in imparting moral education as that of a school master. He wrote in his book *The Christian Doctrine of God.*

   " Doubtless the ethical life of the world has suffered much from religion, but it owes to religion immeasurably more than it has suffered from it. Faulty enough indeed the influence has been, but the ethical life of the world has on the whole been greatly reinforced and purified by its religions."
2. All religions are creations of superb minds. Religious writings are replete with episodes which have great moral lessons far man. It would be lack of wisdom on the part of man not to benefit from the wealth of experience stored in the religious books.
3. We, in India, are not trying to create an irreligious society. What we have accepted is a variously religious society, and not a society which has nothing to do with religion. Therefore, religion cannot be rejected merely on the ground that we are a secular state.

Role of Religion: Those who are opposed to assigning any role to religion in the sphere of moral education may have some of the following arguments in mind.

1. According to Article 28 (1) of the Constitution of India, "No religious instruction shall be provided in any educational institution wholly maintained out of State Fund."

   This, of course, does not apply to the educational institutions run by private trusts. In regard to such institutions, Article 28(3) of the Constitution lays down the following policy.

   "No person attending any educational institution recognised by the State or receiving aid out of State funds shall be required to take part in any religious instruction that maybe imparted in such institutions or to attend any religious worship that may be conducted in such institutions or in any premises attached thereto unless such person or, if such a person is a minor, his guardian has given his consent thereto."

2. Religion is identified by some people more as theology, a set of rituals, fear of God and greed for heaven rather than a code of, conduct evolved over a period of years. Such people see no link between religion and morality. In his work 'Christianity and Hinduism', Bishop Caldwell writes,:

   "We meet with a moral Hindu who has broken altogether away from religion and, what is still more common, still more extraordinary, we meet with a devout Hindu who lives a flagrantly immoral life. In the latter case no person sees any inconsistency between immorality and devoutness."

   'The Karma Theory' which is one of the fundamental principles of Hinduism proclaims the importance of virtuous acts. The following legend in a Hindu sacred- book brings out very aptly the higher place of a kind act than the performance of rituals. A rich man, once, performed the ritual of offering 1000 mangoes to the sacred Ganges. One of these mangoes was picked up by a poor beggar to satisfy his hunger. The same night, the rich man, in his dream saw the goddess Ganges who told him that she had accepted the offering of the mango only! The 'devout Hindus' of Caldwell experience are therefore, not truly religious.

3. People project their moral conceptions in the shape of gods; but once created these divinities react on the conscience of their creators. Examples are not wanting where divinities created by the priest class and other powerful sections in the society have had an adverse influence on the morals of the society. It is in the name of some divinities that injustices are perpetrated on the weaker sections of the society.
4. To many people, religion has meant forcible proselytisation at the point of bayonet or economic and social exploitation of others. Religions have led to feuds among the co-religionists as well as between people of different faiths.
5. Communists as well as many other people have no faith in any religion. Religions like Buddhism make no reference to God. If moral teachings are to be based on religion, it would amount to imparting no moral education to persons who do not believe in religion.
6. Some of these people hold that moral education should be based on rational thinking only. In ancient Greece, where there was no priestly class, the country had no theocratic morality. Aristotle discussed only scientific foundations of morality. In ancient Rome, morality was based on patriotism and not religion.
7. The great Hindu codifier of values, Manu, makes no reference to rituals and supernatural things in his definition of dharma.

   Those who hold that moral education should be imparted independent of religion argue that if some day a person rejects his religion (and this can happen with the growth of materialistic values), he would reject morality also. It would, in a way, amount to throwing the baby along with the bath tub.
8. Today, many societies are pluralistic and have a markedly different value-system arising from their respective religions. Therefore, there is an inherent difficulty in linking morality with religion.

Critics and scholars have also pointed towards several disintegrating factors in various religions. For example, Judaism, Christianity and Islam, which have a common catchment area, believe in an exclusive God. Their God brooks no rival, whereas according to Hinduism, all Gods are manifestation of the same Brahma; only the sages have described Him differently.

The Judaic God commands his worshippers that when they enter the land of their enemies, they will "destroy their altars, and break their images, and cut down their groves, and burn their graven images with fire". (Bible, Deut 7.5). Iconoclasm, temple razing has been preached and practised by Islam to a similar degree. It is told that Walid was sent by the prophet to destroy the idol of al-Uzza at Nakhle worshipped by the tribal people there. Wherever the followers of Christianity went, they destroyed gods and religious places of the 'nonbelievers'.

When America was discovered, the Benedictine monks who came in the train of Columbus boasted of having destroyed single-handed 170,000 images in Haiti alone. Juan de Zummarage, the first Bishop of Mexico, writing as early as 1531 claimed that he destroyed 500 temples and 20,000 idols of the heathens. In our own country, in Goa, Jesuit fathers destroyed many Hindu temples. The Hindus, at one time, had to pay 'Jazia, only because they were Hindus and not Muslims. A law laid down that infidels could not build their temples.

The Laxmi Narain Temple in New Delhi is reported to have come up in the country after a lapse of about 700 years. Various religions, thus, appear to have been reduced to mere denominations only.

In case educational institutions adopt an attitude of indifference to religion, it would mean leaving the interpretation of religion to the reactionaries and half-educated people only and jeopardising the process of social evolution.

The works of the religiously inclined saints and sufi poets and philosophers like Namdev, Tukaram, Kabir, Kurral, Jaisi, S. Radhakrishnan and others in different languages express moral truths in epigramatic phrases. All such works have had a great moralising influence on the society and it would be a mistake not to make use of them for their literary and moral value.

Every religion lays down some code of conduct for its followers and contains in its books numerous legends to inspire its faithfuls to observe certain norms of behaviour. It would be useful to make use of this heritage, for imparting ethical education to students.

Each religion preaches spiritual fulfilment, withdrawing from the lower pulls to higher recesses of mind, prayer, meditation, inculcation of virtues like compassion, contentment, good actions, self-surrender, service of mankind and all that can elevate man and the society.

Whatever be the source of the material employed for moral education, all discussions on the value-system should be on rational basis only and not wrapped in meaningless myths and superstitions. For example, it would be an incorrect approach to say, 'Respect women because it is written in *Manusmriti.*

yatra nariastu poojante, ramante tatra devata,
yatraiatastu na poojante, sarvaatatraphala kriya.

'Homes where women are worshipped become the abode of gods but where women are not given respect, all the actions of the people there end up in failure'.

Instead, students should be told with examples that whenever and wherever women have been given an opportunity in education, services or other spheres,, their contribution has been no less than that of men. On this account as well as on account of the sacrifice which women make as mothers, they are worthy of great respect.

It would be wrong to attribute some of the existing social ills solely to religion. Foreign aggressions, alien rule, present day consumerism and absence of developmental work over long periods are vital factors responsible for moral decay of the society.

Codes of Conduct: To the statement that –

"Students should be given an intelligent understanding of the codes of conduct of various religions", (G-9), the respondents reacted as follows:

S. No.	*Category of Respondents*	*Number Agreeing*	*Number Undecided*	*Number Disagreed*	*Number of persons who expressed no opinion*
1	2	3	4	5	6
1.	Total population (881)	798 (90.6)	39 (4.4)	44 (5)	–
2.	Age-Group 18-25 years (52)	43 (82.7)	4 (7.7)	5 (9.6)	–
3.	Above 40 years (574)	532 (92.7)	20 (3.5)	22 (3.8)	–
4.	High School & equivalent (123)	115 (3.5)	1 (0.8)	7 (5.7)	–
5.	MA or above and equivalent (464)	414 (89.2)	27 (5.8)	23 (5)	–
6.	With income from Rs 1000-1999 pm (98)	88 (89.8)	6 (6.1)	4 (4.1)	–
7.	With income of Rs 4000 pm and above (407)	369 (90.7)	16 (3.9)	22 (5.4)	–

All the categories of respondents listed above lent a high degree of support to the statement.

Religion has played a central role and is still playing an important role in the life of the Indian people. All our works of ancient art, literature, dance, music, etc., are intimately interwoven with religious myths and thought. Sciences such as astronomy and geometry, etc., were cultivated in India initially for religious purposes only. Therefore, it may not be possible to eliminate religion from our lives without the grave risk of cutting ourselves from our roots. According to a news-report, a record number of 19.92 lakh pilgrims visited the holy shrine of Vaishno Devi during 1988, exceeding-the previous year's mark, by 1.35 lakhs. These pilgrims came from all over India. Even a number of politicians who swear by secularism visit the holy shrines located all over India. The visit by these leaders may be politically motivated, but they indicate the 'direction of the wind' in our country. Due to great appeal which religion has for the Indian masses, religion was used as an effective weapon during the freedom struggle of the country. V. Subramaniam writes:

"Annie Besant's use of the *Bhagvad Gita* and theosophy appealed to the urban high-caste Hindu – while Tilak widened the base of appeal through using the Ganesh Puja as an instrument of politico-cultural revivalism quite apart from his Karmayogic (activist) reinterpretation of the Bhagvad Gita. Bengali radicalism drew inspiration from the Mother Goddess right from its early days – and Gandhiji's efforts to appeal to the widest public included the slogan of Ram Rajya and the singing of Ram Dhun. In short, the nationalist movement though never exclusively Hindu nor theocratic, nevertheless used Hindu religion cultural symbols and slogans as the most practical instruments of mobilisation of the Indians - in spite of strong criticism both from the Right and Left, from Liberals such as Sapru or Kunzru and Leftists such as Jawahar Lal Nehru, the from Socialists and the Communists."

The motif 'Yoga is efficiency in action' '(Yoga Karmasu Kaushlam) adopted by the National Academy of Administration and the National Productivity Council is from the holy Bhagvad Gita. Of course, the choice of the motif would have been on account of its appropriateness and eloquence and not religious considerations but this is all the more reason that the students should be given an intelligent understanding of various religions and the useful messages contained in the religious text.

"The Indians," remarks Sir Harcourt Butler, "are as essentially religious as the Europeans are essentially secular. Religion is still the beginning and the end, the alpha and omega of Indian Life". This belief finds expression in a bitter satire of the Urdu poet Akbar, of which the gist is " The East is spiritual, the West is material. Mansur (the Sufi Pantheist who was executed in Baghdad in AD 922 for blasphemy) declared, 'I am God.' Darwin announced " I am the son of an ape".

Religious Institutions: As regards the role of the religious institutions, the questionnaire for the students carried the following statement:

"Religious institutions such as temples, mosques, churches should play greater role in propagating moral values in the society". (S-11)

Value-Dissemination

a S. No.	b Category of Respondents	c No. Agreeing	d No. Undecided	e No. Disagreeing	f No. of Persons who expressed no opinion.
1.	Total population of students. (267)	182 (68.2)	33 (12.3)	52 (19.5)	–
2.	School Students (M) (70)	48 (68.6)	6 (8.6)	16 (22.8)	–
3.	School Students (F) (34)	51 (59.3)	19 (22.1)	16 (18.6)	–
4.	College students (M) (34)	25 (73.5)	3 (8.3)	6 (17.7)	–
5.	College students (F) (7)	51 (72.9)	5 (7.1)	14 (20)	–
6.	College students (M) from Africa in Delhi colleges (7)	7 (100)	–	–	–
7.	Total population of Indian students (when students from Africa are not included in the total population.) (260)	175 (67.3)	33 (12.7)	52 (20)	–

The above score-chart leads us to two inferences.

1. College students agree with the statement to a greater degree than do the school students.
2. Male students are more in favour of the idea that the religious institutions should play a greater role in propagating moral values than the female students.
3. In each case the degree of agreement with the statement is less than 75 per cent.

More than 25 per cent of the respondents were undecided on this issue or were opposed to the idea of religious institutions taking up the work of the propagation of moral values, possibly due to the fact that the respondents were skeptical about the ability of the religious institutions to achieve results. Some of the following steps could be considered for equipping the religious institutions for working effectively in the sphere of value-education.

1. It should be ensured that the temple-priests or other similar personnel involved in the work take a progressive and not

an obscurantist's view of religion. For this purpose, a system would have to be evolved on a national basis for entry to priesthood. Individuals wishing to become priests should go through an adequate course of training and education.

In the USSR, prior to glasnost and perestroika, notwithstanding that communism is antagonistic to religion, the priests; before they could take up priesthood, have had to go through a course of adequate training and education in religious and other allied texts. If government can successfully intervene with the administration of the Vaishno Devi temple in J and K State, there is no reason why a similar system cannot be introduced or at least experimented in India.

2. The education programme of the priests must drill the trainees in the concept of oneness of the Supreme Being and certain degree of the comparative study of various religions. *Ahura Mazda* in Zoroastrianism, Allah in Islam, Heavenly Father in Christianity, Iswara in Hinduism, and Sunyata in Buddhism are only different names given by different people in different geographical and linguistic regions for the same cosmic, creative, infinite and eternal energy. The leaders of religious institutions should be trained to remain free from bigotry.
3. The people in religious institutions, like all other people, should bear in mind that as a society evolves intellectually, spiritually and socially, its value-system undergoes a metamorphosis. In case religious institutions refuse to accept this logic, they would lose their credibility. A couple of examples of a progressive and a rational approach in this regard are given here.

Example-I: Among the Muslims it was held for a long time that the *Zakat* or the *Wakf*, i.e., the money collected for charity purposes, is to be spent, among other things, for religious education only as distinct from secular education.

In recent years, rational Muslims have justified the utilisation of Zakat for secular education. According to these progressive thinkers, the Holy Prophet Mohammad had sent a number of people to India and China to receive education. Evidently these people had not gone to these countries to receive Quranic education. Therefore, it is perfectly in accordance with the Islamic thought to utilise Wakf for imparting secular education.

Example-II: Islamic tenets, on theocratic basis, divide the world into two sections-Dar-al-Islam and Dar-al-Harb' It was said that no taxes be levied by Muslim countries for imports from the former category of countries whereas taxes maybe levied in the case of the second category. The rationalist Muslims have, in recent years, changed this view in this manner. They say that Islam upholds the essentiality of survival. As money is necessary for survival, therefore taxes maybe levied in the case of all categories including the first category.

Example-III: According to Islam, Muslims are not allowed to charge interest from anyone, even from banks. The modern thinking among some Muslims is that banks invest money-deposits of the individuals in various projects and business deals and earn profits. As sharing of profits is not specifically banned by Islam, the depositors can accept these profits. The issue is still a debatable one as Muslims of the conventional types view that trade has an element of profit and loss and risk.

As bank deposits do not have this element, bank interest cannot be equated to trade profits. They argue that this is a circuitous way of accepting the bank-interest by changing its nomenclature; but then if religious leaders refuse to accept these changes, the changing society would just ignore them and their sermons as well.

Role of Mass Media: There was the following statement in the questionnaire relating to mass-media.

"Indu and Joginder Singh were discussing radio and TV coverage of such programmes which are religious in character. Indu justified such coverage whereas Joginder Singh felt that such coverage violated the principle of secularism. Who, in your opinion, was correct?

1. Indu, who favoured such coverage;

   Or

2. Joginder, who opposed such programmes. (G-10)

Coverage of Religious Programmes

A	*B*	*C*	*D*
Option	*No. and percentages of persons Agreeing*	*No. Disagreeing*	*No. Undecided*
(a)	531	5	
	(60.3)	(0.6)	
			68
(b)	274	3	
	(31.1)	(0.3)	

The above statistics show that almost double the number supported coverage of religious programmes by mass media as compared to those who opposed it. The proponents of (a) above may justify their stand on the following grounds:

1. Preventing the mass-media from doing such a coverage would, to some extent, mean working for a closed society. The endeavour, on the contrary, should be to depict all religions, cultures as well as subcultures rather than drawing a curtain on them. India's mission to evolve a society with composite culture and not one which is indifferent to all cultures.
2. Any belief or custom which becomes a part of the mainstream of life no longer remains exclusively religious. It becomes a part of the social life of the community and deserves to be depicted by the mass-media. The immense popularity of the *Ramayana* and the *Mahabharata* TV serials from the Doordarshan network amply establishes the justification of projecting such programmes through the mass-media.
3. Secularism has two forms. There is the 'absolute secularism' which is practised in the communist world where religion has no place in the planned affairs of the country. There the religion is a totally private affair.

The Indian view of secularism is, however, different. In India, all religions can flourish. The government does not give preferential treatment to any particular religion. Therefore, if a balanced coverage of important programmes of all religions is undertaken by mass-media, it would lead to better understanding of all cultures by different communities inhabiting the country.

Those opposed to the use of mass-media for religious programmes primarily may be of the opinion that the Preamble of the Indian Constitution declares India a secular state, therefore the government should not dabble with religion. They may be interpreting secularism as communist societies do this. Some persons in this category also have a feeling that the government mass media occasionally, give a preferential treatment to the programmes of one religion vis-a-vis programmes of other religions. Difficult as it may be to totally ward off such an imbalance or an error of judgement in the selection of programmes for the mass-media, its incidence can be reduced by drawing up a clear and a well-thought out policy. The question is – which is more hazardous in a multi-cultural society – to deprive the people of the chance of having an intelligent understanding of the cultures and religions of other communities and interaction with them, or taking a calculated risk of the consequences which would flow if there is some error in the choice of programmes for dissemination through mass media. Perhaps, the latter course may be a better choice.

It may be argued that humankind had started observing some kind of moral code earlier than it evolved any kind of religion. Merial Downey and Av Kelley held that:

> "morality has to be seen independent of religion. If there is a connection it is not that morality is dependent on religious beliefs, it is much more likely that man's religious beliefs are a result of his moral awareness". As Kant said, "Belief in God is grounded in moral consciousness rather than moral law on belief in God."

The question, however, is not if the moral code preceded the evolution of religion or it was vice-versa; but whether in the present context moral education should be undertaken with or without reference to religion. In this context two things are to be kept in view:

1. Have we evolved adequate secular literature for imparting moral education?

2. If religion is divorced from theology and belief in supernaturalism, is there any harm if its moral code, and fables, stories and other relevant material are used for imparting moral education?

In this connection one cannot overlook that only 532 per cent of the respondents supported the application of religion for moral education, whereas 43.3 per cent supported that moral education should be imparted without reference to religious teachings. However, it is not known what was the picture of religion that the respondents had in mind while reacting to this statement. If the picture of religion before them was that of bigoted priests, performance of unmeaningful rituals, sermonising doctrines, one would agree that religious teachings should be kept aloof from moral education; but if religion means harmony of the individual with all forms of life and matter in the cosmos, religion provides a sound basis for moral education.

In view of the above, it would be desirable, as corroborated by about 90 per cent of each category of respondents (in G-9) to give students an intelligent and a rational understanding of the code of conduct of various religions, so that students are not deprived of the wealth of experience stored in these books.

If our dilapidated value-system is to be restructured and saved from decaying further, it is essential that religious establishments should also play their full role in this regard. For this purpose, it would be necessary to have an educated priesthood which has a comprehensive view of various religions and can see the elements of unity behind all religions. The mass-media should also take a balanced and a rational view while projecting customs, traditions and programmes, etc., connected with various religions and intended to impart information to the viewers on different aspects of the national and cultural life and for inculcation of moral values among them.

Theory of Morality

Value-system and Morality are amorphous concepts. Time, place and social milieu are the chief determinants of all moral codes in the world. Morality, therefore, does not lend itself to any precise interpretation. A few examples would illustrate how man's attitude to moral values tends to change or develop along these variables.

Modern science holds that 'matter' is governed by the theory of 'cause and effect'. Ancient philosophers had looked upon the phenomenon of cause and effect in a wider as well as different context. Indians extended the 'cause and effect' concept to human life-cycle and the world of spirit; and they called it the 'Principle of karma'. According to this theory, the present state of every creature is the *summun bonum* of his or her past actions in the past and the present life.

The Buddhists also subscribe to this view. *Zend Avesta* of the Zoroastrians (Parsees) holds that after death, the soul of a good person is met by a beautiful maiden, who says to him, "I am thy own conscience: I was lovely and thou madest me still lovelier; I was fair and thou madest me still fairer through thy good thought, thy good speech, and thy good deeds". And then the soul is led into the paradise of endless light. On the contrary, the soul of a wicked person is met by a hideous old woman, "uglier than the ugliest thing", who is his own conscience. She says to him, "I am thy bad actions. O youth of evil thoughts, of evil words, of evil deeds, of evil religion, it is on account of thy will and actions that I am hedious and vile". Thereafter, the soul is led down into the hell of endless darkness."

It is obvious that convictions of this nature will have a far-reaching effect on our thoughts,, words and moral behaviour. However, there are many materialists who believe in cause and effect theory but who have no faith in a life after death. According to them, the five elements of air, earth, fire, sky and water, of which every creature on this earth is made up of, merge into the respective five elements of nature after death and this heralds the end of the lifecycle. Actions of such people are, obviously not conditioned by thoughts of 'life to come' and mans soul facing the consequences of his actions. Let us next consider some more specific examples in relation to varying social milieus.

The Zoroastrians declare 'truthfulness' as the highest virtue. The ancient Persians had a great veneration for truth and a strong punishment, was provided for false swearing. Truthfulness, as a virtue, does not have that high place in Japan. This could also be due to the fact that the Japanese, in view of their great veneration for their superiors, could not say unpleasant things to them even if these were true. The Greeks, prior to Socrates, were reputed for their disregard for promises and truthfulness. They could practise fraud freely to achieve their end. It goes to the credit of Socrates to have tried to reverse this trend among the Greeks and finally Raving laid down his life for the ideal of truth.

The 'caste-system' among the Hindus, which was evolved as a division of labour and was nurtured by them for promoting specialisation in trade, industry and various professions among its adherents, stands condemned today by the Hindus themselves. With the cruelties perpetrated by the high-castes on the low-castes in the past, any discrimination based on caste is now a legal offence in India.

Worse than the caste-system was the custom of slavery which was commonly accepted by the Babylonians, the Romans, the Muslims and the Greeks. In fact, slavery is considered by the historians as an important contributory factor for the fall of the Roman civilization. The master had an unquestioned authority over his slave; he gloated over the agony of his slave till the latter died. This kind of insensitivity to morality would, today, make anyone shiver to the marrow of his bone. According to Hothouse, "the recognition of the slave traffic by Mohammedanism has been, and is to this day, a curse to Africa and a source of disturbance to the world's politics".

Aristotle taught to hunt barbarians (all non-Greeks) for purposes of getting slaves and he considered it as right and proper as to hunt animals for food and sacrifice.

Filial loyalty was at great premium in ancient China. A father, with the consent of the son's maternal uncle, could require a magistrate to whip to death his unofficial son. "A patricide is beheaded, his body cut in pieces, his house torn down, his neighbours are punished, his chief teacher is put to death, and the magistrates of the district in which he lived are degraded or deposed" a Filial piety and duty towards the Emperor are the two cornerstones of the Japanese ethics. The latter would invite outright rejection by most modern nations today.

Roman Catholics, among Christians, regard celibacy as a virtue; but among the Zoroastrians celibacy and fasting have no place, Islam goes to the extent of accepting and even justifying polygamy.

For all followers of Christ compassion is a laudable quality. The edifice of Jainism would crumble if the elements of comparison and non-violence are excluded from it. In contrast, the Hellas' motto for justice was 'Do no wrong, and suffer no wrong to self or others', with emphasis on the latter. The Hellas considered revenge a virtue if a person had been wronged. Forgiveness was a considered trait of a timid mind. Hammurabi's code of ethics in Babylon, which is considered to be one of the oldest in the world, recommended "eye for eye and tooth for tooth". If a person killed someone's daughter, the killer's daughter was butchered in retaliation and the society accepted it; it is a matter of conjecture what happened if the killer had no daughter!

The Chinese moralist Mencius called the war marshals as great criminals though are may find the present-day Communist China far removed from this thinking.

The war ethics of today is shrouded with hypocrisy. Today, every war is claimed to have been fought for peace and nuclear weapons are said to have been manufactured for self-defence only The war ethics of our ancestors was, however, more straightforward. In India war was assigned to chiefs. The King could keep an army and it was his duty to protect his people. Manu's laws of war forbade use of poisonous weapons, striking an enemy without armour or an onlooker civilian, or one who was asleep or unconscious, etc. War prisoners could be made to work; but they were to be given proper food. Special care was to be taken of children, women and the old people, and so on. Militarism, in any form has no place in Buddhism. Contrary to this the Assyrians and the Babylonians exulted over the cruelties perpetrated by them in wars. One such account is given below:

" The nobles, as many as had revolted, I flayed; with their skins I covered the pyramid. Some of these I immured in the midst of the pyramid; others above the pyramid I impaled on stakes- three thousand of their captives I burned with fire. I left no one alive among them to become a hostage- I cut off the hands (and) feet of some; I cut off the noses, the ears (and) the fingers of others;

the eyes of numerous soldiers I put out. In the middle (of them) I suspended their heads on vine stemp in the neighbourhood of their city. Their young men (and) maidens I burned as a holocaust".

The brief picture indicates the wide variations in the value-systems of different societies living at different times in the same or different geographical regions.

Transformation of Values: Transformation of values takes place due to several factors – political, economic and social. In the political sphere, constitutionally and democratically elected governments have replaced the rule of the colonisers, the maharajas and the nawabs. The value-based politics of the days of yore de-facto stands condemned today by the political opportunists all over the world. In India too, the principled politics of Mahatma Gandhi, Jawahar Lal Nehru and Jaya Prakash Narain stands abandoned by most of the politicians.

In the sphere of economics, the mercantile industry has been replaced by modern industries bringing a new class of entrepreneurs with new values. The pursuit of heavy industries has led to heavy investments, higher production, consumerism, and so on. It has also led to the concentration of capital in fewer hands. The gap between the rich and the poor in all countries as well as at the international levels has widened, leading to conflicts in several new forms between the rich and the poor. The urge to gain political supremacy in the world has led to the cold-war situation which is altogether a new concept.

In the social sphere, though casteism has been legally banned in India, it gets considerable weightage in the selection of candidates and vote-casting during elections. With India declaring itself a welfare state, formal accountability of public servants has increased manifold compared to what it was during the colonial days of India.

The above scenario keeps on undergoing a continuous process of change. Therefore, the outlook of the people and their values are bound to change so as to adjust to the realities of the new situations created by science, technology, political and other factors.

Value-System: Value-system is the fusion of moral and spiritual values. The Report on the Religious and Moral Education, prepared by the, Committee headed by Shri Sri Prakash defined moral behaviour as the conduct of man towards man in various situations in which human beings come together in home, social and economic fields and in the life of outside world generally. — Anything that helps us to behave properly towards others is of moral value.

Spiritual values are also moral values; but in this case there is emphasis on the inner-self of the individual and his relation with the Supreme Being. Anything that takes the individual out of oneself and inspires one to sacrifice for a great cause for the good of others is spiritual.

It may be conceded here that there is no universally accepted definition of 'good' or 'bad. As pointed out earlier, these terms are related to time, place and persons. Good may, by some persons, be equated with the will of God and evil as an inducement of Satan. Good is also identified with pleasure and evil with suffering. There is hardly any defined frontier between licit and illicit. Such a definition is only possible on the basis of certain socially accepted norms or governmental laws. It is easier to discriminate the lawful from the unlawful.

Morality is concerned, both, with beliefs and actions which are in conformity with the social norms shaped, modified and chiselled over a length of time. In ancient Greece, there was emphasis on 'beliefs' whereas in ancient India, the stress was on 'action'. However, action had to be in conformity with Dharma. Thus action itself had moral spiritual base. Manu, the great Indian codifier, on the strength of the Vedas and the Smritis, says that doing noble actions is the highest duty (dharma) of man.

The belief about what is right and what is wrong; what ought to be done and what ought not to be done is generally defined as moral belief. It is a matter of common observance that the beliefs of the people in any group are not always in consonance with their actions. The fact that adultery maybe regarded immoral by many people in a country, yet some people may by involved in this practice and no law may exist against adultery in the country, can be cited as an example in this regard. Numerous religious customs may not stand the test of a rational debate, yet many people believe in them and adhere to them. One cannot categorise such beliefs as 'right beliefs'. There is, therefore, an inherent problem in identifying beliefs', and 'right actions'.

Further, sometimes an action may appear to be moral, yet it may not be so. Reduction in prices of consumer goods would be moral if it is intended to help .the poor and the general public but not so if its motive is to boost up the sales. Therefore, the 'will' and the 'motive' behind the action is very important. An action becomes moral only if the doer acts in 'desirable way' of his own free-will for the good of others.

At times, an act may not be in consonance with the social mores, yet it may not be immoral. For example, the wide spread students demonstrations and marches in Beijing (capital of China) spread over several days in May, 1989 and in violation of the martial law imposed by the Chinese Government could not be termed immoral, because basically the slogan of the students was "We want Mr. Science and Mr. Democracy".

Therefore, notwithstanding the fact that it is difficult to precisely define the philosophical and abstract concept 'morality' one may attempt to understand this term in the following ways:

1. The basis of morality is right belief and right action.
2. The element of free-will of the doer is fundamental to any moral act. The doer must adhere to the moral act in spite of a temptation to deviate from it.
3. Moral act extends both over physiological and psychological domains.

1. Moral and spiritual values may be classified in several ways. In terms of importance, values maybe divided into the following three groups.
   a. Trivial values, such as the kind of clothes one should wear while going to a restaurant. Today, even the dress that one wears at a funeral or while attending a marriage party has come to occupy a trivial significance, particularly in the urban context.
   b. More substantial beliefs, such as the ones which also effect people other than the belief-holder himself. These include punctuality, cleanliness, etc.

   c. Fundamental or perennial and emphemeral beliefs, such as practice of truthfulness, spirit of patriotism, kindness towards all life etc.

2. The great Indian sage Vatsyayana relates virtues and vices to human faculties and gives the following classification.
   a. Virtues of body: charity, helping the needy, social service.
   b. Virtues of speech: truthfulness, benevolence, gentleness, recitation of scriptures,
   c. Virtues of mind: kindness, unworldliness, piety.
   d. Vices of body: cruelty, theft; sexual indulgence.
   e. Vices of speech: falsehood, harshness, scandal.
   f. Vices of mind: hatred, covetousness, disbelief,
3. In terms of social order, values may be classified as political, economic, social, cultural, spiritual, aesthetic and individual values. Thus, values encompass the entire gamut of life. According to the Indian philosophy, individual interest may be sacrificed for that of the family, the interest of the family for that of the don and all interests for that of the soul. According to Indian spiritual philosophers, individual soul is a part and parcel of the universal soul.
4. There has been no time in the history of man, when he had no moral values. The values, therefore, can also be grouped as ancient, medieval and modern values. Some people hold that there is nothing modern in the value-system of the present age, for example, according to them the so-called modern concept of egalitarianism existed in olden days in the form of tolerance; and scientific temper in the shape of in-depth analysis of the phenomenon of life and forces of nature. It maybe relevant to point out here that when under pressure coal gets transformed into diamond, it is not called coal. It is given a new name, which everyone accepts. The same argument can be applicable in case of ancient and modern values also.

Development of Moral Values

All morality, according to one belief is deemed to have originated from God, His son, His Messengers and His Avtars.

Revealed scriptures and great works are other important sources of dissemination of moral values. It is believed that the sun god presented code of laws to Hammurabi; God gave commandments to Moses; Zeus gave moral sense to humans so that they could cooperate with each other and match the beasts who are stranger and speedier than man. Myths such as the one relating to the dual between the gods and the demons (virtue and vice), where gods are shown victorious in the end help in promoting moral values among the people. These may be lies but they are 'noble lies' which originate and disseminate moral values.

Genetic affinity is considered to be an important factor in parental altruism.

Anthropologists and historians believe that when homosapiens started living in families, its members developed a sense of obligation to each other.

Man may have, as well, imbibed moral behaviour from his animal ancestors. Many animals abide by the norms of mutual cooperation and help. Strikingly, wolves bring the meat of the kill to the members of their group who are not present at the kill; dolphins support their sick to come up to the water surface and breathe. The famous story of the persevering spider which inspired the disappointed King Robert Bruce, to fight once again is included in the school textbooks to instil this quality of the spider among students.

The ancient seers of India, perhaps, gave a very highly rational explanation in this context when they said that cosmic order (rta) was the foundation of human ethics. They felt that the beauty in earth, sky and nature, as a whole, emerged from this cosmic law (rta). "Gradually, the cosmic sense of rta as Natural Law developed into the social sense of rta as Moral Law". In other words, morality was as essential to bring about beauty and harmony in life as the cosmic order in nature. Punishment is not based on whims; but it is the result of wrong actions only. One could enjoy life if one could ensure order in one's activities. Rta, in a way, was the basis of the ancient Indian moral laws.

Great men, or for that matter any group of dominant persons, greatly influence the value-system of the society. The Bhaktas and the Sufis, during the medieval period of Indian history, inspired people towards chastity, renunciation, desirelessness and other similar values. Material aspirations came to be looked upon as undivine. The feudal system and dynastic rules of this age, whipped up sex urge among some classes of people and also produced a class of flatterers and courtiers. In the modern era, Raja Ram Mohan Roy, Swami Vivekananda, Sir Syed Ahmed Khan, Badrudin Tyabji, Madan Mohan Malviya, Lala Lajpat Rai, Swami Dayanand Saraswati, Mahatma Gandhi (1869-1948) and a galaxy of other reformers worked for the independence of the country, better deal for women, social justice for the backward classes and many other values which are enshrined in the Indian Constitution.

The Constitution of India, with its 64 amendments (till 1989), is an important source of the present-day Indian value-system. It lists ten Fundamental Duties for each citizen. The Preamble of the Constitution emphasises certain important values. These may be called national values. Cessation of cold war between countries may be categorised as an international value. Preservation of environment is a national-as well as an international value.

The governments try to uphold and promote these values through laws, penal codes and other measures.

Parmatha Nath Bose divides the evolution of human values chronologically in three stages.

1. During the early stages, the predatory man, like animals, sought comfort in material and emotional gratification. Emotional expression in humans found expression through arts, such as' poetry, painting, sculpture, etc. Thus, this is the first level of achievement of the value-system in human society.
2. During the intermediate stage, intellectual development separates him from the animals. He begins to examine physical and psychical processes. It is at this juncture that science and philosophy are born and scientific and philosophical values take shape.
3. At the advanced stage of his development, man's spiritual faculty has developed and he begins to seek happiness from within rather than from without. Two faculties develop at this stage:

a. spiritual which inspires belief in supernatural beings; and
b. moral faculty which enables a person to perceive moral good or evil independent of expediency, consideration of utility or physical welfare or suffering.

Incidentally this analysis would give students of ethics some idea about the level of cultural heights that India had attained thousands of years ago with her highly developed spiritual culture which remains, even today, unrivalled in the world.

All human values are shaped by our wants. Man has material as well as spiritual wants. These may be termed as wants of the outer and inner life respectively. The former promote qualities of industry, order, perseverence, etc., which have a survival value. The wants of inner life promote cultural values like humility, mercy, self-sacrifice, etc. Neither of these wants should be considered inferior to the other.

A moral code would have a greater appeal for the people in general if it is simple and not complicated. The Buddhism was able to make a mass appeal because its teachings were simple as compared to Brahmanism which in the days of Buddha had become highly complicated. No moral code would be acceptable in the modern scientific age unless it has a rational basis and can appeal to one's reason.

Socrates, the great Greek philosopher, emphasised right knowledge as the true basis for moral actions. Goethe, on the other hand, observed that man comes to know himself not through reflection but through action or conduct only. He said, "Do thy duty and thou wilt know what thou art". According to the ancient Indian thought it is the conduct (Aadiaram) which determines the moral standards of an individual or a group. It is said you are judged not by what you say; but what you are in totality.

Significance of Value-Education: Is the primary aim of moral education to have more scientists, better cricketers, large number of tennis-stars or athletes who can win more gold medals for the country? Perhaps, not. The chief aim of value education is to achieve maximum human resource development so as to improve our total life. One can not do better than to quote here Edwin

Markhani in order to bring out the great importance of value-education. He said:

> "We are blind until we see that in the human plan, nothing is worth the making if it does not make the man. Why build these cities glorious if man unbuiled goes? In vain we build the world, unless the builder also grows".

There is hardly any issue on which one may find complete unanimity of views in the society. The situation is no different in the case of the value- system. Many people feel that there is, at presents a state of total chaos in the society so far as moral values are concerned. However, a number of people do not share deep concern over the so-called deterioration of moral values. The great scientist Darwin had remarked that mankind is continuously progressing on a course of evolution. Undoubtedly, he must have been alluding to the biological factors only. The great spiritual leader Aurobindo Ghosh had said that the homosapien would steadily attain super-manhood and that there is no returning for him to the lower forms of life. Some people hold that the psychological man has, in modern times, been left much behind the physiological man and the cultural march of human race has failed to match its technological progress. On the contrary, there is a class of people who feel that from the predatory man to the present-day civilised homosapien, man's cultural advancement excels his achievement in any other field.

The data collected for the study indicated a convergence of views. Bulk of respondents feel that there has been a decline in moral values. To the statement that "over the past 5-10 years, moral values among Indians have declined", (G-I), the 881 respondents expressed their opinions as follows:

Of the total 881 non-student general category respondents, 88 per cent concurred with the above (G-I) statement, 5 per cent of them expressed their disagreement to it and the remaining 7 per cent were undecided on this issue. The moral crisis has, perhaps, became so obvious that the level of education did not make any significant difference in their view-point on this statement. The highest degree of agreement was expressed by the educationists and the least by the advocates. Reasons for this are, perhaps, obvious! Even in the case of the latter, there is a high degree of agreement about the decline in moral values.

Decline of Moral Values

a S.No.	*b* Category	*c* Number Agreeing	*d* No. undecided	*e* No. disagreed	*f* No. of persons who expressed no opinion
(1)	Total no. of Respondents (881)	775	61	44	1
(2)	Respondents in the age-group 25-40 years (233)	208 (89.3)	10 (4.3)	15 (6.4)	– (0)
(3)	Respondents above 40 years of age (573)	507 (88.5)	39 (6.8)	26 (45)	1 (0.2)
(4)	High School or equivalent (98)	84 (85.7)	6 (6.1)	8 (8.2)	– (0)
(5)	MA and above or equivalent (405)	359 (88.6)	27 (6.7)	18 (4.4)	1 (03)
(6)	Educationists (21)	21 (95.5)	0 (0)	1 (4.5)	0 (0)
(7)	Advocates (10)	7 (70)	1 (10)	2 (20)	0 (0)

Note: (i) Figures in brackets below the columns c to f indicate percentages, whereas such figures below column b give the number of respondents in the corresponding category.

(ii) Though this kind of analysis was done in the case of several categories of respondents, but the entire bunch of statistics has not been given here in order to avoid confusion.

(ii) The above system has been followed all through in this work.

Perhaps people of every generation always feel that the values have declined in their time as compared to what they were in the 'golden past'. Even when the Greek civilization had reached its heights, Plato (427-347BC) stated more than two millennia ago;

"What is happening to our young people. They disrespect their elders, they disobey their parents. They ignore the laws. They riot in the street, inflamed with wild notions. Their morals are decaying. What is to become of them?"

There may be valid reasons to lament over the loss of values in a society; but sometimes it may be difficult to pin-point whether a value-system is undergoing a metamorphosis or whether it is declining. For example, during the Indian freedom struggle of 1930s and 40s, many young men and women left their studies, jobs and families to work for their country against the colonial rule. Many in the older generation had then opposed the action of the youths; but later on it was these youths that were acclaimed as national heroes. In 1967, when the students of the Wisconsin University (USA) staged a massive demonstration against the napalming of North Vietnam by America, they did not receive the requisite general public support in their, struggle; but subsequent events proved that the young students were right.

According to the Rishis of ancient India, gods and demons; creation and destruction; good and evil are the products of the same Cosmic Energy. They have coexisted from the inception of this universe. No Age or society ever had good without evil or evil without good and decline in moral values only means absence of a proper balance between the two. It is the domination of demonic destructive, evil and such like tendencies over the godly, constructive and noble tendencies which amounts to the decline in values.

Moral values have an ideological and a philosophical basis. It would not be wrong to say that during the feudal as well as colonial past, these bases were greatly weakened. The struggle for country's independence did, to some extent, restore the ideological basis, but within a couple of decades after independence the hand of the clock again started reversing. Today, we are at a stage where it is difficult to state categorically if any organised section of the society is seriously and consistently working for upholding moral values.

There are various causes for the decline of values in a society. One can concede that the fall in the Indian value-system is a part of worldwide apathy to moral values.

Further, moral values are generally nourished by the middle class. The rich are generally indifferent to the value-system of the society; and the poor, because of inherent economic and other constraints cannot live up to it. Today, the aspirations of the neo-middle class have increased greatly and the value-system has been subordinated to these aspirations. This has subscribed to the lowering of moral values.

Science and material progress has also greatly contributed to the fall of social and spiritual values. Science has led to industrialisation; industrialisation to capitalism; capitalism to overproduction and concentration of wealth in the hands of the few; and all this to the political and economic exploitation of the many by a few.

The statement contained in the questionnaire in regard to the causes of the fall of moral values in the society read as follows:

The following are the causes for the fall in values in the society:

(a) Absence of proper religious teaching.

(b) Fall in moral values of our political leaders.

(c) Mass media adopting no proper policy to build moral standards in the society. (G-16)

The scores for these statements are given below

Grading Causes of Moral Decline

Statement	*Number of persons who allotted first, second or third positions to the statement.*			*Number persons who left the statement blank.*	*Weighted of score**
	I Position	*II Position*	*III Position*		
(a)	224	233	301	123	54.5%
(b)	328	260	170	123	63.3%
(c)	212	269	277	123	54.9%

Thus among the reasons which were given in the questionnaire, the fall in moral values of our political leaders was considered by the respondents to have contributed significantly to a greater extent than the other two values to the decline of values in the society. It confirms the view-point held by many people that the value-system emerges from the seat of power. Absence of proper religious teaching was given the third place in this regard. Nearly 14 per cent of the respondents did not express any opinion on this statement.

In this respect, Caudwell says, "And the unparalleled increase in the productive power has given birth, not to peace, plenty, and happiness, but to war, famine and misery. Anarchy is the keynote of crisis in all spheres .....Why then have not all the psycho-analysis, Eddingtons, Keynes, Spengiers, and Bishops who have surveyed the scene, been able to locate a source of infection common to all modern cultures. For answer, these people must take to themselves, the words of Herzen: 'We are not the doctors, we are the disease''.

Leadership on Value-Scale: Leadership in all fields tends to influence the value-system of the common man also. This hypothesis is truer when viewed in the context of the politicians, the teachers and the parents. The impact of the politicians, is on a wide cross-section of the society, whereas the impact of the teachers and parents is deeper on the children as among other things, it starts working during the early and impressionable years of the individuals. Therefore, an attempt was made through the questionnaire meant for the general public and the one meant for the students to rate politicians, teachers and parents on the basis of some of the statements that follow.

"Keeping in view the conduct of majority of Indian political leaders, one concludes that their quality is

(a) Of the desired level

or

(b) Average

or

(c) Below the desired level." (G-8)

Of the 881 respondents in the G group, 848, i.e., 96.2 per cent opted for one of the above three options. 3 per cent were undecided and the remaining 0.8 per cent recorded disagreement to these options.

Rating the Politicians

Option	*Number of Persons*	*Agreeing*
(a)	45	(5.1%)
(b)	154	(17.5%)
(c)	649	(73.6%)
Total (881)	848	(96.2%)

The general public have given a clear verdict that the majority of the Indian political leaders are below the desired level.

In this context, one should not forget that the class of politicians during and immediately after the country's independence struggle were highly respected by the public. Leaders like Mahatma Gandhi, Jawahar Lal Nehru, Sardar Patel, Rafi Ahmad Kidwai, Khan Abdul Ghaffar Khan, are revered even today. They made great sacrifices for the national good. The profiles of the politicians who made up the country's Constituent Assembly also fall in the same category. However, while talking of the majority of the present-day politicians, the picture draws a blank.

The Bofors, and the Oil and Natural Gas Commission deals bring a lot of disrepute to the politicians.

No doubt, the charges of nepotism, accumulation of undeclared black-money, etc., are not confined to the politicians alone, but this does not exonerate the politicians from being responsible for malpractices and setting an unworthy example of leadership before their people.

Commenting on the criminalisation of politics with muscle and money power and multitude of corrupt practices, one of the English dailies of national standing had once remarked as follows:

"Every passing day reveals disturbing evidence of growing criminalisation of Indian politics. The results of Sunday's (16.10.88) elections for the pramukhs (chiefs) of block development committees in UP are latest manifestations. In several districts in east UP criminals or candidates supported by them, won elections convincingly at the expense of the candidates backed by political parties. Most remarkable was the victory of a known bandit chief of Banda district. Not only did he win, four of his candidates also won. A well-known mafia don won, unopposed, from Sitapur block, which is right near to Lucknow-the State Capital. All this should come as no surprise. The link between criminals and politicians has assumed alarming proportions in the Hindi belt since 1967, when booth-capturing first occurred on a massive scale in Bihar. But this phenomenon is not confined to the Congress; the links between Janta big wigs and mafia dons of Dhanbad are not even sought to be overt."

The following remark by a scholar- poet-politician, a former Minister in the country's Union Cabinet, and later on Ambassador, is highly significant.

"Of course the present-day politician is rated differently from the luminaries of the freedom struggle, but then he is only elected by the people. Perhaps, no people can rise much above their moral and cultural ethos in elections also."

Statement S-la read as follows:

1. "Keeping in view the conduct of majority of Indian teachers, one concludes that their quality is –
   (a) Of the desired level
   Or
   (b) Average
   Or
   (c) Below the desired level." (S – 10)
2. "The following factors are responsible for lowering the status of teachers
   (a) Lack of scholarship in teachers;
   (b) Teachers' lust for money;
   (c) Absence of sacrifice among teachers for their students."

In the second statement, the respondents were asked to grade the various reasons in descending order of importance.

The guru or the acharya, as the teacher was known in this country in ancient times, had a place of reverence in India. He was the repository of knowledge and a person of exemplary high character. During the period of education of the student, the guru assumed the responsibility of acting as the parent of his students and the students were part and parcel of his family. The mother and the father gave physical birth to the child; and the teacher gave the second, i.e. the intellectual birth to him. Being a religious as well as an intellectual leader of the society, the teacher enjoyed great respect, even in the court of the Kings. The Indian teacher basked in the sunshine of this glory (though somewhat to a lesser degree with the passage of time) till the advent of the British rule. During the British rule, education became procurable and saleable for money. Its past sanctity started vanishing. Any assessment of the present day Indian teachers, must obviously take the above historical background into account. However, the Indian ethos demand a certain level of accomplishment from the teachers. Once they enter the teaching profession, they must come up to the expectations of the society. In order to come up to the expected level of accomplishment, the teachers need to have some idea of their image which they now have in the public eyes.

Assessment of Teachers

Option	*Number of Persons Agreeing*	*Percentage*
Quality of teacher is –		
(a) Of the desired level	32	12
Or		
(b) Average	182	682
Or		
(c) Below the desired level.	46	172
Total	261	97.4%

Six, i.e. 2.2 per cent respondents were undecided and one (0.496) of the school students (male) expressed disagreement with the statement that the teacher's quality was below the desired level. Thus, by and large, teachers have been rated as mediocres by the students. Students' rating of teachers may give teachers some pseudosatisfaction when compared with the following assessment of the politicians by the general public.

It goes without saying that the academic and behavioural excellence of teachers will tend to make their students also likewise. Similarly, the mediocrity of teachers is likely to produce the products of an average quality only.

Comparative Assessment of the Quality

	Politicians	Teachers
OPTION		
(a) Of the desired level	5.1 P.c.	12.0 P.c.
Or		
(b) Average	175 P.c.	682 P.c.
Or		
(c) Below the desired level	73.6 p.c.	172 p.c.

Teachers have, thus, to accept their share of the existing social malaise, especially in respect of their students. It has been aptly remarked, "Teachers can escape from their influence over the moral and spiritual development of their pupils by closing their schools." Teaches are charged with an important responsibility of guiding their students. By entering the teaching profession they, ipso-*facto*, accept this responsibility. In order to fulfil this obligation, they must raise their own level of conduct in their own eyes as well as in the estimation of the public. The Urdu poet was not wrong when he said –

"Rahbar-e-gum gashta ko lazim hai apni ahtiat, Rah pe bane se pahle rah pe ana bhi hai."

'A guide has to be very careful about himself. He has to be on the right track himself, before he can bring others onto it.'

It would be appropriate to diagnose here a couple of causes responsible for lowering the status of teachers.

Grading Causes Responsible for Lowering Teachers Status

Statement	*Number of persons who alloted first, second or third positions to this statement* I	II	III	*Number of persons who left the statement blank*	*Weighted score*
(a)	42	80	142	3	53.4%
(b)	116	82	66	3	72.1%
(c)	106	102	55	4	72%

Thus in the opinion of the college as well as school students it is not so much the lack of scholarship as the other two factors which are responsible for bringing down the status of teachers. Their lust for money and absence of the element of sacrifice among teachers have been considered almost equally important factors for lowering the status of teachers. In this regard a respondent (a colonel in the Defence Services) had remarked very appropriately: "The ethos of the teachers needs to change from those of the merchants to those of the gurus."

In this connection, the students were to react to the following statement.

"Yonger generation will show more respect to their parents, if

1. Parents give greater freedom to their children as children grow in age:
2. Parents spend more time with their children;
3. Parents themselves keep adjusting to changing social values". (S-15)

Students were required to rank the above statements.

Role of Parents

Statement	*Overall scare as given by all student respondents.*	*Scores given by male students in*		*Scores given by female students in*	
		Schools	*Colleges*	*Schools*	*Colleges*
(a)	45.8%	46.6%	51%	42.6%	44.3%
(b)	66.9%	64.8%	66.6%	69.4%	68.1%
(c)	83.1%	88.6%	79.4%	88%	81%

It is interesting to observe that the order assigned, to various statements by the total group and different sub-groups-of students is identical.

All students, whether in schools or colleges, also want their parents to spend more time with them, for this greatly contributes to establishing emotional rapport between the parents and their children. Such a rapport is necessary so as to ward off psychological problems among children. In some cases where the parents are educated, dialogues and meetings : between parents and children are also a source of education for the latter.

However, these meetings can be fruitful only if parents with the changing times keep on adjusting to the changing social values. Present day parents are not what their parents were and their children cannot be what they are. This is a fast changing world where scientific discoveries, mass-media, and international influences are revolutionising the thought-processes which were so far circumscribed when these factors were absent or had a limited impact. In case where the parents refuse to adjust to the transforming social values, the rift between parents and their children is bound to ensue sooner than later. It is worth noting that the young students have not accorded high priority to have greater freedom.

It is difficult to say that the moral values have totally declined. For every treacherous traitor, there has always been a courageous fighter in the world. If there are terrorists, there are Vinoba's and Mother Teresa's also to heal the wounds of the oppressed. Of course, the cases of moral decline are sensationally highlighted through the mass media whereas hundreds of people leading a pious life do not catch the attention of the mass media because they do not create sensation. Notwithstanding all this, a fairly large section of the society feels that the moral values in the present-day Indian society have declined. Other important causes, besides the ones stated above, for the fall in the value-system, maybe summed up as follows.

1. The gap between the material and the spiritual progress is an important cause of the present moral crisis. Nuclear capability is a great (material) achievement, but our failure to coordinate it with moral values poses serious dangers to the human race. We have, somehow, forgotten that there is a psychological man behind the physical man. Stating this idea philosophically, the ancient Indian had declared that the cosmic matter (prakriti) coupled with cosmic spirit (Pursha) alone gives meaning to life. The import of this great thought seems to have been lost somewhere.
2. The fall in values in modern times is attributable to overemphasis on wealth power, and consumerism.
3. The present social milieu, as some people believe, is such that it takes us to the moral downfall. While criticising the

social environs, we should remember that the individual is a block as well as a builder of the social system. The social ethos depend on the ethos of the individuals constituting the group, therefore, why not to start the process of moral regeneration of the society with ourselves?

4. When India became free, the West was highly affluent and was immersed in the consumer-goods civilization.

   It had a glamour for every developing country. Indians also wanted to reach the same stage of affluence. The short-cut approach to it lay through the sacrifice of values. Our weak spiritual and educational background, which was the result of the colonial rule, contributed to our undermining the higher values of life.

5. Western literature introduced some new trends in the Indian literature, some of which were unhealthy. These trends brimmed with sex, crime and violence. This had an adverse impact on the social ethos. What is true of literature, is true of films also, which is literature on a silvery-screen.

6. There has been a sea-change in the political, economic and social structure of the human society during the last about 150 years. Princely states have given way to democratic systems. Altruism has been replaced by self-centredness, acquisition and consumerism. Galloping urbanisation has ushered in the apartment-culture and pushed off the rural life values, including socialisation. With the ever-increasing speed in life and both the parents racing from one appointment to another, there is limited socialisation even at home. All this has brought about changes in our outlook to the existing value-system. The trend needs to be rectified.

7. Democracy has made a great contribution to alleviating the lot of the common man, particularly the downtrodden and the backward. However, one cannot be oblivious to its negative role in regard to nurturing of higher moral values. Winston Churchill once described democracy as the worst form of government till a better alternative was available. Pramatha Bose said:

   " There is, perhaps, no tyranny more incompatible with higher culture than the tyranny of an ignorant democracy.

> The leaders of Greek thought, from Pythagoras to Aristotle, were mostly persecuted some of them sent into exile and some condemned to death."

In a democracy, the lower strata are elevated at the expense of the higher strata. Under democratic process the influence of the 'higher strata', spheres of art, literature, etc., included, gets weakened. Knowledge extends over wider surface but loses in depth. Authors have to adapt to the capabilities of the 'common' man. There is a trend towards writing light rather than thoughtful literature.

All this highlights the need for an enlightened and a fresh approach to the important question of value-education.

Teacher's Role in Harmony

People's life style is the replica of different social values. As is the society, so are the life styles. There have been variations in life styles from time to time. In an age of autocracy, the life styles become too much limited. In democratic times, when everybody has his own way of life, it is but natural that there will be good many life styles becoming popular. At the time of independence of the country, it was a fully integrated and combined type of society. But with the passage of time, there has been some sort of disintegration. So much so that today it has become a popular trend of life. Perhaps, it is coming out as a fashion of life. Only a few individuals advocate it, but majority of people have their disliking for it.

There is disintegration in the personality of an individual. Equally, there is disintegration in the member of a family. It is seen that in a family, different religious beliefs are cropping up. Likings and dislikings also vary from one individual to another in the family. One member of the family wants to have one type of breakfast, another wants a different type and the third one has his own peculiar taste. All this shows a socially disintegrating small unit of a family. Similar is the case of society, the state and the nation when we review the different aspects of life from various angles.

Disintegration is becoming a trend of life. There is disintegration because of different beliefs, customs, traditions, cultures and values of life. Questions arise - Was it so in the past ? Was it so before the independence of the country ? Was it so at the time of independence of the country ? Perhaps, no. Not at all in that spirit as it is now.

Need of the hour in our country is national unity and integrity. Education can play a very significant role. In the words of Dr. Radhakrishnan, "If India is to remain free, united and democratic, education should train people for unity and not localism, for democracy and not dictatorship."

Significance of Education

Education plays an important role in bringing about national integration. Ever since India's independence, many efforts have been made in this direction. There have been commendable achievements, but much more need to be done. Let us visualise the efforts and the achievements.

National Endeavours

Following steps have been taken at the national level to foster national integration:

1. Formation of National Integration committee under the Chairmanship of Smt. Indira Gandhi.
2. Appointment of Emotional Integration in Committee under the Chairmanship of Dr. Sampurnanand.
3. Periodical Conference of Chief Ministers to discuss the problem of national integration.
4. Establishment of National Integration Council.
5. Conference of the Vice-Chancellors to tackle the problem of national integration.
6. Setting up of an organising committee by the standing committee of National Integration Council to conduct organised campaign against communication in the country at a massive scale, with which all the political parties, eminent sociologists and educationists would be associated and so on.

Role of Nationalism

As per Advanced Learners Dictionary of Current English, nationalism is strong devotion to one's nation; patriotic feelings. It is loyalty, love and devotion towards one's nation. A person who possesses the sentiments and feelings of nationalism is called a nationalist. Mrs. Indira Gandhi said, "Even if I die in the service of nation, I would be proud of it. Every drop of my blood, I am sure, will contribute to the growth of this nation and make it strong and dynamic." So feeling of love towards the country, devotion and spirit of self-sacrifice is nationalism. A true nationalist stands far above party politics and is ever-ready to serve the nation and safeguard it from any type of outer dangers. The fundamentals of national unity are co-existence, tolerance, cooperation and unity.

Meaning and Definition: Brubacher says, "Nationalism ordinarily indicates a wider scope of loyalty than patriotism in addition to ties of place. Nationality is evidenced by such other ties as race, language, history, culture and tradition."

According to Humayun Kabir, "Nationalism is that which depends on we-feeling towards the nation."

According to Education Commission Report, (1964-66) "National integration includes a confidence in nation's future, a continuous rise in the standard of living, development of feeling of values and duties, a good and impartial administrative system and mutual understanding."

Dorothy Thompson's view, "National integration is a feeling that binds the citizens of a country."

National Integration Conference Report, 1961. "National integration is a psychological and educational process involving the development of a feeling of unity, solidarity and cohesion in the hearts of people, a sense of common citizenship and a feeling of loyalty to the nation,"

Narrow Concept: Some people talk of nationalism in the limited sense. They are heard saying-my country and not bothering about others or the country of others. When people limit their views to their own limited sphere, to their own nation only in this age of internationalism, that creates hatred, jealousy, conflicts and that leads to destruction of peace and war.

Hitler's views, Hitler used to say that the Germans have been born to rule over the world and others to be ruled. The concept 'My country flood or bad, should be dear to me' is wrong. This narrow concept destroyed the humanity.

According to Bertrand Russell, "The boys and girls are given the education that their greatest worship or devotion is for that country of which they are citizens and the creed of that worship of the country that whatever the government does is desirable. Therefore, they are taught false History, Political Science and Economics so that they may criticise the lesson of worship of countries of other persons."

Mudaliar Commission says, "There is no more dangerous maxim in the world of today than 'My Country right or wrong' the whole world is now so intimately interconnected that no nation can or dare live alone and the development of a sense of world citizenship has become just as important as that of national citizenship."

Pt. Jawahar Lal Nehru said, "Nationalism is such a strange element which while it instils life, development, energy and integration, at the same time makes it narrow because on account of it a person thinks about his own country as separate from other countries of the world."

Nationalism and patriotism are not synonymous. Patriotism is old and nationalism and internationalism are modern. Brubacher rightly remarks, "Nationalism ordinarily indicates a wider scope of loyalty than patriotism."

Broader Concept: True or pure nationalism means love and devotion for one's country but not at the cost of hatred for others. A true nationalist is a well wisher of everyone and he strongly believes in world peace. In fact, the spirit of true nationalism in a person tends to make him a lover of internationalism.

Real Status

It becomes an important study to find out the real causes of the present fast deteriorating social situations. There is more and more of disintegration with the advent of life. The following seem to be the causes:

Role of Unity

In India there are people of different cultures. In many cases, it is seen that there are too many variations among the different cultures. In the absence of conscious efforts uniting them, they will remain separated and will not perhaps share their living together with others. So some type of inter-cultural ties have to be thought of and implemented.

Factors of Language

Different people living in India use different languages for their communication purposes. There is so much of difference that one can hardly be understood properly by the other. It is rather difficult to give equal recognition and status to all the languages. A useful way out has been arrived at through the process of education. The three language formula surely helps in this regard when everybody accepts Hindi as the national language and learns it. It unifies all the people of the country to some extent. Then, English as an international language further strengthens the contacts of the people with one another. The importance of mother tongue remains because it is given the status of first language.

Dr. Radhakrishinan. It the words of Dr. Radhakrishnan, "If India is to remain free, united and democratic, education should train people for unity and not localism, for democracy and not dictatorship."

Pt. Jawahar Lal Nehru beautifully remarked, "We should not become parochial, narrow-minded, provincial, communal and caste-minded, because we have a great mission to perform. Let us, the citizens of the Republic of India, bring about the integration of Indian people. We have to build up this great country into a mighty nation, mighty not in the ordinary sense of the word, but mighty in action, mighty, in culture and mighty in its peaceful service of humanity."

National integration is not a mechanical process, it is rather a psychological process. In fact, emotional integration is the basis of national integration. Emotional attachment links people and persons firmly and strongly.

Humayun Kabir's view, "National integration does not depend on race or language or religion or geography, singly or collectively, though they help, but on the feeling of belonging to one nation."

Pandit Nehru's view: "Let us, the citizens of the Republic of India stand up with straight backs and look up at the skies, keeping our feet firmly planted on the ground and bring about the synthesis, the integration of the Indian people. Political integration has already taken place, but what I am after is something deeper than that, an emotional integration of the Indian people so that we may be welded into one strong national unit, maintaining at the same time all our wonderful diversity."

Factors of Geography

India is a vast country which is spreading far and wide. If we see to the geographical placement of different religions, the South and the North are the two extremes with lot of divergences and variations. People of one region have different ways of life, traditions, conventions which "have hardly any similarity with the ones being maintained in the other region. There is need of making them understand that they are Indian nationals. Their progress and prosperity depend upon their beliefs in true national values.

Teacher and Changing Scenario

Scheduled Growth

The Central government adopted five-year plans with certain important characteristics:

1. Planning was divided into Public Sector Projects and Private Sector Projects.
2. The state reserved large-scale enterprises for manufacture of necessary goods and amenities.
3. Manufacture of consumer goods was left to private enterprises.
4. Agriculture was left in private sector.
5. Trade, regulated by the government, was left in the private-sector.
6. Financing and moneylending was in the hands of individuals or private institutions.
7. Most of the goods were sold and purchased in the open market.
8. In place of barter system, monetary basis of exchange was adopted.
9. Taxation by the government was mainly indirect.
10. A major source of finance for the plans was foreign aid.

Independent India and the Movement

In contrast to the social changes undergone by Indian society during the British rule, the following social changes occurred in post-independent era:

1. The Constitution declared all citizens to be equal.
2. The state was governed by quasi form of federal Constitution with a strong centre and weak state units.
3. The Indian Constitution laid down fundamental rights and the rights in the directive principles of state policy.
4. As the new state aimed at general welfare, it created a massive net work for the purpose at Central, State and local levels. The educational facilities were expanded in all directions. A new demand for education particularly technical was created. More communication with foreign countries started.

Effects of Society

The British Policy of Education resulted into the following social consequences:

Socialisation: Education became the most important socialising agency deciding status and role and over-riding family, caste and religious distinction.

Creation of an Elite Class: The most important social consequences of British educational policy was the creation of a class of WOGS or Western Oriented Gentlemen who had almost no communication with the masses.

Prevention of the Growth of Technocrats: British education was primarily liberal, literary, vocational and non-manual. Therefore, it prevented the growth of technocrat and trained personnel.

Westernisation: British educational policy led to fast westernisation of at least the elite educated sections of Indian society. This resulted in Brain-drain, secularisation and creation of All India Education Cadre. It also created consciousness against foreign rule. It strengthened casteism, communalism, linguism and regionalism. It led to reactionary, communal and linguistic movements on the one hand and secularisation and democratisation on the other.

School Discipline

Change in Merit

If we are to revive a spirit of idealism among students, we must create a favourable social atmosphere based on higher values of life. If humanity is to survive, materialistic conception of life must give way to spiritual values. Moral education in one form or the other must form an integral part of our educational system.

Prof. Humayun Kabir stresses the importance of moral and higher values in these words, "if education trains the future citizens it also determines the shape of future society. The value of such education depends upon the character and competence of the teachers who impart it. It is no exaggeration to say that incompetent and dissatisfied teachers undermine the very foundation of society. Their incompetence and dissatisfaction infect the children and sow the seeds of revolution, disruption and decay. A band of teachers, devoted to ideals and pledged to the continued recreation of traditions, can, on the other hand, ensure conditions of unlimited progress and prosperity for mankind."

In the end we must stress with Sheviakov and Fritz Rede, "discipline is not coercion through force – discipline is a spirit, and a spirit cannot be ordered or punished into or regimented, for true discipline is based on willing cooperation which springs from knowledge, idealism and a sense of duty."

Precautions Taken

1. Come prepared to the classroom.
2. Use a variety of teaching aids, i.e. maps, charts, etc.
3. Modulate your voice.
4. Plan your daily work very systematically.
5. Make the students active participants in the classroom activities.
6. Keep the students always busy in doing some worthwhile work.
7. Be always cheerful.
8. Be humorous.
9. Make your hand-writing legible.
10. Show love, sympathy and affection to your students.
11. Make a judicious use of praise and blame.
12. Put on suitable dress.
13. Teach the whole of the class and not a few students sitting on the front benches.
14. Put thought-provoking questions.
15. Distribute your questions evenly.
16. Put questions to inattentive students.
17. Do not often repeat your questions.
18. Allow reasonable time to the students to answer your questions.
19. Do not put questions in a hurried way.
20. Use precise language in framing your questions.
21. Ask the weak students to repeat the good answers given by others.
22. Avoid sarcastic remarks.
23. Do not waste time in gossips.
24. Do not narrate your college experience too often.
25. Do not discuss your family problems in the classroom.
26. Pay attention to the seating arrangement of the students.

27. Correct the postures of the students.
28. Provide seats on the first bench to the short-sighted.
29. Pay attention to the sanitary conditions of the classroom.
30. Do not play with the piece of chalk.
31. Give reasonable home-work to the students.
32. Take keen interest in co-curricular activities.
33. Do not try to win popularity through cheap methods.
34. Learn to 'ride your eye' through the eyes of the students.
35. Do not get personal work from the students.
36. Visit the home of the sick students.
37. Do not show undue favour to some students.
38. Check the written work of the students very carefully.
39. Stand throughout the major part of the class period.
40. Do not allow yourself to be 'side tracked' by irrelevant questions.
41. Learn the names of the students very quickly.
42. Respect the personality of the child.
43. Do not use abusive language.
44. Learn as much as possible regarding the home conditions of children.
45. Be physically strong, emotionally stable, ethically sound, mentally alert and socially efficient.

The Ideas

In the words of the University Education Commission, "It is important that good discipline be looked upon not as student conformity to arbitrary standards of conduct, but rather as individual responsibility for behaviour."

Narrow and Broader View Regarding Discipline: The concept of discipline may be viewed from a narrow and old or from a modern and broader point of view. From the narrow point of view discipline means subjection to authority, obedience to law and order and bringing the child under control. From a broader modern point of view, by discipline we mean the training of mind, manners and attitudes, sublimation of instincts, bringing the lower impulses of the child under control, formation of right habits and in fact the development of character.

Discipline from the Point of View of an Individual: Discipline viewed from the point of view of an individual is a means of enabling him to bring under control his instinctive urges to reach a position where he willingly and spontaneously identifies himself with a right.

Discipline from the Point of View of Society: Discipline viewed from the point of view of the society is a means of developing a social sense or social conscience in an individual so that he identifies himself with the society and contributes for its betterment to which he belongs.

External and Internal Discipline: According to William A. Yeager, "Historically, it always is associated with the concept discipline, having the connotations of strict mental, moral and physical training, requiring for its achievement, submission to authority, with proper punishment meted out for disobedience in any form."

Thus it implies something 'external', that is conformity to all external stimulus or impulse. More recently, a school control has come to imply something internal, a response to an inner stimulus or impulse.

To quote T.P. Nunn, "Discipline consists in the submission of one's impulses and powers to regulation which imposes form upon chaos and brings efficiency and economy where there would otherwise be ineffectiveness and waste."

S. Bala Krishna Joshi writes, "What is discipline? To put it in a nutshell, it is decent and decorous conduct which contributes to harmony, joy and success, and exalted sense of responsibility, respect for authority, love of orderliness, eagerness to discharge duties with regularity, promptitude and efficiency, a desire to be agreeable and helpful to others by exercising, if necessary, a wholesome check on individual proclivities and a capacity to maintain equipoise in the face of the most trying circumstances — these constitute discipline."

Discipline and Freedom: Divergent and conflicting opinions have been expressed by the leading educationists from time to time on the question of 'freedom in schools'. There is the extreme view put forward by Rousseau and the persons of his way of thinking that the child should be left free to act practically whatever he likes and free not to do whatever he does not like. This is a revolt against the old conception of 'discipline' and 'freedom' which puts stem restrictions on the child and shuns completely all ideas of 'freedom' and self-discipline'. The protagonists of such an idea believe in the efficacy of the 'rod' as an instrument of discipline. However, the truth lies somewhere between these two extreme views. Ryburn writes, "Freedom in school should bear some relation to the freedom that is found in the world at large." It would be very harmful to leave the child at the mercy of his environment. The theory of 'Natural Consequences' or 'Laissez-Faire', "Children should never receive punishment as such - it should always come as a natural consequence of their fault, is fraught with grave consequences".

Unregulated freedom can be given only at our peril. Bagley rightly puts it as, "The pupil is immature and helpless and he must not be given a long rope with which he may hang himself " Absolute, freedom is a myth. It did not exist, does not exist, will not exist and should not exist.

Excessive Restrictions are Equally Bad: A child who is constantly loaded by many 'dos' and 'don'ts' is unlikely to develop into a well-balanced personality. He will not get sufficient opportunities to do his best. His initiative and drive will be checked. His faculties will remain stunted. His creative powers will remain unharnessed. Authority which derives its strength and sanction from 'fear' paralyses the human mind and spirit. The 'fear atmosphere' will simply create hindrances in providing a suitable environment to the child to grow and blossom. "The man whose tongue is constricted by laws or taboos against free speech, whose pen is constricted by the censorship, whose laws are constricted by an ethic which considers jealousy a better thing than by affection, whose childhood had been imprisoned in a code of manners, and whose youth has been drilled in a cruel orthodoxy, will feel against the world that hampers him with the same rage that is felt by the infant whose arms and legs are held motionless. In his rage he will turn to destruction, becoming a revolutionary militarist, or a persecuting moralist according to temperament and opportunity," writes Russell. It is wrong to believe 'what the whip was to do to the horse, the rod was to do to the child.' 'Compulsion' kills spontaneity.

Discipline is not synonymous with 'class order.' We usually make the mistake of identifying discipline with the orderly behaviour in the classroom teaching and other forms of school activities.

School discipline cannot be conceived in terms of military discipline which is based on:

There is not a reason why
There is not to make reply
There is but to do and die.

Three Conditions

Dr. Adams has marked three distinct stages in the development of ideas of discipline.

First Stage -'Flogging': Flogging was the order of the day in the first stage. Rod was the chief instrument to educate the educant. Fear atmosphere prevailed in the school. The student had to abide by certain rigid rules and regulations and any branch of these meant penalties. The rod and instruction were deemed inseparable. Discipline was enforced from above and known as 'external discipline.'

Second Stage - "Impression rather than Repression: The second stage was when teachers believed that 'impression' rather than 'repression' should be the basis of discipline. They did not support the Flogging Theory. There was a scope for light corporal punishment. According to Ross, "The compelling power of the educator's personality takes the place of punishment; it is his personal influence and that of the school system which he plans and governs that are effective in ensuring that desirable modes of behaviour are followed. There is a reign of respect and love rather than one of terror."

Third Stage of Laissez Faire: The doctrine of Laissez Faire or Free Discipline which constitutes the third stage is the outcome of the teachings of educationists and psychologists like Rousseau, Froebel, Montessori, Dewey, Neill and others. 'Save the child' is the slogan of these educationists.

Repression is Dangerous: Some masterminds contend that the repressive measures only help splitting up the personality of the child into two, i.e. the outer one orderly and obedient and the inner one frustrated and rebellious.

Discipline and Order: J.E. Brown writes that discipline like honour and peace has almost as many different meanings as it has uses. He defines order as, "an outward semblance of good behaviour not in itself to be despised, since it permits work to be carried on smoothly." To achieve order nothing is needed but an authoritative presence with a voice to match, failing which a strong arm is effective.

By discipline he means, "a cooperative mental attitude in which each member of the class freely gives of his best because he feels himself a member of a corporate body whose aims are recognised as worthy; and misbehaviour on the part of any member is condemned by the whole body because it is recognised not only or even chiefly as a crime against the whole 'Community.' The aim of such discipline is to produce self-control led men and women who will work without supervision. This is the ideal stage and known as constructive discipline. Constructive discipline is the outcome of the activities and experiences that inculcate in the individual virtues of self-control based on reason and not on force. It is the outcome of persuasion and not of compulsion. It comes out of doing rather than of talking. Like religion it cannot be taught but can only be caught and practised."

Importance of Discipline: P.C. Wren states, "As in the army, the navy, or the State, so in the school, the prerequisite, the very condition of existence is discipline." Discipline gives the real power and self-control by which potentialities can find their full development. Discipline enables an individual to undertake and discharge his share of responsibilities worthily.

Discipline and Democracy: Discipline is the essence of democracy. In democracy it is not forced from above. It grows from within. It is based on the realisation by the individual of the worth of all other individuals. It is the result of "training of conscience which consists in the cultivation of good will and the development of moral insight."

To quote- the Secondary Education Commission. "Discipline is the fruit, the valuable by-product of cooperative work willingly and efficiently undertaken."

Positive Aspect of School Discipline: An eminent educationist has suggested, "The discipline employed in our classrooms should be designed to place upon the child more and more responsibility for his own choices, purposes and behaviour as he grows in the ability to shoulder such responsibility. Such 'discipline' instead of being repressive and utilising punishment and repraisal for mis-steps will plan with the children the purposes to be achieved and through the social control of group approval will teach the child to discharge creditably the responsibilities assigned to him by the groups."

Discipline is the fruit of cooperative work willingly undertaken and efficiently completed. Discipline from without is always temporisation.

Discipline through the Influence of Social Group: Discipline in the school will not be a matter of arbitrary rules and regulations enforced through the authority of the teachers, helped by the lures of rewards or the fear of punishment. The students will be given full freedom to organise functions, to conduct many of the school activities through their own committees and even to deal with certain types of disciplinary cases. In this way, discipline be maintained through the influence of the social group and it will gradually lead to the development of self-discipline.

Checking Measures

A review of the causes of indiscipline shows that the problem of indiscipline is not an isolated one. Many-sided attempts will, therefore, have to be made to tackle this problem. The parents, the political leaders, the teachers and the government must fully cooperate with each other for the creation of an ideal atmosphere. The following measures should be taken to check indiscipline:

1. Restoration of the lost leadership of the teachers.
2. Improvement in the economic lot of the students.
3. Reform in the system of education.
4. Revival of the sense of values.

Restoration of the Lost Leadership to the Teachers: The salaries of the teachers must be raised to ameliorate their economic lot. High salaries are bound to attract right type of persons to the teaching profession. To raise the social status of the teachers, special measures should be adopted.

Refresher courses and seminars help the teachers to know the current educational thoughts and practices.

Holiday Homes should be established so that with moderate expenditure, the teachers are in a position to enjoy their holidays.

Improvement in the Economic Lot of the Students: A large number of scholarships and stipends should be given to the meritorious students who are economically handicapped. At nominal prices the State should take steps to supply tiffin to school children belonging to poor families. There should be provision for supplying free books, etc. to the students.

Reform in the System of Education: Far reaching changes in the curriculum are needed. Secondary education should be diversified to meet the varying needs of the adolescents. Youthful activities should be provided in large numbers. Programmes which offer excellent opportunities of developing character and citizenship should be undertaken.

"The problem of discipline must be looked at from the point of view of proper utilisation of the abundant energy of the youth. If youthful urges and energy are canalised and fields are found which will utilise all their enthusiasm and devotion, there will be little occasion to impose restrictions from above. Discipline must be achieved by giving proper direction to the energy of the youth and not by suppression," observes Maulana Azad.

Examination system should be changed radically so that the students work throughout the year. The work of a student should be assessed after taking into account the record of his achievements throughout the year.

Our methods of teaching require a great transformation. The students should be made active partners and not passive listeners.

Personal contact with the students should be established to understand and solve their individual difficulties.

Autocratic attitude on the part of the authorities should be replaced by democratic ideals. An atmosphere of love, affection and sympathy is very conducive to the development of the personality of the child. Cooperation of the students should be secured in utilising boys' funds.

Students and teachers should keep aloof from politics and the political leaders should make it a point not to exploit students for the furtherance of their political cause.

"At the time of election, members who contest election do not hesitate to utilise students for the furtherance of their objective, namely the winning of the election. The utilisation of immature minds for purposes of campaigns with or without slogans attached thereto is not calculated to promote sound discipline among students," observes the Secondary Education Commission.

Significance of Self-discipline

It is very erroneous to think that free discipline or self-discipline or creative discipline can be had by resorting to external discipline. At the same time it must be remembered that the goal of self-discipline cannot be achieved in a day or so. It can be had only with increasing watchfulness. It requires patience of a very high order. Cooperation of the various agencies of education is absolutely essential to inculcate right types of attitudes and habits in the students. A school is said to be a cooperative society where all work for the welfare and happiness of each and each for the whole. The rules and the regulations of a cooperative society are framed to a considerable extent, by the members themselves and are not imposed from above. All the members of this society are expected to respect and honour them. Discipline is not the business of school authorities. Why? It is, as a matter of fact, the business of the whole society. The Secondary Education Commission observes, "Discipline, they say, should be a responsibility of parents, teachers, the general public and the authorities concerned."

Student Government: This is considered to be a very effective way of securing the willing cooperation of the students. By participating in various committees formed to govern themselves they realise that rules and regulations and their enforcement are very essential. They learn that no society can function smoothly if the members do not obey its rules. They get opportunities to understand and appreciate the significance of tolerance, open-mindedness, cooperation and fellow-feeling. They learn to appreciate that rights and responsibilities go together.

Games: Students learn that for the success of a team, they must cooperate with each other and also must subordinate their individual interests. Every player knows that the rules of the game must be obeyed if he wants to participate in it. Thus the students learn to discipline themselves.

The Secondary Education Commission has suggested that "Another important method of bringing home to the pupils the value of discipline is through group games. It is on the playing fields that team spirit can be cultivated. Extra-curricular activities will promote a proper spirit of discipline."

Cooperation among the Staff Members: Children are imitative and suggestive by nature. They acquire many habits simply by imitating their teachers. Lack of cooperation among the members of the staff and between the staff and the Headmaster, is bound to develop attitudes of non-cooperation in the students. This unhealthy aspect of the life of the institution has a great demoralising effect on the minds of the students.

Methods of Teaching: Good methods of teaching facilitate learning. Use of audio-visual aids, black-boards, story telling, etc., brings life in the dead-matter of various subjects. Methods like Dalton Plan, Project, the Heuristic and the Basic Scheme develop habits of constant work among the students, besides sharpening their power of thinking. Learning by doing is a device which keeps the students busy. The students make mischief only when they are passive listeners. Rightly it is said that the best method of keeping the students disciplined is to fill the time with work.

Sympathetic Attitude: 'Love the child and the child will love you, hate him and he will hate you' is an old saying. A sympathetic teacher is sure to win the hearts of his pupils. Once this is done, there is no reason why they should go astray. Quite a large number of troubles arise due to the harsh and unsympathetic behaviour of the authorities towards the students.

Personal Relationship: Loss of personal relationships between the teacher and the taught is fatal for creative education. Without it, we cannot think of students developing ideals of a creative citizen.

Punishment: It has a definite place but should be used very carefully and judiciously. It must suit the nature of the offending child. 'Just rebuke' may be sufficient in some cases while in others, even corporal punishment may prove to be futile.

Co-curricular Activities: These provide them suitable channels to utilise their surplus energy. They are also very helpful in sublimating their instincts. Sultan Mohiyuddin thinks, "The various activities and pursuits will furnish their motive power, work will be done for its own sake, the mutual relations of the members of the school will be properly appreciated and the rules and laws of the school will be recognised as necessary for smooth functioning of the school as whole and for the effective participation of each individual member in the school life, and in consequence the needs of the individual and of the group will be properly adjusted."

Material Conditions of Work: Good' furniture, library, laboratory, sufficient classroom accommodation, hall, playgrounds, good arrangement for light, water, ventilation and sanitation, etc., present a congenial environment conducive to self-discipline.

Moral Education: A programme of moral education stimulates the interests of the adolescents in the social aspects of religions. It helps them to fortify their faith in the conviction that there are certain fundamental values in life which are very essential for a gracious and harmonious living. Albert L. Ayars writes, "The school programme of moral and spiritual values should not be thought as a course of division of instruction. It is an integral part of the curriculum, emphasised in all courses and activities."

Rising Indiscipline

We can hardly minimise the gravity of the problem of indiscipline in our educational institutions., "No amount of improvement and reconstruction in education will bear much fruit if the schools themselves are undermined by indiscipline," observed the Secondary Education Commission. In the candid opinion of Prof. Humayun Kabir, "Failure to take effective steps at this stage can so aggravate the problem that it may shake the very foundations of our national life." In the absence of discipline in a school, there is bound to be chaos and confusion, waste and inefficiency. Discipline is the life-blood of an institution. An indisciplined life is like a boat without rudder tossing every now and then at the passing current.

Prof. K.G. Saiyidain attributed these causes:

1. Sense of frustration among students.
2. Lack of sufficient interest in studies.
3. Overcrowding in schools and colleges.
4. Undignifying examples set by politicians.

Shri K.M. Cariappa observed on January 6th, 1966 that students were being exploited by unscrupulous politicians who encouraged them to strike and indulge in acts of rowdyism.

A number of factors are responsible for the growing sense of indiscipline in our students. The fault lies partly with the system of education, partly with the teachers of educational institutions, partly with the existing social, economic and political conditions and partly also with the conditions prevailing in our homes. Prof. Humayun Kabir in a pamphlet Student Indiscipline has described the following causes of indiscipline in our students:

1. The loss of leadership by teachers.
2. Growth of economic difficulties.
3. Defects in the existing system of education.
4. General loss of idealism.

Loss of Leadership by Teachers: Failure on the part of teachers to take active part in the struggle for freedom, sweeping criticism of the present system of education and of teachers; inadequate salaries of the teachers and frustration caused by it, entry of unqualified persons in the teaching profession, control of politicians over educational institutions and the acceptance of tuitions on an almost commercial scale by some of the teachers are considered to be some of the major factors which have led to their loss of leadership among the student community. Strained personal relations between the staff and the head have also an adverse effect on the minds of the students. The Secondary Education Commission observes: "Discipline among students can only be promoted if there is discipline among the staff both within the school and in organisation connected with the teaching profession. The teacher has always to realise that all his activities are being watched by his pupils to that extent, therefore, both in his personal conduct and his general attitude to all his problems concerning the country, he has to realise that there are limitations within which he must act for the best interest of the profession."

Economic Difficulties: Another reason, though to a very limited extent, of indiscipline in some educational institutions is that some students who otherwise may be topmost are economically distressed. On the one hand they feel that they are superior to the other children in studies and on the other hand find that their economic condition is far inferior to that of some well-to-do but mediocre students. This leads to discontentment with the existing order and in the absence of any soothing influence, they gradually become bitter and indisciplined.

Defects in the Existing System of Education: It would not be unfair to say that the present system of education is rather indifferent to the development of character among pupils.

The progress of a child is judged by the results of the annual examination. The energies of the students are not properly utilised during the major part of the year and the students seek outlets in activities which are anti-social. Co-curricular activities hardly exist to canalise their energies. They are considered as sheer waste of time. Frances W. Parker writes, "The fundamental reason why children do not act is because they do not have the conditions for right action." Maulana Azad has also stressed this point : "I am convinced that if the young are at times restless and turbulent, it is not due to any intrinsic defect in them. Their restlessness is largely due to the fact that they do not have enough channels for the expression of their youthful urges."

Education not being in accordance with the age, ability and aptitude of the students, develops frustration among them.

The running of most of our educational institutions more or less on commercial lines fails to establish moral and spiritual links between the teacher and the taught.

The authoritarian attitude of the authorities in our educational system is also an important factor in the growth of unrest and indiscipline in our students.

The students have no say in majority of the cases in the disposal of Boy's Funds and it raises suspicion in their minds. Lack of imagination on the part of the authorities to understand the growing awakening among the students aggravates the problem all the more.

Classes being overcrowded, the individual needs of the students remain unattended to and the personal contact between the teachers and the students does not develop.

Too much talk of self-discipline and liberalism in the field of education has also done some harm. Loud talks of student government have sometimes led the students to believe that there are no rules for them to be obeyed.

General Loss of Idealism: There appears to be a general fall in the standard of morality in the different walks of life. It will not be wrong to say that the society is undermined by indiscipline to a greater extent. Discipline is greatly affected by the tone of the society as a whole.

Reasons of Tussle

1. Demand for removal of a teacher on the grounds of inefficiency from the point of view of students.
2. Retention of the teacher whom the management intends to transfer or retire.
3. Refusal of the authorities to pen-nit some students to appear in an examination owing to shortage of attendance.
4. Demand for grant of holiday in the memory of some important personality or for the celebration of some public event.
5. Demand for a change in the date of examination.
6. Stiffness of the examination paper.
7. Demand for the establishment of the students' union.

8. Demand for the remission of fine to particular student who has been fined due to his behaviour.
9. Demand for certain facilities (library, etc.) in the school.
10. Enhancement of funds.

Common Types

1. Disrespect for authorities, i.e. rudeness.
2. Disrespect for school rules and regulations.
3. Disrespect for teachers, i.e. discourtesy.
4. Coming late in the class.
5. Deliberately not doing assignment.
6. Unruly behaviour in the class, to be noisy and disturbing others.
7. Making noise in school assembly and public gatherings.
8. Damaging and spoiling the school property.
9. Using indecent and abusive language.
10. Making uncalled for remarks to the fair sex.
11. Forming gangs.
12. Organising strikes.
13. Aggressive behaviour, e.g. bullying and teasing.
14. Using unfair means in the examinations.
15. Dishonest dealings, i.e. stealing, lying, etc.
16. Deliberately not paying the fee in time.

Physical Training

The Theories

Psychological and physiological principles form the basis of physical education and it is but obvious that physical education should include activities pertaining to these principles. Following points should be borne in mind while organising a programme of physical education:

1. Undue emphasis should not be given to those physical activities which primarily develop strength of muscles.
2. Activities which are suitable for the different age groups should be provided. The children should not be judged by adult standards.
3. Too much emphasis shall not be laid on inter-school competitions. A large number of students should be encouraged to participate in various physical activities.
4. Classroom physical activities should be encouraged.
5. Physical activities pertaining to the cleanliness of the school should be organised off and on.

Physical education is not merely to be confined to the playground but should pervade the classroom. Physical education in the classroom may take the following forms:

1. Direct instruction emphasising the necessity of having a good physique.
2. Suggestions regarding the maintenance of good health.
3. Emphasis on right postures.
4. Provision of good seating and lighting arrangements in the classroom, thereby impressing upon the students the importance of studying under healthy surroundings.
5. Providing ample opportunities to the children for physical activity.

The last point requires elucidation. It should be borne in mind that physical development and mental development are inseparably allied to each other. Classroom should not be devoid of physical activity. Instruction in a play-way manner affords ample opportunities to the students to be physically active and a wise teacher would always bring this spirit of play-way in classroom work. The students should play an active role in the instruction work. They should not remain merely as passive listeners. For pre-primary classes, Kindergarten and Montessori methods afford opportunities for the physical development of the children. Basic system of education is based on the principle of learning by doing. This involves many physical activities. Project Method and the Dalton Plan are the other examples which require many activities on the part of children. Paper cutting and folding may be associated with Elementary Geometry and Arithmetic. Students may learn Nature Study and Geography with the help of clay modelling. A variety of programmes may be introduced in the classroom. Reading, writing, figuring, drawing, etc. should be profitably attempted to provide practical activities. A few minutes drill or music after every lesson of the class may introduce bodily activity among the children.

We may sum up by quoting J.F. Williams, "Of all the activities of school curriculum, none is as rich with educational outcomes as the plays, games, sports and athletics of physical education."

Athletics and Gymnastics

Gymnastics and athletics are two important forms of physical education.

The chief aim of athletics is recreation. Gymnastics on the other hand stimulate normal physical development, promote good carriage and secure general efficiency in the individual. The effect of gymnastic exercises is internal and primary. They are based on sound principles. Each exercise has its own value for a specific purpose. Gymnastic exercises are very helpful in teaching correct postures. Gymnastic exercises with apparatus (Bars, Horse, Ladder, etc.) are greatly liked by the boys as these involve a great degree of skill and difficulties. Gymnastic exercises like marching, easy exercises in jumping and skipping, aesthetic dancing and folk dancing appeal to the girls.

Athletic activities include running, jumping, disc throwing, hammer throwing and weight throwing, etc.

In carrying out gymnastics, the following points should be taken into consideration:

1. Lessons and exercises should be purposive and not at random.
2. A shirt and shorts are sufficient.
3. The postures should be good.
4. The boys should not be held in a straight position for a long time.
5. The gymnastic exercises should be correlated with material and play.
6. All material should be kept in order.

Modern educationists believe in freedom of children. They dislike every sort of compulsion as they think that the element of compulsion robs the child of the enjoyment which he would otherwise derive.

A child derives immense pleasure in free play. He wants to choose games and other kinds of activities according to his interest. He does not like that any time limit should be imposed on him while he is at play. Free play has direct appeal to his natural urges and it satisfies his psychological needs. "Play is a biological and social necessity for children. It is the most fundamental thing about a child - play for the child is one of the most serious facts of life; it is a form of work for the young, and the basis for all natural education," writes Davie.

It is in the nature of the child to play. He is interested in it from the very birth. Stern defines play as "voluntary self-constrained activity". The values of play may be classified as under:

- Educational.
- Intellectual.
- Physical.
- Social.
- Emotional.
- Developmental.

Physical Drill: Physical drill should be organised regularly. It should be properly graded, 'simple to complex' and 'easy to difficult' should form the basis of physical drill. Violent exercises may lead to heart strain. The duration of the period should depend upon the age and strength of the pupils. A good system of physical exercises would give beneficially exercise to all parts of the body, e.g. muscles, legs, neck, trunk, etc. Following types of exercises will make the programme interesting and instructive:

1. Preparing or warming up, running in a circle, marching, etc.
2. Corrective exercises.
3. Educative exercises.
4. Recreative exercises.
5. Physiological exercises.

The playground is said to be the cradle of democracy. Various co-curricular activities and especially the games and sports contribute a lot for the development of all the major qualities needed to be an ideal citizen.

Games Teach Cooperation: Team work is the pivot round which the wheel of games revolves. If the members of the team do not work for the team but for their individual distinctions, the team is sure to go to the walls. Games and sports bring home this fact to the students that loyalty and cooperation are the important contributory factors for the honour of the team. These serve to eliminate selfishness and teach the students to subordinate their own interests for the sake of a broader aim of winning the game.

This lesson is very important and every citizen is expected to follow it:

Preparation for Life Situations: The players have to play sometimes against heavy odds. Courage, patience, steadfastness and perseverance are needed to play well and effectively. The players get accustomed to face very critical situations and this stands in good stead when they enter life. We cannot think of an ideal citizen without possessing these qualities.

Providing Opportunities for Leadership: Games and sports provide opportunities for leadership of a very high order. The captain of the team has to put right players at their right places and has to bring harmony among the different members of the team. Only a man of self-confidence, imagination and enterprise can lead others.

Development of Various Senses: The games and sports call for a variety of movements — physical and mental. "School games involve a wide range of activity. Most of the senses are called into action. Comparison and judgement are needed," says William Gowers. The mind has to be kept alert to meet the changing situation to the ball. Body and mind work in harmony.

Physical Development: Games and sports promote good health, which is perhaps more important than wealth. Good health is also a sign of a good citizen.

Emphasis on Struggle: They teach the lesson that struggle is more important than success. Baron de Conbertin states, "The important thing in sports is not to win but to take part. The important thing in life is not triumph but struggle. The essential thing is not to have conquered but to have fought well. To spread these precepts is to build up a stronger and more scrupulous and more generous humanity."

Satisfaction of Various Urges of Children: Games satisfy one of the important urges of the children. Play is a biological and social necessity for the children. It is the most fundamental thing about a child - play for the child is one of the most serious facts of life; it is a form of work for the young and the basis for all education.

Development of Esprit de Corps: Tournaments develop in the minds of the students love for the school. 'We feeling' comes to the forefront. Tournaments if properly conducted help in developing the idea of corporate life in the minds of students. The players play for their respective schools and the other students of the respective schools cheer up. How thrilling it is to witness the students clapping and encouraging the players of their sides! The love for the institution is clearly manifested in the minds of the students.

Tournaments are of great help in raising the standard of sports of different institutions.

However, a few objections have been raised to the inter-school tournaments:

1. They benefit too few students,
2. They are expensive in time and money,
3. They cause physical injuries,
4. They cause emotional injuries,
5. They foster over-specialisation,
6. They encourage professionalism and commercialism,
7. They give rise to unsocial feelings,
8. They develop poor sportsmanship.

"To suffer defeat cheerfully and not to burst into rowdyism or even resort to discourtesy, to do one's best against odds and not to lose heart, to be fair to the opponent and not to take any mean advantage of him, to play on equal and honourable terms for the sake of play and not try to win by hook and crook, in short to love the game above the prize, this is the spirit which should prevail in these inter-school tournaments."

Profitable Use or Leisure Time: Leisure time is utilised in a very profitable way and thus these games fulfil another function of education.

Training in Character: Lastly they afford a valuable training in character. Gandhiji has stated, "What is education without character?" Similarly, we ask, "What is character without self-control, courage, steadfastness, perseverance, obedience, morality, nobility and health?" For promoting all these qualities of character, games and sports are very potent and effective.

A glance over the educative values of these games and sports is apt to lead to the conclusion that playground is another school and its function is equally important.

There is no rose without a thorn. If we are not cautious enough to pluck a rose, thorn is sure to prick us. In the same way if games and sports are not scientifically planned they may do more harm than good.

We may sum up the importance of games and sports with a quotation from Aldous Huxley. "Like every other instrument that man has invented, sport can be used either for good or evil purpose. Used well, it can teach endurance and courage, a sense of fair play and a respect for rules, coordinated effort and the subordination of personal interest to those of the group. Used badly it can encourage personal vanity and group vanity, greedy desire for victory and hatred for rivals, an intolerant 'esprit de corps' and contempt for people who are beyond a certain arbitrarily selected pole. In either case sport inculcates responsible cooperation."

Game Organising Theories

1. Keeping in view the different needs of children, a variety of games should be provided.
2. Every child should be induced to take part in one or the other game. Our motto should be 'Games for All'.
3. Every team should consist of members having more or less the same skill.
4. Games time-table should be framed. Regular time should be given to the games.
5. Indian as well as western games should find a place.
6. Supervision of games by the teachers is very essential to have their benefits. 'Unsupervised playgrounds often become hot bed of vice.'
7. The attainments of the students in this field should be mentioned in their progress cards.
8. The teaching periods of those teachers who conduct games should be lessened.

9. Games fund should not be spent on a few selected stars.
10. Tournaments should be organised off and on.
11. Winning of trophies should not become the end and be all of activities.

The Development

Recommendations of the Secondary Education Commission 1952-53

1. Physical activities should be made to suit the individual and his capacity for physical endurance.
2. All teachers below the age of 40 should actively participate in many of the physical activities of students and thus make them a lively part of the school programme.
3. Full records of physical activities of the students must be maintained.
4. The training in physical education should be comprehensive enough to include all aspects of health education.
5. The teachers of physical education should be associated with the teaching of subjects like Physiology and Hygiene and given the same status as other teachers of similar qualifications.
6. The existing facilities for training of teachers of physical education should be expanded by increasing the seats in the existing colleges, by opening new colleges where necessary and by recognising some of the institutions as All India Training Centres to which aid may be given both by the Centre and the States.

Recommendations of the All India Seminar

The All India Seminar was held at Mahabaleshwar from 16th to 30th May, 1958 under the chairmanship of Shri D.G. Wakharkar. *Inter alia*, the seminar made certain recommendations regarding physical education at the school level. Among the important recommendations are:

1. Physical education should be a curricular subject in the schools at all levels and should be on par with other subjects.

2. The programme of physical education and recreation should cater to the needs, interests and capacities of the pupils, and should have 'carry over' value. It should promote normal growth and development, maintenance of health, acquisition of skills and desirable social attitudes and behaviour.
3. Leadership in the field of physical education should consist of: a) qualified staff, b) specialist coaches, and c) student leaders.
4. Any of the following qualifications should be considered as approved qualification for a person to work as a physical education teacher in a secondary school: a) A Degree in Physical Education; b) A University Degree with a Diploma in Physical Education; c) A pass in Intermediate or its equivalent with a Certificate in Physical Education; d) A pass in Matric or S.S.L.C. or S.S.C. or S.F. Examination with a Certificate in Physical Education.
5. In primary schools, classroom teachers should teach physical education.
6. Periodical refresher courses should be organised for in-service physical education teachers.
7. Special coaching camps should be conducted for school physical education teachers at Government cost.
8. Playgrounds should be provided by schools as laid down in the National Plan of Physical Education and Recreation. Schools may, however, have playgrounds with the following minimum limits:

Category	*Boys*	*Girls*
(a) High Schools	5 acres	3 acres
(b) Middle Schools	3 acres	2 acres
(c) Primary Schools	½ to 1 acre	½ to 1 acre

9. Schools having excess open space may be required to permit the use of such open space by the neighbouring schools.
10. Each school should have an indoor gymnasium with the dimensions of 60' x 15'.

11. Schools should provide daily one period for physical education in the time table.
12. The syllabus given in the National Plan of Physical Education and Recreation should be followed in all schools with suitable modifications wherever necessary.
13. Medical inspection should be compulsory for all pupils.

Supervision of Health, Physical Education and Recreation in Schools: In order to make supervision serve its purposefully, the following staff may be provided in each state:

1. Deputy Director of Education for Physical Education and Recreation;
2. Two State Physical Education Officers for men's branch and women's branch separately;
3. Regional or Divisional Physical Education Officers (Men's and Women's branches separately), each in charge of a unit of about four District Physical Education Officers;
4. District Physical Education Officers (Men's and Women's branches separately), each in charge of about 50 high schools.

Report of the Ad Hoc Enquiry Committee on Games and Sports

The Government of India, appointed a Committee in 1958 to investigate the persistence of low standard in sports in India and the performance of the Indian teams in international contests, such as Olympic and Asian Games, and to recommend measures for improvement.

Major References

1. More facilities and better opportunities for training and competition should be provided and greater administrative efficiency achieved.
2. Greater facilities should be provided in educational institutions in the form of equipment, playgrounds and funds.
3. Incentives in the form of credit for achievements in sports and games should be provided.
4. Health, power of endurance, physical well-being of young people should be developed by improvement in nutrition.

5. Sports and games should be organised in rural areas through Vyayamshalas, Vyayam Mandals, Akharas, etc. and in cooperation with the Community Projects. Sports festivals should be organised and sports events encouraged on the occasion of fairs. Indigenous sports like Kabaddi and indigenous style of wrestling should be encouraged.
6. If schools and colleges and universities have to play their part in the development of sports and games in the country, they must have the minimum requirements in respect of playgrounds and equipment. The following standards have been recommended:

A College (with a student population of 1000 to 1500)	:	10 acres for playground
A High School (with a student population of 500 to 1000)	:	5-6 acres
A Middle School (with a student population of 200 to 500)	:	3-5 acres
A Primary School	:	1 acre

7. Where separate playgrounds cannot be made available for each educational institution, a common pool for a group of institutions should be created.

Recommendations of the Education Commission 1964-66: Writing about the concept of physical education, the Education Commission 1964-66 felt, "It must be emphasised that such education contributes not only to physical fitness but also to physical efficiency, mental alertness and the development of certain qualities like perseverance, team spirit, leadership, obedience to rules, moderation in victory and balance in defeat."

Five Forms of Physical Activities According to the Commission: According to the Education Commission 1964-66, physical education should include:

1. Development exercises.
2. Rhythmic activities.
3. Sports and games.

4. Outing activities.
5. Group handling activities.

Simple and Advanced Forms: The Commission further observed that all these have simple and advanced forms. The simpler activities should be introduced in the early classes, the more advanced ones should be gradually provided as boys and girls become more and more mature.

Principles of Developing a Programme of Physical Education: The Education Commission (1964-66) suggested the following eight principles for developing a satisfactory programme of physical education:

1. The physical education programme should be planned for desirable outcomes keeping in mind the interests and capacity of the participants.
2. The traditional forms of play and physical activities that have developed in our country should receive due emphasis in the programme.
3. The activities promoted should develop in each child a sense of personal worth and pride.
4. A sense of sharing responsibility in a spirit of democratic cooperation should grow from experience on playground and also in the gymnasium.
5. The programme offered should supplement other programmes of education and not duplicate them.
6. The programme should be within our financial means.
7. The programme should reach all rather than a selected few.
8. Special instruction and coaching should be provided for students with talent and special aptitude.

National Policy on Education and Sports and Physical Education

Sports and physical education are an integral part of the learning process, and will be included in the evaluation of performance. A nationwide infrastructure for physical education, sports and games will be built into the educational edifice.

The infrastructure will consist of play fields, equipment, coaches and teachers of physical education as part of the School

Improvement Programme. Available open spaces in urban areas will be reserved for playgrounds, if necessary by legislation. Efforts will be made to establish sports institutions and hostels where specialised attention will be given to sports activities and sports related studies, along with normal education. Appropriate encouragement will be given to those talented in sports and games. Due stress will be laid on indigenous traditional games. As a system which promotes an integrated development of body and mind, yoga will receive special attention. Efforts will be made to introduce yoga in all schools; to this end it will be introduced in teacher training courses.

The Reputation

"The physical welfare of the youth of the country should be one of the main concerns of the State and any departure from the normal standards of physical well-being at this period of life may have serious consequences," observed the Secondary Education Commission.

Hall has very emphatically observed, "A ton of knowledge bought at the expense of an ounce of health which is the most ancient and precious form of wealth costs more than its value."

Similar views have been expressed by Carlyle when he writes, "We manufacture clever devils by the thousand because health is not the object of party politics."

Our great saint Swami Vivekananda has also stressed the importance of well-built bodies when he remarks, "What India needs today is not the Bhagwad Gita but the football field." Our Indian schools must give due importance to this aspect of education. There is a great need of a general philosophy of physical education in India, though it appears to be a very strange in a country famous for ancient Yogic system. There is no denying the fact that of late we have been ignoring this side. This has led W.M. Ryburn to remark, "We need in Indian education a general physical education — a conception of education in which physical education takes its rightful place and in which its vital importance is recognised."

Regarding the significance of physical education, H.C. Buck has observed that a properly directed physical education should result in health, happiness, efficiency and character.

Froebel says, "If we wish to develop the whole being, we must exercise the whole human being."

Rousseau states, "It is the sound Constitution of the body, that makes the operation of the mind easy and certain."

Spencer is of the view, "To be a good animal is the first requisite to success in the life and to be a nation of good animals is the first condition to national prosperity."

Montague writes, "physical education does neither train up the soul, nor body but the whole man."

Meaning and Concept: In the words of C.L. Brownwell, "Physical education is concerned with strength and endurance (the principal objectives of physical training). But physical education regards these qualities as a means to an end — the means of obtaining greater satisfaction in a specific activity, and the end which represents the all-round educational development associated with participation in the activity. In short, physical education means the physical activities that have characterised the immemorial history of mankind."

According to Delbert Obertenffer, "Physical education is the sum of those experiences which come to the individual through movement."

Jesse Feiring Williams thinks, "Physical education is the sum of man's physical activities selected as to kind and conducted as to outcomes."

In the words of Jay B. Nash, "physical education is that field of education which deals with big muscle activities and their related responses."

"Physical education is an integral part of the total education process and has as its aim the development of physically, mentally, emotionally and socially fit citizens through the medium of physical activities which have been selected with a view to realising these outcomes."

Charles A. Bucher: "Physical education is the social process of change in the behaviour of the human organism, originating primarily from the stimulus of social big-muscle-play and related activities."

C.C. Cowell: "Physical education is that phase of education which is concerned, first, with the organisation and leadership of children in big muscle activities, to gain the development and adjustment inherent in the activities according to social standards, and second with the leadership of the activities so that the educational process may go on without growth handicaps."

Clark, W. Hetherington: "Physical education should be defined as that phase of the whole process of education which is concerned with vigorous muscular activities and related responses and with the modifications in the individual resultant from these responses."

Nixon and Cozens: "Physical education is that part of education which proceeds by means of, or predominantly through physical activity, it is not some separate, partially related field."

Edward F. Voltmer, Arthur A. Esslingor: "Physical education is but one aspect of the larger problem of education in general, and any system which divorces or tends to divorce, the physical from the moral and intellectual aspects of life, is thoroughly unsound."

The Secondary Education Commission made it clear "that unless physical education is accepted as an integral part of education, and the educational authorities recognise its need in all schools, the youth of the country, which forms its most valuable asset, will never be able to pull their full weight in national welfare". The old concept of physical education as 'mere drill or a series of regulated exercises' has been rejected. "It includes all forms of physical activities and games which promote the development of the body and mind." The Commission recommended that physical education should be comprehensive enough to include all aspects of health education; full records of physical activities should be maintained; teachers of physical education should be given the same status as other teachers of similar qualifications; and other teachers of the school along with the physical instructor should actively participate in the physical activities of students. Regarding health education, the Commission emphasised the need for a properly organised school medical service in all States, and a thorough medical examination of all pupils with follow-up and treatment where necessary.

The Education Commission (1964-66) points out: 'There has been a tendency in recent government schemes of physical education to emphasise only the physical fitness value of physical education and ignore its educational value.' The concept of physical education has been made broader, as it should contribute 'not only to physical fitness but also to physical efficiency, mental alertness and the development of certain qualities — perseverance, team spirit, leadership, obedience to rules, moderation in victory and balance in defeat.' The Commission was aware of the hard realities which one encounters while preparing programmes of physical education in schools and colleges, and, therefore, it suggested that the programmes 'should take into account not only what is useful but also what is possible in view of limitations of facilities, time and number of teachers.' It also emphasised the need for re-examining and redesigning the programmes of physical education in the light of certain basic principles of child growth and development.

From the views expressed above it will be obvious that physical education is not only concerned with helping the child to grow and develop physically but learning to fit in with his social environment and adjusting to life around, acquiring the capacity to be mentally alert to all environmental responses, expressing emotions without prejudice to others and otherwise reaching his maturity progressively.

Targets and Goals

1. Conservation of health.
2. Development of well-built bodies.
3. Development of qualities like endurance, self-control, courage, etc.
4. Development of qualities relating to society, e.g. obedience, cooperation, leadership and followership, etc.
5. Development of regular habits of exercise and play.
6. Development of regular health habits.
7. Development of the whole man. Montague rightly remarks, "Physical education does neither train up the soul nor body, but the whole man." Froebel aptly stated, "Early education

must deal directly with the physical development and influence the spiritual development through the exercise of senses."

The Curriculum

The types of activities considered essential are as under:

Developmental Activities

1. Exercise tables, 'dands', 'baithaks' and yogic exercises.
2. Fundamental movements such as walking, running, throwing, jumping, climbing and balancing.
3. Mimetics and story plays.
4. Stunts, pyramids, weight and conditioning exercises.

Rhythmics

Rhythm fundamentals, rhythm games, folk dances, social dances, singing games, community singing, Indian rhythmics, 'garha', 'phugdi', 'himma', 'tipri', etc.

Games, Sports, and Athletics

1. Major Games, such as 'kabaddi', 'kho-kho', volleyball, basketball, football, hockey, cricket, etc.
2. Dual games such as tennis, table tennis, badminton, ring-tennis, etc.
3. Recreative games, minor games, relays, social games, group games, lead-up games, etc.

Sports: Cycling, canoeing, shooting, riding, skating, etc.

Athletics: Running, jumping, throwing, walking and relays.

Formal Activities

Drill and marching, light apparatus, calisthenics, mass P.T. exercises.

Apparatus: Parallel bars, vaulting, beam, roman rings, ropes, pommel horse, single bar, 'malkhamb', etc.

Combatives: Wrestling, boxing, judo, lathi fight, dagger fight, farigadga, sword fight, simple contests and mass combatives based on 'attack and defence'.

Aquatics: Swimming, diving and life saving.

Self-testing Activities: All types of tests.

Camping and Outdoor Activities: Hiking, cross country, camping and mountaineering, picnics, excursions, etc.

Special Activities: Demonstrations, ceremonial parades, singing the National Anthem, flag salutations, practical projects, citizenship training, etc.

Health Education

Locke's famous saying 'a sound mind in a sound body' is true for all ages. Regarding the importance of health Ben Johnson has stated. "O Health! Health! the blessing of the rich! the riches of the poor! Who can buy thee at too dear a rate, since there is no enjoying this world without thee." Similarly Herbert Spencer writes, "The preservation of health is a duty few seem conscious that there is a thing physical morality." The Secondary Education Commission has greatly stressed the importance of physical well-being in these words, "The physical welfare of the youth of the country should be one of the main concerns of the State, and any departure from the normal standards of physical well-being at this period of life may have serious consequences." Health education should form all integral part of education.

Precautionary Measures

1. The student should be asked to take regular exercise to strengthen muscles.
2. Suitable furniture should be provided.
3. Good postural habits should be developed. The students should be told that the head, neck, trunk, thigh and legs are in a straight line in a good standing posture. While writing, the students should be asked to keep their note-books at a

distance of one foot. While reading, the books should be held vertically so that the top and the bottom of the books are at an equal distance from the eyes. The distance of 12 inches is an ideal one.

4. Stools should be provided for smaller children so that they may learn to sit without reclining against the chair.
5. Suitable corrective postural exercises should be recommended to the students.
6. Students having defective eyesight and hearing should be seated on the front benches.
7. Rooms should be suitably ventilated and sufficient accommodation should be provided.
8. Bold type books should be selected.
9. The aid of school medical officer should be sought.

Diseases by Infections

Causes of Infectious Diseases: These are caused by germs which are organisms that are either invisible or visible only under a very powerful microscope. They invade the body and multiply rapidly. The poisons manufactured by the germs circulate in the blood and give rise to symptoms of particular diseases. Germs are carried from one person to another and the diseases spread. Germs can be carried by flies and other insects, human beings, articles used by the infected person and public conveniences.

Prevention of Infectious Diseases: The following steps should be taken to prevent the spread of the disease.

Notification: The health officer or the municipal committee should be informed at once when a case of infectious disease occurs in the home.

Isolation: The patient should be separated from healthy individuals.

Quarantine: Neighbours and relatives of the patient and all those people who have come in contact with the patient should be separated for a specific length of time, equal to the incubation period of the disease.

Disinfection and Preventive Measures: Disinfectants are agents that destroy germs. Some of the chemical disinfectants are lysol, potassium permanganate, carbolic acid, iodine, phenyl, sulphur dioxide, formaldehyde, etc. Heat and sunlight are natural disinfectants.

Education: Public should be educated about the disease — how it is spread, how to prevent it and what steps they should take to control its spread.

Stages of Diseases: There are three distinct stages in every disease caused by germs: i) The incubation stage, ii) The acute stage of the disease, and iii) Convalescence.

Description of Various Diseases

Disease	*Incubation period*	*Symptoms*	*Affected Age*	*Precaution to be taken in the School*
1. Measles	One or two weeks	Cold, rise in temperature, reddish rash on the body	Usually before 10 years of age	1. Consultation of the doctor 2. Sending the child home 3. The child to be kept away from school for at least 3 weeks.
2. Mumps	14 to 28 days	Swelling from ear to ear, painful eating	Common among school children	Child to be separated from the school for about 20 days.
3. Whooping cough	6 to 18 days	Common cold	Childhood before 5	Send the child home for at least two months.
4. Diphtheria	2 to 10 days	White patches on the soft palate, tonsils and throat.	Before 2 or 3 years of age	Until the child gets cured, he should not be allowed to attend school.

Contd...

Disease	*Incubation period*	*Symptoms*	*Affected Age*	*Precaution to be taken in the School*
5. Chicken Pox	11 to 19 days	Rashes consisting of red spots, blisters, scabs	Generally upto 12 years of age.	1. Student to be sent home 2. Student not to be allowed to attend school for about 3 weeks.
6. Small Pox	10 to 15 days	Severe headache, backache, high fever	All ages	1. Vaccination 2. Student to be sent home.
7. Influenza	A few hours to a few days	Pain in the head, back and limbs, shivering, rise in temperature, running of eyes and nose, sneezing and coughing.	Children and Adults	1. Students to be advised not to visit crowdy places. 2. Use of handkerchief 3. Students to be separated from the school.
8. Cholera	A few hours to a few days	Severe pain in the abdomen, vomiting, diarrhoea.	All ages	Cleanliness of urinals and lavatories.
9. Typhoid	12 to 15 days	Severe headache and vomiting, high temperature	All ages	1. Inoculation 2. Cleanliness and disinfection.
10. Malaria	7 to 21 days	High fever, shivering	All ages	1. Boiled water to be arranged. 2. Less eating.

First Aid: First Aid is the immediate and temporary care given to the victim of an accident or sudden illness. Its purpose is to preserve life, assist recovery and prevent aggravation of the condition, until the services of a doctor can be obtained, or during transport to hospital or the casualty's home.

The First Aider's responsibilities end as soon as medical aid is available; but he should stand by after making his report to the Doctor in case he can be of further assistance.

First Aid is definitely limited to the assistance rendered at the time of emergency with such material as may be available. It is not intended that the First Aider should take the place of the Doctor and it must be clearly understood that the redressing of injuries and other such after-treatment are outside the scope of First Aid.

The Origin: The term "First Aid" was adopted officially in England for the first time in 1879 by the St. John Ambulance Association. The expression "First Aider" was not coined till 1894 and was intended to designate any person who has received a certificate from an authorised association that he (or she) is qualified to render first hand.

The originator of First Aid was Esmarch (1823-1908). He was born in Schleswing Holstein, became a distinguished surgeon and was appointed Surgeon General in the German Army on the outbreak of the Franco- Prussian War. Later he was appointed Consulting Surgeon to the large military hospital near Berlin and was recognised as one of the greatest authorities on hospital management and military surgery. However, no part of his work was more widely valued than his two manuals, entitled First Aid on the Battlefield and First Aid to the Injured. The triangular bandage was invented in 1831 by Dr. Mayor of Lausanne, Switzerland, but was later popularised by Esmarch.

First Aid Equipments

Set of splints with metal connections	6-inch kidney basin
Splint straps for securing splints in lieu of bandages	Dressings forceps
Triangular bandages	Note-book and pencil
	Torch, electric (with spare battery)

1-inch roller bandages	Small size prepared sterile dressings
2-inch roller bandages	
3-inch roller bandages	Medium size prepared sterile dressings
1/2 oz. packets of cotton-wool	
1/2 oz. packets of lint or gauze, plain white	Large size prepared sterile dressings
Grey (unbleached) wool (for padding)	Glucose sweets or lump sugar Assorted adhesive wool dressings
Adhesive plaster, 1/2 inch 5 yards	Constrictive bandage (rubber)
Scissors, 5-inch, blunt pointed	Small square of mackintosh
Medicine glass, graduated, or	or plastic sheeting bake lite measure
Safety-pins (assorted, rust-proof, in box)	Sal volatile or smelling salts (the latter if no water is carried)

Management of the Case

1. Respond quickly to calls for assistance.
2. Give artificial respiration if breathing has stopped - every second counts.
3. Stop any bleeding.
4. Guard against or treat for shock by moving the casualty as little as possible and handling him gently.
5. Do not attempt too much — do the minimum that is essential to save life and prevent the condition from worsening.
6. Reassure the casualty and those around and so help to lessen anxiety.
7. Do not allow people to crowd round as fresh air is essential.
8. Do not remove clothes unnecessarily.
9. Arrange for the removal of the casualty to the care of a Doctor or hospital as soon as possible.

Clinic at Schools

Every school should establish a school clinic to look after the health of the pupils and for the treatment of minor diseases. Several schools in a town may combine and set up a dispensary under the charge of a qualified medical officer.

Medical examination should be conducted free of charge. In case any teacher finds, a student suffering from some disease, he should report it to the doctor and ensure that the treatment at the clinic is carried out. Parents of the student should be informed accordingly.

Medical Service: An efficient school medical service is now regarded as an essential part of the public system of education in all progressive countries of the world. In India the problem has acquired all the more importance in view of the poverty of the masses and low hygienic standards.

Health Service Agencies: The health service can be provided by means of:

1. School Medical under the charge of a school medical officer.
2. School Dispensary or clinic.
3. Red Cross units.
4. Physical education department.

Programme of Health Service: This will consist of:

1. Medical inspection of the students.
2. Maintaining records of medical inspection and health of the pupils.
3. Sending notices to parents regarding the physical health of the pupils.
4. Clinical treatment of students who suffer from some diseases.
5. Recording of history and defects regarding special cases.
6. Follow-up work regarding medical inspection.
7. Provision of midday meals.
8. Attending to the healthful school conditions.

Health of Mind

Importance of Mental Health: There are laws of mental health just as there are laws of bodily health. Any disregard of these rules leads to mental disorders and conflicts which ultimately lead to misery and unhappiness. It is of paramount importance to give due recognition to mental laws which result in healthy mind.

What Constitutes a Healthy Mind?

(a) Cheerful and optimistic outlook.

(b) Well-regulated instincts or habits.

(c) Well-regulated and energetic will.
(d) Normal appetite.
(e) Normal sex-consciousness.
(f) Healthy philosophy of life.
(g) Free from prejudice.
(h) Calmness.
(i) Good temper.
(j) Receptivity to new ideas.

Mental Disorders

(a) Irritability.
(b) Depressed and pessimistic outlook.
(c) Abnormal interest in sex.
(d) Lack of courage.
(e) Full of prejudice.
(f) Easily embarrassed in the presence of others.
(g) Low intelligence.
(h) Undeveloped habits and will.
(i) Bad temper.
(j) Undue anxiety.
(k) Moodiness.

It is a matter of great relief that our educationists have begun to realise the importance of mental health. 'Feeling of insecurity' and the 'feeling of inferiority' are the two great enemies of mental health. A knowledge of mental hygiene helps us to kill these two demons. A psychological approach is needed. Our attempts should be to provide suitable emotional, physical and intellectual environments in which a child may have the 'feeling of security' and the 'feeling of equality'. He should feel that his personality is respected and is given a suitable place.

Close Pupil-Teacher Contacts: The teacher should carefully observe the child in and outside the school and should know the child and his home conditions. This will develop the feeling of 'oneness' in the mind of the child who feels that the teacher is interested in his welfare.

Favourable Home and School Environment: Unfavourable home and school environment leads to mental disorders. Parents should be guided to adopt good methods of upbringing. The child should be free from unsatisfactory family relationships and strict discipline. Treatment by the parents should be just and impartial. Too much fondling may also lead to emotional maladjustment. The treatment of the teachers should be just and fair.

Medical Examination: There should be provision for the medical examination in schools and remedial measures be adopted to safeguard the health of the child. Defective physique becomes a contributory factor of mental disorders. Cases requiring special treatment should be sent to child guidance clinics.

Intellectual Life of the School: Sound methods of teaching suited to the individual needs of the child should be adopted. Activity Method, e.g. Play-way, Project Method, etc., should be encouraged. Audio-visual aids develop interest in the lesson. Special time and attention is to be devoted to weak students.

Provision of Educational and Vocational Guidance Centres: Schools should start such centres. It is not necessary to appoint psychologists in schools. Trained teachers may be asked to undergo short educational and vocational guidance courses and the work of guidance be entrusted to them. For specially difficult cases, intelligence, aptitude cnd personality tests be conducted.

Provision of Co-curricular Activities: Properly planned activities are very helpful in providing much needed and useful training in civic sense. Sublimation of instincts is also achieved.

Freedom and Self-discipline: Unnecessary rules and regulations greatly upset the mental equilibrium of the child. A child who breathes in an atmosphere of freedom develops initiative and courage. Severe punishments result in mental retardation. Let us be wise and remember the useful words of Hobbes, "The fool cannot be mended by flogging, and he who flogs is the greatest fool." Hence the right approach would be to give freedom to the child. A.S. Neill says, "We could abolish caning by an act of Parliament, but no act of Parliament can abolish the fear of teacher or a system."

Teacher's Mental Hygiene and His Dynamic Personality: The teachers should be mentally alert to develop mental alertness in the students. They should be painstaking, sympathetic, appreciative and trusting. They should not have any prejudice which may have an adverse effect on the emotional and intellectual conditions of children. They should have always higher ideals of life before them.

The Development

Report of the School Health Committee

The School Health Committee was appointed by the Government of India in February 1960 under the chairmanship of Shrimati Renuka Ray to assess the standard of health and nutrition of school children and suggest ways and means of improving them.

Terms of Reference: 1. To examine the present position of school health programme in the country in all its aspects (excluding physical education, games and sports), e.g. prevention of diseases, medical care and follow-up service, nutrition, health, education, healthy environment, etc. of the students at all stages of education and to suggest: i) further survey of studies if required; and ii) how the work of various agencies such as medical, social and welfare associations can be coordinated to assist in the promotion of health of school children.

2. To examine studies and surveys so far made to assess the nutritional standard of school children and to indicate: i) further survey of studies needed in any specific areas; and ii) to give concrete suggestions to institute appropriate measures to improve standards of nutrition among school children recommending, *inter alia,* ways and means for financing and organising such a programme.
3. To examine and recommend the possibility of entrusting Primary Health Centres and other organisations for conducting a comprehensive and realistic school health programme in association with the local education administration. The recommendation should include measures to develop an effective school medical service suitable to the country.

4. To examine the present facilities available for promoting nutritional standards of pre-school children and to suggest practical measures to improve the present position.

Major References

School Health Services: 1. All children should be provided with school health services. However, with the limited resources available at present, school health services may be made available to primary school children, i.e. children between 6-11 years.

2. The functions of the school health services should be the provision of health measures both preventive and curative. These should include the detection and treatment of defects and the creation and maintenance of a hygienic environment in and around the school.
3. All newly admitted children should have medical examination first and then again after four years, as the limited facilities available at present do not permit medical examination at frequent intervals.
4. Prevention and control of communicable diseases in schools should be the responsibility of public health authorities.
5. Emphasis should be laid on compulsory primary and revaccination against smallpox immediately. Immunisation against diphtheria, whooping cough and tetanus should be made compulsory in the immediate future.
6. With adequate training in health education and school health services, it should be possible for the teacher to undertake certain functions connected with school health services such as: a) observation of children with a view to spot out any deviations from normal health; b) recording of height and weight and simple testing of vision and hearing; c) maintaining of health records of children; and d) giving first-aid.
7. During the Fourth Plan period, school health services should be provided to: a) all children in the age-group 6-11 in rural and urban areas; and b) the children of middle and high schools in areas where facilities exist.

School Meal: 1. The primary aim of the school meal programme should be to improve health and encourage sound dietary habits among children.

2. The school meal should be based on cheap nutritions and locally available foods. A sample menu may comprise a minimum of: cereals and millet :- 2.5 oz. : pulses - I oz. : non-leafy vegetables I oz. : oil - 1/4: and condiments and salt.
3. Every school should be provided with protected water supply and facilities for drainage; sanitary environment; facilities for storage; preparation and distribution of food; adequate space for feeding of children; and sanitary disposal of garbage.
4. It is necessary that the Government should support the school meal programme besides the contribution of the community at the rate of 50 per cent of the total cost.

Pre-school Child: 1. A comprehensive health and welfare service for pre-school children should be introduced.

2. Services of 'Balwadis', 'Mahilā Samitis', maternity and child welfare centres, health centres, clinics and nursery schools, the pre-primary schools, pediatric centres of hospitals and social welfare and similar organisations should be utilised for the distribution of milk to pre-school children.

School Health Education: 1. Health education should be included as a part of general education in the primary, middle and secondary schools.

2. The State Administration should take immediate steps to publish textbooks on health education and to have health lessons included in other appropriate textbooks.

Training, Studies and Research: 1. In teacher training programmes, health education and school health should be a required part of training. The teacher should have the knowledge of the growth and development of children, personal health, community health, school health practices and methods of health education.

2. For the teachers who are already in service, special short term courses should be organised by the local school

organisations with the technical assistance from the health personnel.

3. Future school health and school meal policies and programmes should be developed from the results obtained through scientific surveys and studies. Studies and research are quite essential for making school health programme efficient, effective and economical.

School Environment: 1. School buildings should be simple, safe, attractive and sanitary.

2. Every school building in urban areas, where public water supply is available, should have water supply connection and adequate number of taps. In rural areas, an independent water supply system is desirable for each school.
3. In urban areas wherever drainage facilities exist, these should be extended to all schools. In rural areas, drains should be constructed for the removal of waste water.
4. The sale of food by hawkers in and around the school should be prohibited.

School Health Administration: 1. At the Centre, there should be National School Health Council. Such a Council will facilitate cooperation and coordination of many individuals and groups that are concerned with the health of the children.

2. Each State should have a State Council of School Health. The Director of Education and the Director of Health Services should alternatively be Secretary and Joint Secretary of the Council.
3. At district level, School Health and School Meal Committees should be set up as sub-committees of the District Development Councils.
4. The district health and education organisations should be strengthened appropriately to plan, implement and supervise this additional work.

Healthy Diet

Importance of Nutritive and Balanced Diet: The quality and quantity of food taken by a person has an important bearing on his development. In fact nutritive and balanced diet provides the body with the required energy for doing everyday work.

Balanced Diet of a Normal and Healthy Person: The diet of a normal and healthy individual should consist of edibles in the following proportion:

Food Item	Vegetarian Diet	Non-vegetarian Diet
1. Bread	14 oz.	14 oz.
2. Milk	14 oz.	10 oz.
3. Vegetables without leaves	6 oz.	6 oz.
4. Vegetables with leaves	4 oz.	4 oz.
5. Meat and fish		3 oz.
6. Eggs		1 oz.
7. Cereal	3 oz.	2 oz.
8. Sugar	2 oz.	2 oz.
9. Fruits	2 oz.	2 oz.
10. Liquids	2 oz.	2 oz.
	47	**46**

Changes should be made in the above list according to the profession, body build, sex, age and climatic conditions.

Report of the Secondary Education Commission points out "At no period of life does malnutrition play such a large part in causing ill-health or in promoting defects of growth as in the periods of adolescence."

Undernourishment

Lack of Sufficient and Proper Food: When a person does not get proper food according to his age and nature of work, his health is adversely affected and malnutrition is caused.

Defective Atmosphere: Lack of fresh air, sunlight, physical exercise and unhealthy situations of school building also lead to malnutrition.

Over Work: Over work also adversely affects health.

Lack of Sleep: Lack of sleep also proves harmful for health.

Irregular Meals: Irregular and untimely eaten meals cause indigestion, dyspepsia and constipation.

The Diagnosis

Physical Conditions

(i) Bad postures.
(ii) Laziness.
(iii) Easily Fatigued.
(iv) Susceptibility to disease.
(v) Pale and charmless face.
(vi) Drowsiness weight.
(vii) Under-weight

Mental Conditions

(i) Gloomy nature.
(ii) Unenthusiasm.
(iii) Forgetful memory.
(iv) Lack of concentration.
(v) Slow comprehension.
(iv) Irritability.

Meal in Schools

Why School Meals: It is now generally recognised that in the wake of under-nutrition and malnutrition of the most of the Indian children, the school must take up the responsibility to make up this deficiency. This will not only assist in improving the health and physical development of the child but also assist him in making quicker and sounder progress in his studies because a child who is better-fed and healthier makes rapid progress. It is, therefore, essential that we must develop a universal programme of school meals as an integral part of its programme of universal, free and compulsory primary education.

Free Milk: With the help of United Nations International Children's Emergency Fund (UNICEF) which gave milk powder free of charge, milk was distributed to about 7 lakh primary school children.

Contents of Midday Meals: The School Health Committee (1960) recommended that it should be based on cheap, nutritious and locally available foods. A menu may comprise a minimum of cereals and millet 2.5 oz.; pulses - 1 oz.; non-leafy vegetable - 1 oz.; oil-¼ oz. and condiment and salt.

Subsidy by the Government: The Committee recommended that the Government should support the school meal programme besides the contribution of the community at the rate of 50 per cent of the total cost.

Storage, Preparation and Distribution Arrangement: It must be stressed that food should be prepared and served under proper – hygienic conditions. There should be adequate storage facilities and also adequate space for feeding of children.

Assistance of the Central Government: In order to assist the development of the programme, the Government of India approved a centrally sponsored scheme of grand-in-aid to State Governments in 1962-63. Under this scheme, assistance is offered to State Governments to the extent of one-third of the total expenditure incurred by them in school feeding programmes.

Supply of Gift Food: The Midday Meals programme known as Nutritional Support to Primary Education was launched on August 15, 1995 on a nationwide scale.

The Behaviour

We can hardly ignore the seriousness of poor postures. It affects health, physical efficiency, mental attitude and appearance of an individual. Most of our diseases are the outcome of poor postures. A teacher can do much in the classroom work and physical instruction period to prevent bad postural habits in the students. As a result of poor postures says Dr. Mosher; "constipation, diarrhoea, flatulence, disturbance of the circulation, nervous irritability and, most marked of all fatigue out of proportion to the effort expended lessen the efficiency of the individual and often make life a burden." Some of the main defects of poor postures are given below:

1. Interfere in the normal working of respiration, circulation and digestion.
2. Badly affect the eyesight.
3. Spoil handwriting because the students will not be able to hold the pen properly.

4. Lead to round shoulders and drooping body.
5. Decrease physical efficiency and develop laziness.
6. Develop crooked bodies which are not normal in shape, and look very unpleasant.
7. Result in undesirable traits, e.g. timidness, lack of courage, etc.

The Reasons

1. Weakness of the muscles which may be due to lack of exercise.
2. Wrong postural habits due to lack of information regarding correct position.
3. Defective desks and seats compelling the students to stretch or cramp their bodies.
4. Wrong writing positions.
5. Wrong reading positions.
6. Defective eyesight.
7. Defective hearing.
8. Illegible writing of the teacher on the blackboard.
9. Wrong postures of the teachers leading to depressing effects on the students.
10. Illness of the students.
11. Wrong type of dress of the students.

The Categorisation

1. Standing postures.
2. Sitting postures.
3. Writing postures.
4. Reading postures.
5. Walking postures.

General Aims

1. To make the student realise the necessity of having good health.
2. To give information regarding health rules.
3. To develop health habits among children.

4. To develop certain skills concerning health, e.g. training in first aid, etc.
5. To enable students to understand the educative value of sanitation, cleanliness and healthful living.
6. To develop a will to listen to rules relating to health and to observe them.
7. To develop better human relationship in matters concerning health.
8. To acquaint them with the causes and remedies of general diseases.
9. To influence parents and other adults to better health habits and attitudes through the health programme of schools and to make the school an effective agency for the promotion of the social aspects of health education in the family and community as well as the school itself.

Meaning of School Health Programme: According to a report of the Committee on Terminology in School Health Education in America, the school health programme is defined as "the school procedures that contribute to the maintenance and improvement of the health of pupils and school personnel including health services, healthful living and health education."

Scope of Health Education: School health education is a vital part of general education. It includes all such instruction that enlightens a student about activities and functions contributing to preservation, promotion and restoration of health. By means of a health education programme the spread of diseases in the school-going children can be checked and their eradication can also be attempted. A thorough knowledge of health rules underlines the needs of the study of anatomy and also the symptoms of common diseases of children. Practical knowledge of causes and diagnosis is equally essential. School health education also includes knowledge about the environment, equipments and routine of the schools as well.

Health Programme in School

1. Health Appraisal or Medical Inspection.
2. Health Counselling and Follow-up.

3. Emergency Care in Schools.
4. Communicable Disease Control.
5. Identification and Education of the Handicapped Children.
6. Health of School Personnel.

Personal Cleanliness

Personal hygiene teaches the individual how to keep himself in health by paying attention to his cleanliness, exercise, rest and sleep, etc. The personal habits of an individual may be either important aids to the promotion of health and prolongation of life, or they may be powerful predisposing causes of disease. It is of the greatest importance to our well-being that we should form habits that are beneficial and not which as are hurtful to us.

Personal hygiene includes:

1. Cleanliness of the hair, the teeth, the nails, the eyes, the ears, etc.
2. Sound habits of bodily exercise.
3. Adequate rest and sleep.
4. Periodic medical check up every six or twelve months so that any disease may be detected at its very beginning and be properly treated before it has taken root.

Examination Medically

Systematic medical examination in one of the most important means of taking care of the physical well-being of the students. Although this system has been in existence for many years, it has failed to achieve the desired results.

The Secondary Education Commission has observed the following defects in the prevailing system:

1. It is done in a very superficial manner.
2. The remedial measures suggested are often not carried out.
3. Follow up work is practically absent.
4. Effective cooperation has not been established between the parents and the school authorities.

The Recommendations

Medical inspection to be effective should be done in the following manner:

1. It should be thorough and comprehensive and should not be treated as a mere routine. It should not merely concern itself with the height, weight and chest measurements but should also concern itself with ears, teeth, eyes, nose, heart and lungs, etc. In fact no-part of the body should be left unexamined as far as possible. The first inspection should be at the time of admission of the child in a school. If it is found out that the child is suffering from some chronic disease, he may be refused admission. Child should be examined every year. The last inspection will be just prior to leaving the school which reveals the strength and weakness of the child and helps him to choose some vocation suited to his physical development also.
2. Students with serious defects should be examined more frequently.
3. Remedial measures should be taken to remove defects.
4. Three copies of the report should be prepared. One should be sent to the parents, another should be kept by the teacher-in-charge and the third one should be kept by the medical officer.

The Support

A few words may be said regarding 'follow-up' work. It has been rightly stated that medical inspection is of little or no use unless proper 'follow-up' work is undertaken. In many cases, it does not call for any extra burden. A slight care of the child brings about good results. The parents and the teachers should cooperate. Immediate action should be taken after the medical inspection is over. When the parents are unable to take remedial steps due to poverty, school should take upon itself the responsibility of looking after the health of the child. The State may arrange mobile hospital ambulances for the purpose. "In any case such remedial measures as the school medical officer may suggest should be adopted, and the school authorities should see that they are carried out," thus remarks the Secondary Education Commission.

Apart from medical inspection by the physician, daily inspection of the general cleanliness of the child should be made by the teacher.

This costs nothing and can be made in a few minutes.

School Staff and Health of the Students

Personal Cleanliness: The daily morning inspection of the cleanliness of the students by the teacher is very helpful in enforcing personal cleanliness. A rapid survey of the class should be made. Competition may be introduced among the students. Cleanliness chart may be prepared and marks allotted to them.

Development of Habits Regarding Air: Stress should be laid on the need of fresh air at all times and especially while sleeping. The students should be asked not to cover their mouth at night. They should be taught to breathe through their noses.

Training in First-aid Habits: The students should be instructed to give immediate attention to cuts and bruises.

Vaccination and Inoculation: At times of epidemics, precautionary measures should be suggested to them and they should be vaccinated and inoculated.

Development of Habits of Hygienic Feeding: The students should be taught to take right type of food in a suitable quantity. They should be warned of the dangers of overeating. They should be asked not to take sour food. The students should be made to understand the importance of drinking plenty of water.

Selection of Suitable Physical Exercises: A variety of physical activity programmes should exist in a school so that the students may choose activities to their linking.

Formation of Good Classroom Habits: A wise teacher would always pay due attention to the postures of the students. The students may be instructed to keep pens and pencils out of mouth and to use handkerchiefs when coughing. Such other matters should be attended to.

Development of Better Human Relations in Matters Concerning Health: Every child should be asked to make it a point to do his best for the betterment of the health of his friends, relatives, neighbours and the whole community.

Medical Inspection and Follow-up Work: Medical examination should be thorough and the follow-up work taken seriously.

Special Procedure

Apart from verbal talks, a good deal of health instruction can be imparted to the students in an interesting manner through the methods as suggested below:

Health Posters: Posters depicting washing of bodies, about various diseases like plague, malaria, etc., and about food, sleep and exercise, etc., can be made and pasted on the school walls. Health authorities may be requested to supply these. Each poster should illustrate one idea only. Striking headings catch our attention. Students may be asked to help in preparing simple charts and posters.

Health Projects and Weeks: Once a year, a week may be set apart for the purpose of health education. Cleanliness campaigns in the school and locality go a long way in instilling ideas about health. Various committees of the students regarding different aspects of personal cleanliness, i.e. teeth, hair, nails, etc., may be formed. One teacher may serve as an adviser to each committee. The good posture committee should arrange posture competition and the participants should be asked to show proper posture. Prizes may be awarded to the best ones. Similarly, exercise competitions etc., may be arranged. Data regarding height, weight, chest measurements, etc. may be collected by respective committees. Special lectures on general hygiene may be arranged. The Panchayat Health Department or the City Health Department, as the case may be, should be requested to help.

Health Book: Each student should be asked to maintain a health book. One important health rule should be pasted on the top of each page. Pictures illustrating certain health rules may be pasted in it. It should also contain his health records.

Healthy Environment: Attempts should be made to make classrooms and the school building very attractive and conducive to health. This has a direct bearing on the child. 'As is the environment, so is the individual'.

Film and Film Strips: Well-made health films and film strips are valuable in the teaching of health education.

Excursions: 'Seeing is believing' is a true saying. Excursions to good dispensaries, water-supply centres, etc., may be planned for health educational purposes.

Health Clubs: Like literary clubs, health clubs should be organised in schools. A definite weekly or monthly programme may be chalked out in coooperation with the school Red Cross Society. Debates and declamation contests on health matters may be arranged. Plays depicting health rules be staged.

Radio: Special programmes for children relating to health should be broadcast.

We may conclude by quoting the Secondary Education Commission, "This approach to the maintenance of school children's health may appear impracticable at first sight. But a clearer appreciation of the factors involved and a better coordination of the agencies concerned with the promotion of health will show that the adopting of such measures can produce tangible results within a reasonable time."

Health Counselling and Follow-up: The main aims of this service are:

1. Giving pupils the information about their health status as revealed by appraisal or medical inspection.
2. Acquainting parents with the significance of health problems and encouraging them to obtain needed care for their children.
3. Motivating pupils to seek and accept needed treatment.
4. Promoting each pupil's acceptance of responsibility for his own health in keeping with his stage of maturity.

Teachers, nurses and parents have to play an important role in the follow-up programme as actual improvement in the health of children depends more on follow-up than on any other school health activity.

Significance of Environment

Bharat H. Desai rightly points out in an article "We are in the midst of a deepening environmental crisis triggered off by unprecedented growth and development of the human race. The unbroken history of rapacious exploitation of natural resources and the continued neglect of the need for regeneration and conservation have begun to boomerang", observes a High Powered Commission in its report submitted to the Government of Gujarat recently.

The twelve-member High Powered Commission (HPC) headed by R. Parthasarathy, Chairman of Vadodara Urban Development Authority (VUDA), was constituted "to study the problems of people affected by large undertakings in Gujarat". However, the findings reached and the recommendations made by the Parathsarathy Commission have wider ramifications, meriting attention for environmental protection in India as a whole especially its recommendation to set up a statutory environment protection agency.

In the post-independence era, urbanisation in the wake of large-scale industrialisation has brought about widespread environmental degradation. Industries sprang up all over Gujarat in the sixties in an unplanned fashion which uprooted hundreds of small and marginal farmers following land acquisition. "The plight of the land losers", according to the HPC, "has been aggravated partly by inadequate negligible compensation and partly by the failure of existing policies and programmes to rehabilitate them adequately, economically and socially." Apart from this, most of the villages affected by land acquisition are suffering from inadequate or near absence of basic minimum needs. The rapid felling of trees, disappearance of greenary, destruction of village forests, indiscriminate disposal of solid and semi-solid wastes by industries in and around affected villages are leading to serious health hazards for the people. "There has been nearly no rehabilitation worth the name of the land losers' families", laments the HPC.

The world is facing or rather passing through many crises but the most dangerous crisis is that of gross and constantly increasing pollution of the environment. Needless to say that if immediate attention is not paid, ways are not rooted out; plans are not implemented in their right direction to put a check on the growing hazards of pollution, the entire humanity may be in the grip of destruction, devastation and it maybe a sign of doom and loom for all of us. For this, proper environmental education is inevitable if we are to attack the problem, not only at the roots but also with a view to have a final solution to our growing gigantic problems of the devilish pollution.

Let us, first of all, see as to what is meant by Environment. In an article-Crisis of Environment-Environment is explained as under:-

Environment refers to surroundings - those natural things around us, from the essentials which sustain human life, such as the earth's atmosphere or healthy air or drinkable water, to the non-essentials that nevertheless make life sustainable, such as wild animals, clean places or human living space.

Thus, the environment is not just pretty trees and tigers, threatened species of birds, animals and plants and the ecosystems. It includes the entire entity on which we live and on which our agricultural and industrial development depends. Saving or preservation of the essential ingredients of life and of the rich natural diversity of the planet is consequently necessary for healthy existence.

The compulsions and complexities of life sometimes require us to make a dent into natural wealth; but everyone now agrees that the fewer such dents human beings make, the better for them and for the coming generations. Certain actions become inevitable, but several others are advisable for man. Continuous destruction of the vital environment certainly robs us, and also the succeeding generations, of variety and beauty in nature.

Undeniably, the environment has become the world's common problem. The environmental health of a country is in fact an indicator of the quality of life of the people. The need for an environmental ethic is now universally accepted. The environment is in grave danger, but it can certainly be saved. Conservation has necessarily to be adopted as a long-term strategy : it must be made a mode of life.

We need air, water and adequate land of sufficient quality to sustain life. Continuous research and monitoring have to be done to ensure that these precious resources are preserved. The importance of their preservation is apparent from the fact that air, water and land are finite, limited sources, and can be exhausted. To use a Term of economics, air, water and land must be regarded as capital, not as income. Even the Vatican and the Holy Sect, representing the Pope, said: "Stewardship of the resources of the physical world has always been a key concern of religion."

Besides this, it will be worthwhile to note that broadly speaking atmosphere that implies both-natural as well as social-in natural atmosphere generally, air, water, trees, vegetables are included. Again it is divided in two parts-biological and non-biological. There may be further sub division-such roots of bioatmosphere in the forms of generator, consumer and destroyer. Under natural atmosphere all the living beings fall under the head of consumer. The second atmosphere takes into its compass — social, economic, political and family relations.

Important Elements

Y. Naidumna has rightly stated that the unlimited exploitation of the natural resources has lead to dangerous consequences and now there are only two ways left before the entire human race for its existence-one is to make the environment useful keeping the needs of life while the other is to put a check on waste material along with the use of natural resources. Following are causes of pollution:

Rapid Rate of Development. The editor of *Competition Master* rightly says:-

"The irony of the situation is that the more the economic and industrial development in the world, the more the danger to the environment". At many places, "development" has acquired a sinister dimension – pollution. It threatens forests and farms, human health and aquatic life. Disposal of hazardous wastes is another allied problem.

The United Nations Economic and Social Commission for Asia and the Pacific (ESCAP) warned early in February, 1985, that the Asian environment, already in a critical state, is likely to be burdened with additional load resulting from development activities. Statistical data compiled by this UN agency indicated that from 1970 to 2000, the volume of-solid wastes will increase five times- dissolved solids, pesticides, biochemical oxygen demand, and particulates.

These statistics mean that every environment has what is termed "carrying capacity", or the amount of pollution or damage an environment can sustain or "carry" without further degradation. A lake that is ten times larger than another one can carry roughly ten times the pollution load. If the loads are not minimised or the environment upgraded to an extent that it will be able to carry them, the environmental degradation will inevitably worsen. As for the size of the expected future loads, solid wastes refer mostly to garbage, there is hardly any Asian city where garbage collection is efficient enough to avoid piles of refuse on the streets.

Biochemical oxygen demand (BOD) is a measure of the quality of oxygen required in the natural decomposition and recycling process. BOD is expected to increase four times by 2000, but there are no more sets of clean rivers, lakes and seas to accommodate the additional waste. Many Asian water resources are already at, or past, their carrying capacities.

Chemical Pollution. The editor again throws light on the evil effects of chemical pollution- "There are even more dangerous chemicals in use in India than MIC which caused havoc in Bhopal in the world's worst disaster of this kind. The plastic industry uses a chemical closely related to MIC known as toluene di-isocynate (TDI) to make polyurethane foam. TDI is used more extensively than MIC and is far more dangerous to human beings.

"A group of chemicals called polychlorinated biphenyis (PCBs) are highly toxic. These are widely used in the electronics industry and there is no control on PCB use in India. But only when these chemicals are discharged into water can the Water Pollution Act apply to them.

"There are other equally hazardous chemicals which are being manufactured, sold and used in India, and about which there is no information at all.

"Oddly enough, there is no law in India authorising the Government to collect information on the number of chemicals imported or produced in the country. In terms of tonnage at least 70 per cent of the pesticides used in the country have been classified as highly toxic or hazardous by WHO. Protection and improvement of the environment became a priority issue only in the Fifth Five Year Plan (1974-79)".

Acid Rains. Out of the smoke and other waste material a by product of mills and factories, there is a lot of acid rain which not only damages the outer surface of earth but gives birth to many fatal diseases -amongst human beings and life on this earth.

"Acid rain", which contains 65 per cent sulphuric acid, 30 per cent nitric acid and 5 per cent hydrochloric acid, is caused by pollutants which fossil fuel-based industries emit. It has destroyed considerable vegetation. Sweden and Canada are the worst victims of acid rain which is no respector of national boundaries.

Disturbing the Nature: The pollution caused by machines, motor vehicles, mills, factories, petroleum products, etc., the felling of trees, the digging of the hills and such other fearful devices have given birth to a lot of problems such as soil erosion, the presence of dangerous gases and compounds the layers of smoke and dust prevalent all around are some of the major problems we are facing under its impact.

Population Pressure: In 2000 AD there will be 3.4 billion people to feed instead only of 2.6 billion in the early eighties. It is clear, therefore, that if current tends are allowed to persist, Asians will face a grim future-not just zero development, but regression. Undeniably, population pressure is the root cause of virtually all pollution and environmental damage. A realistic national timetable for population stabilisation is clearly indicated.

Role as a Checker

Before we discuss the role of education in the eradication of pollution let us keep in mind a few things like its impact on health, the radio active waves, rise in respiratory and eye diseases, the growth in diseases caused by virus, the gastroenteritis diseases, various diseases relating to noise resulting in deafness, and other diseases of lungs and heart. The growing adverse effect on all types of vegetation cannot be ignored.

Now it shall be worthwhile to discuss the role of education in the eradication of pollution. Following are the measures if adopted in letter and spirit in the right carnest, may bear fruitful results.

1. New ways of looking at the environment so that its value can be reflected in the national accounts, better planning and legislation, more careful and wider use of existing and new environmental technologies, including the all-important environmental impact assessment-a way of appraising the effect of any proposed project on the environment before it is launched.
2. The new Environment (Protection) Act, 1986, is far better in approach than the earlier laws. The Water (Prevention and Control of Pollution) Act, 1974, and the Air (Prevention and Control of Pollution) Act, 1981, were weak and merely regulatory in character.
3. The aim of the new measure is stated to be: 'To provide for the protection and improvement of environment and for matters connected therewith.' The Act contains provisions for tackling the inter-relationship between nature and human beings and the diverse kinds of pollutants. Section 6 (b) empowers the Central Government to make rules for 'the

maximum allowable limits of concentration of various environmental pollutants (including noise) for different areas'.

4. There is a section on hazardous industries and environmental disasters. Thus, hazardous industrial pollution is also covered. A hazardous substance is defined as "any substance or preparation which, by reason of its chemical or physio-chemical properties or handling, is liable to cause harm to human beings, other living creatures, plants, micro-organisms, property or the environment.
5. There are stringent measures to check hazardous pollution. Section 8 of the Act states clearly: 'No person shall handle or cause to be handled any hazardous substance except in accordance with such procedure and after complying with such safeguards as may be prescribed.' Section 6 (f) empowers the Central Government to make rules for 'the procedures and safeguards for the prevention of accidents which may cause environmental pollution and for providing remedial measures for such accidents.' Moreover, it is now mandatory for a person responsible for the discharge of any hazardous substance in excess of the prescribed norms to immediately inform the concerned authorities and to render all possible assistance. Earlier there was no such responsibility.
6. Vigilant citizens can initiate proceedings against an establishment that is polluting the water supply or otherwise ruining the environment. The penalties for defaulters have been made more stringent. The Water Act provided for a maximum imprisonment of six years and/or a fine upto a total of Rs 5000; in the Air Act the limits were a maximum imprisonment upto three months and/or fine upto a total of Rs 5000. The new Act provides for imprisonment of defaulters for upto a total of seven years and/or a fine which may extend upto Rs 1 lakh.
7. However, there are some flaws even in the new Act. One, all power and authority is vested in the hands of the Central Government.
8. (i) There is no provision relating to forests, even though it is open knowledge that in India about 50 per cent of the energy consumed is non-commercial or collected from fields, trees and bushes.

(ii) Secondly, supplementary legislation in respect of enhanced penalties and for tightening the enforcement of the provisions has yet to be brought up. Nor is it clear whether the new Act supersedes or supplants the two earlier laws. The enhanced punishments may or may not be deemed applicable to cases which fall under the purview of the other Acts. The areas of jurisdiction have not been clearly demarcated.

(iii) Thirdly, there is no clear provision for public participation which is vital for preserving the environment. The relevant issues are left to official bodies (Air and Pollution Control Boards) and other regulatory agencies. Any individual can file a complaint with the Government against a factory management, but it requires the complainant to give 60 days' notice, which permits the offending management to bring its emissions within control. The role of the public, especially voluntary bodies, needs to be enhanced considerably under the Act.

9. Section 6 (e) of the Act empowers the Government to make rules for "the prohibition, restrictions on the location of industries and the carrying on of processes and operations in different areas". But there is no mandatory provision for the industry to prepare and submit to the concerned authorities a suitable environmental impact assessment report before the location is approved. The US National Environmental Policy Act, 1969, requires that an environmental impact assessment must be prepared prior to any federally financed project. In India all that a government-financed industrial unit needs is a simple "no objection" certificate from the concerned Pollution Control Board.

10. Addressing the first meeting of the National Land Use and Wastelands Development Council on February 6, 1986, Prime Minister Rajiv Gandhi called for a nationwide "people movement" to protect the country's ecological balance. He suggested a time bound land reclamation and afforestation programme. The approach to this problem could not be departmentalised or compartmentalised but had to "respond to the differing needs of every section."

An integrated approach, not hemmed in by internal contradictions, would ensure sufficient food, maintain nutrition levels, meet fuel and fodder needs and raw material requirements of industry and help preserve natural habits. 'We will have to mobilise not just the Government, but we will have to mobilise absolutely everyone. Stressing the need for decentralisation of nurseries, tree growers' cooperatives, he called for the involvement of farmers, youth and women in the programme. The landless and the marginal and small farmers should be the key elements in the programme.

11. Having experienced the ill effects of industrial development, it is high time a long-term strategy for environmental protection is evolved. In this respect, the Parthasarathy Commission has strongly pleaded for a Regional Development Strategy and a National Urban Development Policy with a view to contain metropolitan chaos, for developing secondary cities and to ensure development of existing small and medium towns as well as establishing new ones, as part of a regional strategy generating employment and promoting decentralised urbanisation. In addition, a clear industrial location policy will ensure setting up of specific large industries at specific locations with a predetermined time-frame. It will ensure not only systematic industrial growth but also facilitate in taking measures for environmental protection economically and in a coherent manner.
12. All State governments, semi-government bodies and municipalities as well as social organisations have been propagating "grow more trees" campaign. To boost the idea of growing more and more trees, the government has taken up the project of "social forestry" on a large scale. The project aims at planting trees singly or in groups wherever they can be grown.
13. Apart from increasing the forest wealth, the programme generates additional earnings to the Panchayats, more employment to labour, and it provides cheap fuel to the village poor. In Dhanoli, a village in Valsad district of Gujarat, social forestry has achieved remarkable progress. By adopting

the scheme of raising village forests in only four hectares of land a net income of over Rs 43000 was generated.

14. Social forestry not only prevents felling of trees but also tries to distribute the produce of the project directly to the people of the area. The scheme also aims at growing more trees and forests on unused land and promotes research in the science of trees and their varieties.
15. Community lands in villages are wasted and used only for grazing village cattle. This unproductive use of land yields the village panchayats hardly Rs 4000 to Rs 5000. But the same land, if utilised for a cluster of trees for which the Government provides free seedlings, can fetch a much higher income to the Panchayats. The Gujarat Government has decided to give 50 per cent of the net profit realised from the sale of village wood-lot to the Panchayat. Crores of trees are required to strengthen and support agricultural and animal husbandry, to combat pollution and to attract adequate rains and also to stop erosion of fertile soil.
16. But social forestry, especially the growing plantations of eucalyptus, has been criticised by several ecologists, sociologists and economists. The environmentalists claim that social forestry is encouraging monoculture, and in particular the plantation of eucalyptus, which makes up 80 to 90 per cent of all the trees planted so far under these programmes: Eucalyptus, it is contended, degrades the soil and permits nothing to grow beneath it. It is a heavy consumer of water and lowers the water table.
17. The Government of India has launched a Rs 292-crore project to clean up the mighty Ganga, which has been greatly polluted as a result of the inflow of effluents and dirt from various sources. There are about 100 cities situated along the banks of the river, in the States of UP, Bihar and Bengal. Nearly 4200 small and medium units are responsible for polluting the holy river. The Ganga Project is the largest and most ambitious of all the environmental protection plans launched in the country.
18. The cleaning up work began at Rishikesh and Hardwar in September, 1985. Cleaning the Ganga is also in progress at

Varanasi waterfront, which is heavily polluted. A Central Ganga Authority had been constituted under the chairmanship of the Prime Minister himself.

19. The wanton destruction of natural wealth, including forests, and the indiscriminate setting up of chemical industries endangers the lives of both human beings and animals. The greed for personal gain, the general decline in values, the knowledge that one can flout the laws with a vengeance and get away with it, or at worst to pay a small fine, have cumulatively rendered ineffective the agencies entrusted with the duty of protecting the environment. There are poachers galore, but it is only rare that legal action is taken against such offenders.
20. Besides, there are wide variations between official data and the actual position. For instance, the Forest Departments in the States have been spending crores of rupees during the past 30 years and claiming that a large area has been brought under forest cover. The Union Minister of State for Environment and Forests Mr. Z.R. Ansari, said in the Lok Sabha that only 13 per cent of the country's geographical area is under "forest cover" according to satellite pictures, whereas the revenue records show the area to be 22.7 per cent.
21. In February, 1986 the Supreme Court directed the Union Government to examine the possibility of setting up environment courts. The court judgement in the Shriram Foods and Fertilizer Industries case may well provide a basis for action by the Government to safeguard the environment in areas where potentially hazardous industries are located. The court has in fact set out a framework for appropriate governmental action. It has also set up a monitoring committee to ensure that the expert bodies recommendations are implemented. Even more significant is the suggestion that measures should be taken to educate the workers and provide early warning systems for the public.

While the increasing awareness and rethinking about the importance of preserving all aspects of the environment, including forests, clean air, and wild life is welcome, there is an urgent need for earnest implementation of declared policies. So far, the implementation has been poor and, consequently, the environment has been deteriorating; forests, in particular, are disappearing at a disconcerting pace. It is time to recall the farsighted Chanakya's observation in the 4th century BC that "the stability of an empire depends on the stability of its environment:" Strong and committed machinery is needed and it must have sufficient resources.

Ecology also has some effect on poverty. Undeniably, an ecologically and scientifically sound afforestation programme can provide a solution to the problem of India's poverty, if it is not based on the profit motive alone. More research is undoubtedly needed to evaluate the costs of monoculture based social forestry. Unless afforestation programmes are linked with the basic needs of the rural poor, they will prove economically counterproductive and ecologically disastrous.

Obviously, the plunder of what nature has built over billions of years has to be stopped. We need a new lifestyle with environmental ethics as an integral part of it, not only for this generation but also for the future generations to live and enjoy the freedom of this planet and beyond. It is important in this regard to reduce the rate of population growth to one per cent from the present 2.2 per cent, as China has done. Industries generating high pollution should be moved out of the perimeters of cities. Environmental education should be made compulsory at every level of learning.

For the rapid protection of environment the following measures should be adopted:-

1. Aesthetic sense among the citizens be developed.
2. Attitude towards cleanliness be evolved.
3. Civic sense must be prevailed.
4. Social forestry be adopted.
5. Religious attitudes towards trees be scientifically developed.
6. Eco club be established.
7. Research in Environmental Studies in every subject be promoted.

Fundamental Issues

"Surveys have revealed that India has suffered greater havoc by destruction of natural wealth and pollution of the environment than other countries. India as a whole is adding about 4 million tonnes of sulphur dioxide, 7 million tonnes of particulates, one million tonnes of carbon monoxide, besides nitrogen oxide, hydrocarbons and several other toxic substances. Bombay illustrates the catastrophic dimensions of air pollution in the country: With all its industries, it emits daily 1000 to 1700 tonnes of pollutants. In Calcutta about 1300 tonnes of pollutants are discharged every day.

Because of the three thermal power stations and massive burning of domestic fuel, Delhi has suspended particulate matter as high as 640-1000 micro-gram per cubic metre one of the highest in the world. Delhi is a topper in respiratory diseases. The other badly affected towns are Kanpur, Ahmedabad and Coimbatore.

Dr. S. Dillon Riply, an eminent environmentalist from Smithsonian Institute, said at a seminar in Delhi last year that in India "massive exposure of land, the soil and water and the air to the fruits of technological advance and development without regard for essential biological precepts can only hasten the degradation of what has been a fair land and a marvellous one for all manner of life."

Grim evidence of this came through the well-documented World Conservation Strategy prepared by the International Union for Conservation of Nature and Natural Resources in cooperation with the United Nations, Environment Programme and the World Wildlife Fund. This revealed that more than half of India suffers some form of soil degradation.

A recent study of the Doon Valley indicates that the once beautiful area is fast becoming an ecological disaster. The region's 2000 mm rainfall has percolated into its limestone belt-a vital cog in the ecological cycle of hills. Thoughtless limestone mining over the past 20 years has resulted in a 50 per cent drop in agriculture productivity and the drying up of several perennial streams which once watered the land. Very few commercial concerns have benefitted from the "rape of the land", but thousands of residents continue to suffer.

Life and Death Issue. An even more ominous warning was given in November, 1985, through the Second Citizens, Report on the State of India's Environment (1984-85) released by the New Delhi based Centre for Science and Environment (C.S.E.). The C.S.E. has a high reputation. Its first report in 1982 was hailed by the United Nations Environment Programme as "a model for other countries to follow."

The rapid pace of environmental destruction in India through soil erosion, deforestation, pollution and urban decay is already affecting the lives of millions of poor people; the country faces social, economic and ecological disaster if its environment is not properly managed. The report seeks to establish a link between environmental destruction in rural areas and urban decay. Many slum and pavement dwellers in India's cities are 'ecological refugees'.

A five-year study of air pollution in Bangalore city has shown that pollution due to automobile emissions and domestic firewood consumption (cars and kitchens) pose a greater danger than industries.

The construction of dams and power stations, the growth of the mining industry and the destruction of forests and grazing land have displaced large numbers of people. The World Bank financed Narmada Valley Project involving the construction of 329 large dams at a cost of 3.5 billion will displace a million people.

The report is not merely a catalogue of catastrophes. It points out that, proper environmental management can provide India with opportunities to tackle poverty. Government-controlled wasteland, which covers between one-third and half of the country, has enormous agricultural potential. But where wasteland development is taking place, few attempts are being made to involve the landless. Most afforestation schemes, for example, are designed solely to meet the industrial requirements of paper mills and fibre manufacturers.

In a signed statement at the end of the report, the authors call for a new 'social order' for resource management. Government policies have served to create' a strong sense of alienation' among village communities which should be left to manage forests, grazing lands, rivers and lakes themselves.

'Environmental activism' has increased dramatically in India. The building of two dams has already been stopped as a result of public protests-the Silent Valley Project in Kerala and the Bedthi project in Karnataka. The Munda people of Chhotanagpur are fighting against a third project-the massive Koel Karo Scheme in Bihar. A coordination committee and the participation of local leaders of various political parties from probably the strongest popular anti-dam movement in India."

Many dangerous chemicals are used in India. The Plastic Industry uses chemicals Toluene-diiso-Cynate which is closely related to MIC which caused havoc in Bhopal Gas tragedy in 1984. Needless to say that this (TDI) is more fatal for life. Similarly a group of chemicals called Polychlorinated biphenyis (PCB) which are highly toxic are widely used in electronic industry. Besides this there are other hazardous chemicals which are being manufactured sold and used in India. In terms of tonnage at least 70 per cent of the pesticides used in the country have been classified as highly toxic or hazardous by WHO.

Development and Growth

Balanced use of Natural Resources: There has been a prevalent misconceived notion that more use we make of available natural resources, more the progress of the world. Actually there becomes an imbalance in the nature if there is an unrestricted exploitation of available natural resources. Y. Nondumma is right when she points out that this misconceived notion of the exploitation of the natural resources under the pretext that they are meant only for exploitation by and for human being, will take the entire humanity to a point of destruction. As it will lead to the entire change in the environment.

Control over the Waste Material: In every industry there is left enough material which is nothing but waste. This waste is either thrown into the water or somewhere on the ground. In both the cases the atmosphere becomes polluted either through water or through air. To have a control over such a waste material is inevitable if we want to preserve the environment or face pollution.

Check on Industrial Development: Industrial development brings with it environmental degradation and may be a menace for the humanity if no check in the right direction is made on this. Industrial development adversely affects the community and surrounding atmosphere all around.

Proper Utilisation of Natural Resources: Nature has given us coal, gas, oil and many other minerals, etc. As there is no limit to the greedy nature of the human being, he has started extracting every thing mercilessly and putting the same at his disposal without caring for its proper utility and the limit to which the same should be exploited, according to need and limit. The result is explicitly clear. At certain places there is drought while at other place there are heavy rains and floods. It brings untold miseries but man has still not learnt a lesson to make a balanced use of natural resources.

Pollution: A Worldwide Problem: The United Nations has repeatedly expressed deep anxiety over the ceaseless pollution all over the world and the innumerable problems it creates. In the initial discussions on environment there were wide differences on the issue. The UN Conference on Environment, held in Stockholm in 1972, became known for controversial approach. Two leading US environmentalists openly contradicted each other over whether too many people or too few resources were responsible for the world's deepening ecological crisis.

The Eastern bloc, led by the Soviet Union kept aloof because the UN had not fully recognised the German Democratic Republic. The Third World accused the industralised nations of using the "pollution problems" as an excuse to keep it underdeveloped; and well-known anthropologist Margaret Mead warned of the need for a "Copernican Revolution" in thinking if we were not to irreversibly damage the natural world.

Since the Stockholm session there have been the UN Habitat Conference on Human Settlements in Vancouver in 1975 and the UN Desertification Conference in Nairobi in 1977. In 1972 only 10 nations had environment programmes; today the number is nearly 100. Third World attitudes have changed dramatically. As the concern has mounted, so has the Doomsday syndrome.

Scientific agencies issue urgent warnings to emphasise the gravity of the population crisis-four births and two deaths every second; 10,000 new chemicals a year are being introduced into the world some deserts are encroaching at the rate of 30 kilometres annually; a century ago 96 per cent of all energy used was either human or animal and now the figure is 1 per cent; the oceans are dying and the earth's protective ozone layer is being broken up by aerosols and supersonic aeroplanes. The list of disastrous deeds is endless.

The need to teach people about the environment has become increasingly obvious. In October, 1977, nearly 400 delegates from 74 countries gathered in Soviet Georgia for a major intergovernmental conference on environmental education organised by UNESCO in collaboration with the UN Environment Programme (UNEP). They heard UNEP Executive Directors' blunt warning: "Environmental education is now a matter of life and death." Dr. Amadou Mahtar M'Bow, UNESCO's Director-General, cautioned that the problems of the environment were "jeopardising the development of mankind."

There is a growing number of hopeful examples : 15 out of 18 nations surrounding the Mediterranean signed a "Save the Mediterranean" agreement; Tanzania had invited international environmental experts to advise on the design of the country's new capital; the USA and Canada were cooperating to revive the Great Lakes. The Chinese have been conserving energy by the widespread use of bio-gas collectors, which produce gas for cooking and generators, and the Soviet Union is minimising the effluence from the pulp plants around Lake Baikal, which contains one-tenth of the world's entire fresh water supply.

An international conference to consider the question of saving trees and forests was held in Paris in January, 1986. The meeting was convened by President Mitterand and brought together for the first time Heads of States and senior government leaders from 36 nations to discuss forestry issues.

Because the pollution envelops the entire world and as such no country- remains aloof from its evil effects, there is an awakening throughout the world to save it from the fatal clutches, of the fearful dragon of pollution.

Cultural Factors

Significance of Education

The intimate relationship between culture and education is evident from the fact that one of the major aims of education is to impart to the child his cultural heritage, the social heritage. In any human group, the various elements and parts of culture evolve after thousands of years of the experience, and these are handed down as a whole to the succeeding generations. Hence, every individual is born into a particular culture which provide him with definite patterns of behaviour and values which guide his conduct in different walks of life. He has thereby saved the necessity of making fresh experiments every time. Obviously, then, culture plays an important part in man's life. But understanding the nature of its importance, it will be easy to understand how the education of various elements of culture can help man. The main features of the contribution of culture to man's life are the following:

Adaptation to the Natural Environment: Everywhere, man lives in a definite natural environment to which he must necessarily adapt himself. Without doing this, he cannot exist. All the experiments and inventions that he makes in the process of this adaptation form an important part of the culture. Due to differences in the natural environment of different communities, there arise differences in their cultures also, and it is on this basis that a distinction is made between primitive and developed cultures. In all the tribes of India, the members behave in certain distinct and specific ways in order to adapt to their respective environments. These modes of behaviour are taught to the younger generations. It is these modes of behaviour which go to make up culture.

Adaptation to the Social Environment: Culture also includes customs, traditions and the pattern of current behaviour, etc. Inherent in it are our beliefs and ideas, decisions, values and social institutions. All of these help the individual to adapt to his social environment, but it must be remembered that all these elements undergo gradual changes as the social environment itself changes. Culture determines the patterns of social control, through which the individual is subjected to the coercion of the group. Hence, the advantage in communicating the culture of the group to the child through education is that he is thereby acquainted with the traditions, customs, values and patterns of conduct prevailing in his group. This knowledge enables him to adapt to the social environment and thus achieve his socialisation.

Development of Personality: The personality of an individual is manifested through his pattern of behaviour. The behaviour is always profoundly influenced by the culture of his group. Anthropologists have established as a fact that one finds differences in the basic behaviour patterns of individuals belonging to different cultures and that differences of behaviour correspond to differences in culture. Some people are more aggressive while others are submissive. One can find the clear imprint of Indian culture on an Indian and the imprint of Western culture on a European or American. Culture influences the physical, mental, social, emotional, moral and aesthetic aspects of the individual. Individual efforts lead to important changes in culture, but the behaviour of the average individual is determined by culture.

Socialisation: Culture plays an important role in socialising the individual, and for this reason the quantity and direction of socialisation differs from one society to another. Every society has its own ethos, and this is communicated to the individual in many different ways. Ralph Linton has pointed out three ways in which the individual can participate in culture. In the first place he participates universally in culture, that is, he adopts the habits, ideas and emotional patterns that prevail among the adults of that group. In the second place, the individual specifically participates in culture by adopting those elements of culture which are found among some specific organisation or specific group of people. And finally, in third place, the individual's participation in culture turns to that alternative elements in which he adapts those elements which are found only in a small number of individuals. It is this participation in the third, the alternative aspect, that leads individuality to the personality of each person. George H. Mead expresses the opinion that in adopting his culture the individual's ego passes through three stages analogous to the three stages of education. In the first stage, the individual imitates other people around himself, normally unconsciously. He is found smiling at others. In childhood, the infant acquires his culture through imitation. In the second stage, the children imitate different individuals in society in their play. Play of this kind introduces many different kinds of qualities in the child's personality. The third stage of acquiring culture is the stage of games where the individual learns to control his behaviour. In the social environment of the playground, the individual cannot behave wilfully, since he has to conform to the social norms. Hence, he gradually begins to adopt the ideals, principles and beliefs of his group, and it is only this kind of individual who is called cultured.

Culture and Education

Education of Culture in Family: The child's cultural education begins at home, and it is in the family that he participates in the elements of culture and he passes through the various stages of culture development explained by Mead. The parents and other members of the family educate the child in the various means of culture such as traditions, customs, values, belief, etc. It is in the family that the child first learns to distinguish between right and wrong. The various impressions impinging upon his mind in the family environment help to make the child cultured. In Indian society a variety of religious ceremonies are performed to initiate the child into cultured life. Comparable religious practices are found in other cultures also. Patterns of moral and religious behaviour are also learnt in the family. Good behaviour is imbibed from the behaviour of adult members of the family, because the child invariably imitates the behaviour of the adults and brothers and sisters. One can find the clear imprint of family influence upon the lives of the greatest men who have contributed to their respective cultures. A part of the cultural training in the family is unconscious, but a large part of it is consciously imparted to the child by the adults.

Cultural Education in School: Nowadays, it is the school which has taken over the function of culturally educating the child, just as it educates him in every other way. Schools in different countries educate the child according to their own cultures because through their text books they seek to acquaint the child with their own values, mores, ideas, customs, etc. Various extracurricular programmes are also intended to impart culture to the child. These programmes take the form of games of various kinds, dramas, community songs, dances, discussions, tours, of various parts of the country, etc.

Cultural Education in Society: Generally speaking, of course, both the family and the school undertake the task of communicating the society's specific culture to the younger generation, but nevertheless one does find minimal differences between the cultures of individuals belonging to different ranks of the same society. Hence, this education in culture is limited not only to training in the culture of the society as a whole, but also of a more limited culture belonging to different strata of society. Hence, cultural education comprehends both the general or extensive culture as well as the numerous subcultures existing within the extensive culture. Culture education is important inasmuch as it helps the individual to adapt to his natural and social environment, to develop his social personality, to enable him to conduct himself fruitfully in this intercourse with other members of the society. Apart from this, the individual is also assisted by culture in his livelihood and other important functions of life. Through this culture he adopts social institutions and learns to conform his behaviour to the accepted norm. He finds in this culture distinctive patterns of behaviour designed to meet the various contingencies of social life. It is through this training that he becomes a useful member of society.

Education in Liberality to Other Cultures: Cultural education must supplement knowledge of one's own culture with the liberality of approach for other cultures which is so essential for understanding and sympathising with them. In the absence of this liberality members of one culture believe themselves to be either superior or inferior to members of other cultures, with the result that tension is enhanced. This tension can even find violent expression. This is a major cause of many communal riots that frequently disrupt the peace in India. It is, therefore, desirable that the children should not only be taught their own culture but also be taught to appreciate other cultures. This is essential if the organisation of society and world peace is to be maintained.

For this, some attention should be paid to other cultures also while imparting training in the various aspects of one's own culture. While leaching the child about the religion of his own group for example, it is necessary to tell him that despite the obvious differences the same elements are also to be found at the root of other religions. The child should be made to understand that cultural differences arc the manifestation of the different natural environments, but that this is no reason to believe one culture to be superior or inferior to another. There is no magnificence or denigration attached to differences in the natural environment. It is more creditable for every human group to lead its life according to its own culture. Therefore, it is never proper to foist the culture of one group upon another. When the child comprehends the true causes at the root of cultural differences, he can adopt a more liberal and sympathetic attitude to other cultures, and also avoid the mistake of considering his own culture to be the best one.

Education in the Proper Use of Leisure: One important aspect of cultural education is training in the proper use of one's leisure. That man is a cultured animal can be judged from the manner in which he spends his leisure, and it is only this which really distinguishes between the cultured and the uncultured individual. Hence, children should be educated to use their leisure for cultural attainments, such as literature, music, art, self-development, etc. It is for this reason that educationists have insisted upon supplementing education in science with some education in humanities also.

The relationship between education and culture is clear from the foregoing account.

While Karl Marx looked upon the economic factor as the most important factor to bring about social change, the German sociologist Max Weber emphasised that the economic phenomena themselves rest upon culture, particularly religion. Max Weber showed that there is direct relationship between the practical ethics of a community and the character of its economic system. He confined himself to the analysis of one particular economic phenomenon, namely capitalism, and one particular religious phenomenon, namely Protestantism. Weber asserted that the development of modern capitalism could be attributed to the Protestant Reformation, particularly Calvinism. A description of the various contributions of Protestantism to capitalism may now be given.

The first important aspect of Protestantism which led to development of modern capitalism is a changed attitude towards work. The Catholic outlook emphasised leisure rather than work. It also subscribed to the biblical story that God condemned Adam and his sons to earn their bread by the sweat of their brow. Thus, according to the Catholic ethics, work is a burden; it is a punishment; it is reminder of the original sin. On the other hand, the Protestant ethic emphasised that work is virtue, it is something good and it is something done for its own sake.

Though Calvinism believed in the doctrine of predeterminism, it also asserted that success in one's work or "calling" is a sign that one is marked for ascent to heaven. So Calvinism emphasised that one should work hard in one's calling, even if such calling is the pursuit of private economic profit. Thus, success in one's efforts to become rich was looked upon as a sign that God had marked one for heaven.

Calvin also changed the attitude of the Christian towards collection of interest on loans. The official Catholic doctrine looked upon usury as a sin but it did not differentiate between legitimate interest and excessive interest. Consequently, by the time of the Reformation, the terms usury and interest were looked upon as being synonymous because the Jews lent money and charged high interest. So the Jews were looked down upon with contempt.

Weber showed that this attitude towards interest discouraged the accumulation of capital which is necessary for the success of a business enterprise. In 1545, Calvin gave sanction for the collection of interest on loans. This brought about a big change among the Protestants and they lent money to men who wanted to establish new business.

Another important contribution of Protestantism to the development of modern capitalism is its favourable attitude towards an austere life. It was against the consumption of alcohol and so the money that was wasted on the purchase of alcohol was now available for the accumulation of capital.

Another very important aspect is the encouragement of literacy. The Protestant Church asserted that every man could read his own Bible. This led to the translation of the Bible into the various European languages and to the promotion of literacy among the masses. Mass literacy, as we have seen, is one of the important characteristics of the modern industrial society.

Finally, Protestantism discouraged holidays. The Catholic Church believed that one should pay exclusive attention to religious observances on holidays; but because of the change of attitude towards work. Protestantism discouraged holidays. In passing, it may be observed that one of the chief difficulties in the Indian ethic is the emphasis on innumerable holidays which cuts the national output.

Thus, Weber showed that the new ideas of the Protestant Reformation prepared the way for increased production of economic goods. The worldly asceticism promoted by Protestantism emphasised the virtues of hard work, thrift and savings. All these, according to Weber, lead to conditions appropriate for the development of the earlier phases of capitalism.

The aim of Weber was to determine the origin, the propagation and the perpetuation of a distinctive type of social organisation, the "rational organisation" linked with science and technology. Such an organisation is dedicated to completely impersonal ends and all the status-roles within it are defined in terms of contribution towards that impersonal end. In other words, the characteristic of such a rational organisation is that individual actions and human relations are accurately and efficiently controlled in a bureaucratic way to attain the impersonal end.

Max Weber's work is a very important contribution towards the understanding of the phenomena of the social change. His emphasis that ideas, ideals and attitude towards work, savings and life are very important to bring about the unique phenomenon of economic development in Western Europe and America is of great value, but this should not be taken to mean that other factors like the economic, technological, demographic, etc., are not important. Weber himself was quite cautious. Secondly, we cannot look upon this as a causal relationship implying that unless there is change in religion there cannot be change in economic development. The non-Protestant countries like Japan and the USSR have shown that economic development can take place without a change in religion; but they also proved that a change in attitudes, ideas and ideals is very important. It is because Japan gave up its feudalistic organisation that it was able to build up a new economy. The same was the case with respect to the USSR.

Modern View

The need for a change in outlook of the individual and a change in the social norms in order to bring about economic development has been emphasised by Tinbergen. He asserts that the present attitude of indifference to material conditions among the people in Asian, African and other underdeveloped countries should be changed to an interest in material well-being. It is true that in India people do not attach much value to material comforts and to wealth. This ideal is quite in order as far as the wealthy man is concerned. But Indians as a whole have to develop an attitude of horror towards the poverty of the millions. So long as one remains indifferent to the poverty and squalor prevailing in the slums of the big cities and the poverty in the villages it is impossible to work for an improvement in the wealth of the nation which will improve the living standards of each person in the country.

There must be a change from aversion to complicated techniques and an inclination to routine habits, to an interest in technological innovation. So long as the people at large are content to do things in the same way as their ancestors were doing, there cannot be any economic development. It is necessary for the people of the developing countries to welcome and to foster technological innovation.

Another very important outlook that pervades the underdeveloped countries is short-sightedness and a desire for quick returns. This attitude is pervasive among the merchants in particular and citizens in general. The merchant is India wants to attain quickly as much wealth as possible. Similarly, people are eager to subscribe to lotteries, benefit schemes, etc., so that they can get wealth without work and effort. The same shortsightedness could be seen among the backward castes and classes in India. They want to send their children of eight or ten years to work and earn. This attitude prevents the education and development of the children; they will not have higher ambitions and aspirations. All these attitudes inevitably lend to poverty. On the other hand, our aim must be to give up immediate gains and to look ahead. This is particularly true of large scale industries. Installation of capital industries will produce results only after a considerable time.

Another prevailing feature in the Indian society, as in other underdeveloped countries, is a desire for security and certainty. This is one of the reasons why, generally, the educated person as well as the illiterate person seek jobs in government service. They know that government service does not offer attractive terms but they are sure that the little that is offered is secure. Economic development on the other hand implies a willingness to take risks.

Finally, the strong individualism has to be replaced by the willingness to collaborate with other people and to observe certain rules and regulations. Modern social and economic life depends upon cooperation with others and the willingness to observe certain rules. A new outlook is necessary in this regard. Generally, the Indian cooperates with others if they belong to the same caste or creed and he is willing to obey rules for fear of punishment by the elders. This has to give place to a new outlook where one works with other people in the factory, office or other such organisations and where rules are obeyed not because of any fear of punishment by the elders or by those in authority but because of a sense of discipline emanating from within.

Another very important change that is necessary in the outlook of individuals is with respect to time. In modern life, the entire series of activities are linked with time, according to the clock. This is one of the important results of schooling, where the child is taught to attend the school according to time and to work according to a time schedule. No organised institution could function if the individuals composing it do not have a sense of time.

It is true that during the last 20 years, the poor countries have shown a marked desire for economic development. But a mere desire cannot produce results. Economic development can take place only when large sections of the people change their outlook and seek better ways of doing things and more comfortable ways of living.

We can now describe briefly another way in which changes in culture can take place. The American psychologist McClelland and his colleagues have done considerable work in what is called the need for achievement McClelland has tried to show that when there is an emphasis on the need for achievement there is economic growth, and there is stagnation and decline when this need for achievement is absent

Actual Issues

The immediate world-problem is the great disparity between the developed nations and the developing nations. While 7 per cent of world's population in North America enjoy about 43 per cent of the world's wealth, 55 per cent of the world's population in Asia have only 16 per cent of the world's wealth.

McClelland puts forth the hypothesis that it is the achievement motive or the need for achievement that is responsible for economic growth. He tried to develop a method to measure the individual differences in achievement motivation. He used the spontaneous thoughts, the waking fantasies and free associations in order to measure this motivation. He gave pictures depicting a variety of situations connected with work and asked the people to write stories about these pictures within five minutes. He found that there was a marked variation regarding the stories produced. The individual with strong achievement motivation made references to standards of excellence, wanting to do well, etc. Further, he found contrasting behaviour between those with high achievement scores and those with low achievement scores. It was found that the people with high scores came more often from the middle class homes than from the lower or the upper class homes. They were more resistant to social pressures. There was also a big difference in "task orientation". The people with high achievement scores tended to work hard and reach the standards which they set for themselves.

In another study, eight-year-old boys were tested and their mothers were interviewed in order to find out if there was any difference in the upbringing between these two groups of children — those with high achievement score and those with low achievement score. Interviews revealed that the mothers of the high scorers expected their sons to be active and encouraged them to make their own friends and to go about by themselves, to study by themselves and to try hard to get things for themselves, to do well in competition and so on. On the other hand, mothers of low scorers reported that they wanted their sons to play with the children approved by the parents; they did not want their children to make important decisions by themselves and so on. The study revealed that the score on the achievement was thus related to the way in which the mothers bring up their children; those who were given freedom generally got higher scores than those on whom many restrictions were imposed.

McClelland says that there is a close relationship between Max Weber's hypothesis and the findings of this study.

McClelland developed a programme of training on the basis of this hypothesis. He assumed that it is possible to train people so that they become achievement-minded, with a desire for a standard of excellence. The first systematic experiment was carried out in India at the small Industry Expansion Training Institute (S.I.E.T.I.) at Hyderabad in 1964. The original plan was to select 60 persons from each town with approximately one hundred thousand population and give them intense training for ten days to develop their achievement motivation. A comparable group was taken up as a control group. Comparisons were made not only between the experimental group and the control group but also between the performance of the experimental groups before the training and after the training in their respective business concerns. Fifteen potential entrepreneurs were taken at a time for training. Four such groups were taken from one town making a total of 60 people from that town. The training consisted in influencing the fantasy of the participant with achievement oriented imagery. They were given training to examine their current behaviour and their possible future plan in the achievement-motive framework.

They were encouraged to work out for themselves future achievement plans and possible ways of collaborative and cooperative endeavour. The results showed that the programme had influenced the entrepreneurial activities of the participants; there was a significant difference between the preprogramme period and the post-programme period in the business activities of the participants. Further, the business activities of the trained people was significantly higher than the business activities of the control group. It was also found that there was a great improvement not only in self-development but also in insight into themselves and into their work among the trainees. McClelland reports that it was found that within two years, two-thirds of this group showed signs of inventive business activities, for example, starting a new product or taking a course in accountancy or doing something which brought them a big salary rise. As McClelland asserts "the significant thing is that this is neither due to material aid nor to technical instruction but because of motivation".

There is a social component in this need for achievement. The aim of these people is not only to improve their own prospects but also to bring about a significant change in the economic position of their town or of the country. Thus, there is not only a concern for excellence but there is also a concern for the welfare of others. McClelland reports that this theme of concern for the common good was also found in the children's textbooks in the countries which achieved rapid economic development. On the other hand, in the stories for children from the underdeveloped countries, there were more references to traditions or to habitual ways of doing things. This concern for the welfare of others is an important aspect of modernisation. This is why, he says, there are large investments on public health and public education which lead to economic growth.

Thus, according to McClelland, the need for achievement on the one hand and a concern for the welfare of others on the other are the psychological ingredients essential for modernisation. To quote, "The impulse to modernisation under ideal psychological terms seems to consist in part of a personal virtue — need for achievement — and in part of a social virtue — interest in the welfare of the generalised other fellow". Thus, technological innovation by itself is not enough. A change in attitude is also necessary for economic growth.

McClelland gives an illustration from a Government of India programme. The fishermen of Kakinada were given nylon fishing nets which required less mending and also because they could be untangled easily. The idea behind the programme was that the fisherman would catch more fish, make more money, buy more consumer goods and thus lead to economic expansion. As anticipated, the fisherman got more fish with the nylon fishing nets. But, two unexpected things followed. Some of the fishermen stopped fishing as soon as they had caught the usual quantity. In other words, they now worked less and relaxed more. The other group worked more, caught more fish and made more money; but they spent all the extra money on bootleg liquor, instead of purchasing consumer goods. So, the new fishing nets did not increase the need for achievement in the fishermen. They did not have any desire to work more, to save and to invest the savings.

Prayag Mehta has also done some work to improve the need for achievement among the high school boys. He found that the boys whose fathers had high education and those whose fathers had low education showed a lower level of need for achievement than the boys of the fathers with secondary school education. Thus, these two Indian studies — one among the entrepreneurs and the other among the high school students demonstrate that need for achievement could be developed through training.

Udai Pareek asserts that there are three important motivations which have to be taken into account with respect to economic growth. He uses the term "expansion motivation" for what McClelland calls the concern for the common good. He identifies, besides these two, namely the achievement motivation and expansion motivation, a third motivation which he calls the "dependence motivation", which contributes negatively to development. This may be reflected in excessive dependence, seeking support and guidance from other people or in excessive counter dependence, the aggressive rejection of authority. Both of these manifestations could be found in the traditional behaviour among Indians. According to Udai Pareek, just *as* the achievement motivation and the expansion motivation could be improved with training, similarly the dependence motivation could be reduced or eliminated with training (Kuppuswamy, 1975).

We have reviewed here the contributions of Max Weber, Tinbergen and McClelland. All the three of them have shown that ideals as well as ideologies are powerful sources in social change. The belief of the people and what they think have a profound influence on what they have and what they want.

According to Becker, as noted above, secularism by definition is readiness to change. A significant aspect of this is the desire for innovation and readiness to try innovations. The two most significant innovations are in the technological field, invention, and in the administrative field, innovations in goals as well as in procedures.

Before proceeding further we may, in passing, refer to the hypothesis of "cultural lag" formulated by the American sociologist Ogburn. He distinguished between the material and the non-material aspects of culture. He believed that when changes occur in the material culture, they will stimulate changes in the non-material culture in the ways of utilising these material changes. The changes in the non-material culture may be slow to respond to the changes in the material culture. For example, when the factory system was introduced there was a good deal of ugliness and squalor. Workmen had to face many kinds of accidents and they were also victims to many kinds of industrial diseases. Factory laws to regulate the working conditions and the working environment were passed long after. This is the lag to which Ogburn refers. But the difficulty about his hypothesis is that he assumes two things – a clear distinction between material and non-material culture. It is really very difficult to distinguish between these two. He also assumes that the material culture is always in advance which is not a correct assumption. In fact, one of the great difficulties faced by the traditional culture is the technological lag. We may accept the products of the forest but fail to maintain the forest itself. If we take the illustration of the use of the computer in modern India it is difficult to tell whether the delay in the introduction of the computer is due to a technological lag or a cultural lag. The Indian technology has not yet reached the stage when it could manufacture computers. Of course, we can always import the computers. But the management should be in a position to understand the relative advantage of the computer in organising the data at its disposal to arrive at the necessary decision. There is also the problem of the attitude of the workers towards computers. It is well known that the workers in the LIC have been agitating against the introduction of the computer because they are sure that many of them will be thrown out of 'employment even though management is assuring that none of the workers on the rolls will be thrown out because of the introduction of the computer. Thus, the resistance may come from either source because there is a lack of development in technology or because the vested interests are against the introduction of technological development In fact, there is the supreme illustration of Gandhi who was against the introduction of industrialisation in India because it was anti-cultural.

So it is not possible to assert dial the technological change always takes place first and the cultural change takes place later, often with considerable lag. Anyway, the merit of Ogburn is that he showed that there may be cultural resistance to technological change.

The contemporary situation in the developing countries clearly shows the influence of the cultural factor on social change. New techniques are available but they cannot be imported because of the low availability of capital, which in turn is due to cultural factors which are in favour of expenditure of vast amounts on marriage ceremonies, rites, rituals, etc. There is also the other obstacle which arises out of a lack in education and a lack in training. Even when machines are brought there may not be the personnel to repair the machines. Finally, there is the problem of obsolescence. By the time the government sanction is obtained to purchase the machine and orders are placed and shipping space is obtained, that machine would have already become obsolescent because of the rapid technological change in the developed countries. This is the reason why it is necessary that there should be a great cultural change in the developing countries. They must develop the ideal to manufacture machines for the purposes on hand with the raw materials available instead of trying to imitate the advanced countries by importing the machine and the know-how. This is one of the most important cultural changes which is necessary at the present time.

Emphasis in this section has been regarding the cultural factor as it affects changes in economic life. It is true that there are so many other changes. For example, it is well known that the contact with the British through colonialism influenced more the educational and social aspects rather than the economic aspects. The liberals of the nineteenth century were greatly impressed *by* the idea of parliamentary democracy, freedom of women, uplift of the lower castes and classes, advancement of education and so on rather than by any ideas of great changes in the economic condition of the people. This is one of the reasons why it was easy to bring about a political change rather than the economic change with the end of colonialism. This is in great contrast, as we have observed already, to the Japanese response to the Western culture. Japan emphasised technical education and technological advancement and has now become a leading industrial country. But India is one of the poorest countries in spite of the efforts to bring about an economic change through planning.

The emphasis on the economic aspect is justified by the preoccupation of all the developing countries today, and of India in particular, to bring about economic growth by planning. The contemporary situation emphasises the need for economic change because of the most rapid economic advancement of the developed counties since World War II. The impact of the growth of the media of mass communication is to emphasise the economic aspect. The other values will have a meaning today only if the people in the villages and in the slum areas of city have adequate food, clothing and shelter. It is vain *to* expect them to respond to the other values of culture when these basic needs are not met in a world of affluence.

Understanding the Theory

In anthropological literature the term culture is used in many senses, but in general writings it is used to indicate social charm and intellectual superiority. Even some sociologists believe cultured individuals to be the leaders of society. According to Sorokin and MacIver, culture implies man's moral, spiritual and intellectual achievements. In the words of Bogardus, "Culture is composed of integrated customs, traditions and current behaviour patterns of human group. Culture is the stock in trade of group. It is an antecedent complex of value into which every individual is born. It is a medium within which individuals develop and mature." In Indian Society the individual is prepared for performing various functions in society at a very early age by a series of impressions deliberately made upon his mind. For example, the ceremony of marriage places upon the individual's shoulders the responsibility of procreating and thus ensuring the continuity of the race. Culture includes all those elements for which ceremonies and their consequent impressions are required. It is the process of purification. In ancient India Sanskrit was believed to be the language of the educated people, and this too is intimately concerned with culture, because the Hindi synonym is 'sanskriti'.

Heritage of Culture

In the words of Kroeber, "In short, a cultural fact is always a historical fact, and its most immediate understanding, and usually the fullest understanding of it to which we can attain, is a historical one. To a large degree calling culture super-organic or super-individual means that it yields more readily to historical interpretation than to organised or psychosomatic explanations." Thus, Kroeber calls culture super-organic and super-individual in the sense that it is amenable to a historical interpretation or more apt interpretation of culture. This viewpoint makes it amply clear that although human beings create culture, it is not the creation of single individual. The same thing has been stated by Majumdar and Madan in these words "Human beings, it must be realised, are perhaps equally the creator of cultures as they are its creatures and careers." Hence, culture guides mankind, and while it renders him free from many causes, it also, to certain extent, enslaves him It is evident that Majumdar and Madan have also accepted culture

as super psychic and super social. Kroeber's viewpoint on culture is considered to belong to the category of cultural determinism according to which culture is the determinant of man's activity, not itself dependent upon man. But this concept of cultural determinism is no less unbalanced and one-sided than biological or geographical determinism Kroeber's belief that culture is super organic and super individual is acceptable only to the extent that culture is not the creation of any one individual but of a community of human beings. But it is difficult to agree with him in the belief that culture is the final determinant of all human activity.

Human Development

The sole aim of education is to bring an all-round development in the personality of education. Educational Psychology, being a science and technology of education, should help in the realisation of this aim. As you may be aware, human life starts from a single fertilized cell. The constant interaction with the environment results in the growth and development of the innate capacities, abilities and potentialities of the child.

The task of formal as well as informal education is to help him in this path of growth and development. Therefore, it is imperative that the individuals, supposed to be connected with the task of helping the child to grow and develop satisfactorily, must be acquainted with the nature of growth and development.

It is only with a knowledge of growth and development of the learner at each stage of his life that it is possible for the teachers to render proper guidance, arrange the learning situations and plan the instructional programmes for bringing desirable harmonious development in their personalities.

In the following pages, we would try to understand the process of growth and development with its various aspects.

Worth of Reading

The above mentioned principles of growth and development carry wide educational meaning for the children, parents and the teachers. It can be explained in the following way:

1. Knowledge of the principles of growth and development tells us that there are wide individual differences among the children with respect to their rate of growth and development. Therefore, we must pay attention to their individual pattern and growth rate while planning the course for their education and development.
2. Its knowledge helps us to know what to expect and when to expect from an individual child with respect to his physical, mental, social development, etc., at different stages of development. The correct knowledge of the growth trend of a child helps the parents and teacher not to under or overestimate the future competency or expectancy of their child.
3. It helps us to know the direction as well as the general pattern of development. It guides us to locate the degree of abnormality in our children and students and to take likewise remedial steps. The knowledge that development starts from whole to parts and then from parts to whole helps us to plan the learning procedure and set the learning methods accordingly.
4. Principles of interrelation and interdependence of the various aspects of growth and development help us to aim for the harmonious growth and development of the personality of the child and warns us not to develop a particular aspect at the cost of one or the other.
5. The knowledge of the uniformity of pattern with respect to growth and development makes it possible for the parents and teachers to plan ahead of time for the changes that will take place in their children. Children will also get benefitted if they can be acquainted with these changes beforehand.
6. The knowledge that heredity and environment both play a joint role in the process of growth and development helps us to pay sufficient attention over the environmental conditions in upbringing the children.

In this way, the knowledge of the principles of growth and development helps much in the well-being of the youngsters.

Development of Society

The Definition: Human beings Nossess a unique characteristic which separates them from animal beings. Their behaviour is social. Society is as essential as food to them. They believe in the maintenance of social relationships and try to adjust with others. But this does not mean that the child is born with such social behaviour and social qualities. Like other aspects of growth and develoment, he develops the necessary social characteristics in him.

The process of the development of such qualities which brings desirable changes in his social behaviour is referred to as social development or socialisation of the child. Social development occupies very important place in the overall process of growth and development. We cannot even describe an individual as a person if he has not passed through the process of socal development or socialisation.

Let us try to think over further. What does this term social development (also described as socialisation) mean? Varous thinkers have tried to define it. Some of the definitions are given below:

1. *Sorenson:* "By social growth and development we mean increasing ability to get along well with oneself and others." (1948, p. 50)

   In this way Sorenson explains that during the process of social development there is a progress in the social abilities of an individual. With these increasing abilities he tries to bring improvement in the maintenance of social relationships. He tries to mould his behaviour and seek adjustment and harmony with others.

2. *Freeman and Showel:* "Social development is the process of learning to conform to group standards, mores and traditions and becoming imbued with a sense of oneness, intercommunication and cooperation."

   This definition lays stress on the following:

   a. Social development refers to the process by which a person acquires the necessary knowledge, skills and disposition that makes him an acceptable member of his own group.

b. It develops group loyalty and encourages mutual dependence, cooperation and cohesiveness.

c. It is the process which helps an individual to behave in accordance with social traditions and mores and thus makes him able to adjust in his social environment.

3. *Mrs. Huriock:* "Social development means the attaining of maturity in social relationships." (1959, p. 257)

   This brief definition carries a wide meaning. It asserts that as in the case of emotional development, the goal is to attain emotional maturity, similarly there is the case of social development, the goal should be the attainment of social maturity. An individual should have all the opportunities to modify or improve his social behaviour so that he may be able to maintain proper social relationships and can adjust himself to his social environment.

4. *Garrett:* "Socialisation or social development is the process whereby the biological indiuidual is concerted into a human person." (1968 p. 555)

This definition is based upon the distinction between the term 'individual' and 'person'. We cannot name each and every body as person. The person always possesses some personality. The personality is the product of social interaction between him and his social environment. Socialisation and social development — the process of social interaction — helps the individuals to attain essential personality characteristics.

In the light of all these views we can come to the conclusion that social development or the socialisation is a process.

1. Which begins with the infant's first contact with other people and continues throughout life,
2. It is the net result of his constant interaction with his social environment,
3. It helps in learning and acquiring various social qualities and characteristics, and
4. With the result of such learning the individual becomes adjusted to his social environment and can maintain proper social relationships.

Development of Social Behaviour during Different Stages of Development.

Various Stages: The behaviour of the human infant is not social at birth. He is too much self-centred. He is only concerned with the satisfaction of his physical need. He does not even distinguish between people and inanimate objects.

Social behaviour is said to be taking its birth when the infant first distinguishes between persons and objects. He is dependent upon the adults for the satisfaction of his needs, therefore, normally the baby's first social contacts are with an adult.

Mrs. Hurlock in her book '*Child Psychology*' has beautifully explained the process of socal development during the first two years as a result of the contact with adults. Below we give the summary of her findings.

Duration of Age	*Pattern of Social Behaviour*
During first Month	Cannot differentiate between the human voices and other noises.
Second Month	Recognises the sounds of human beings and gives smiles to the person.
Third Month	Recognises its mother and feels unhappy on separation.
Fourth Month	Shows selective attention to the human face and feels happy in company.
Fifth Month	Reacts differently to smiling and scolding and distinguishes between friendly and angry voices.
Sixth Month	Recognises familiar persons with a smile and shows definite expressions of fear of strangers.
Eighth and Ninth Month	Attempts to imitate the speech, simple acts and gestures observed in others.
Between the tenth and twelve Month	Plays with his image and even kisses it as if it were another person.
At twelve Month	Can refrain from doing things in.
At two Years	Response to 'no-no' or some other form of request.

Can cooperate with adults in a number of routine activities and becomes an active member of the family.

Social development of infants as a result of contact with other infants and children – With regard to an infant's social reactions to another infant or child it has been observed that his early behaviour is egocentric and selfish. He cannot share his toys with others. He wants to have all things for himself and does not tolerate any external interference. From the thirteenth to the eighteenth month the young child's interest shifts from play materials to the playmates. There is a decrease in fighting for toys and increase in cooperative use of them. Up to 3 years he learns to divide and share his possession with others and to cooperate with them. They are now in a position to engage themselves in the cooperative and organised plays activities. Up to 7 years or so the children seek companionship regardless of sex of the other children. Usually the boys and girls play together at this stage.

Like emotions the early stage of social behaviour during infancy is characterised by negative social characteristics. Imitation, timidity, shyness, rivalry and desire for possession dominate the first two years of development. Between 2 to 6 years both negative and positive aspects of social behaviour are seen. Negativism, rivalry, quarrelling, teasing and bullying, cooperation, sympathy and social approval are some of the new social behaviours which are learned at this stage. As we have seen that during the period 2 to 6 years a child progresses from being relatively unsocial to distinctly socialised individual. He learns to share, to cooperate and to do things with others. But the circle of his social contacts is limited at this stage. Therefore, we cannot expect much from him regarding his social development.

With the entrance in childhood most of the children begin to go to school. The area of their social contacts is now widened. We note the following changes in the social behaviour of a child:

1. This period is marked by greater degree of social awareness. There is a great expansion of child's social world. Most of the important types of social behaviour; necessary to adjustment with others, begin to develop at this stage.
2. He tries to seek independence from his parents and other elders and spends less time with them. In actual sense he

now drives no enjoyment from them. Thus interest in playmates of his own age gets increased.

3. He becomes an active member of a 'peer groups' and this group gradually replaces the family group in its influence over his behaviour and attitudes. The members of such a group are almost of the same age. They believe in group loyalty and thus try to conform to the rules and the values maintained by their group.
4. We find a sort of segregation among boys and girls of this age. They form their group among members of their own sex because of a definite and clear differentiation between their habits, interest and atitudes, etc.
5. The interests and values of the peer group often have a clash with the interests and values of the teachers and parents. The child at this age is caught between the two. On the one hand he aspires for the social values of his own group; on the other hand, he is equally anxious to win the love and affection of his parents as well as of teachers. Therefore a proper balance between these two influencing forces — peer group, parents and teachers — is essential. Being neglected by either side he may develop himself into a maladjusted and anti-social personality.
6. Up to the end of the stage of childhood, *i.e.* 11th or 12th year the child enters the peak of "gang age" with increasing loyalties towards his own gang and conflicts with other gangs, parents and teachers. The gang life develops so many good and bad social qualities in the child.

Adolescence is a period of rapid change and adjustments. In the social sphere also it holds a greater significance. The social development of this age is marked by the following characteristics :

1. Adolesecence is marked with too much sex consciousness, sexual development and the accompanying attraction for opposite sex. Boys and girls of this age try to attract and hold the attraction of each other through their style of dress, manner of talking and other forms of social behaviour. They also try to seek friendship and even sexual relationships. In

this way the social behaviour pattern of the adolescence is almost dominated by sexual needs and desires.

2. During this stage group loyalty becomes very much pronounced. Like childhood, it does not confine itself to the gang only but extends to the school, the community, the province and to the nation. Martyrs and patriots are the product of this age. Cooperation reaches its peak during this period and the individuals are in a mood to sacrifice their own interest for the greater cause of the group, society and nation.
3. Adolescence is also marked with the increase in friendly relationships. The nature of friendship maintained at this stage differs much from that of childhood. While in the childhood the friends are generally chosen from the neighbourhood or class, in adolescence there is no such bar of distance. The adolescents tend to choose friends of their own age, mental level and from the same socio-economic group to which their own family belongs. Their friendships are based on their common interests, hobbies and skills or the satisfaction of their mutual needs and subsequently tend to last longer than the friendships made in early childhood. It sometimes ties them in life long relationships.
4. Adolescence is a period of intense emotions. Emotional behaviour dominates the social characteristics and qualities of adolescents. An adolescent is highly sensitive, idealist and social reformer by nature. He feels strongly for the weak and sufferers. He is always ready to do some sort of social and community service. From time to time he exhibits his desire for bringing reforms in the social set-up and is highly critical of social evils and injustice.
5. There area of specific interests and social contacts gets widened during adolescence. Besides individual characteristics the culture, socio-economic status of the family, sex education — all effect their social interest and contacts. We find too much diversity in the adolescents regarding their interests and sociability. While some are highly extrovert and sociable the others like to remain aloof and shirk from social contacts and participations.

In the end we can say that adolescence is a period of maximum social awareness, increasing social relationships and intimate friendships. During this age the individual is provided with wide area of interests and opportunities for making social adjustment and learning so many social qualities. During this age an individual prepares himself to play a role of adult in his social life. Up to the end of this stage, the social behaviour of the child becomes almost matured.

As we have seen earlier, the aim of social development is to gain social maturity. The child while passing through various stages from his very birth strives to attain it. Let us see what does this term social maturity indicate or what are the characteristics which are supposed to be present in a socially mature individual ?

1. A socially mature individual likes to mix up with people. He is capable of making and keeping friendships.
2. He is not self-centred. He is always ready to sacrifice his interests for the greater cause of groups, society and nation. While demanding and asserting for his rights, he always cares for the social obligations.
3. He possesses the ability for sharing and shouldering the social responsibilities. He is prepared to play the role of a leader or of a staunch follower as the situation demands from him.
4. He is able to make proper decision and take suitable action at the time of any social crisis, problem or situation in which his help is needed.
5. He is very much cooperative. He believes in maintaining relationships and working with others. He does not do anything which hurts the feeling of others. He possesses the social virtues like the feeling of sympathy and kindness, courtesy and cheerfulness. He believes in justice, equality and fraternity and never does anything which disrupts cohesiveness and unity of the social structure.

Actually speaking he is imbued with all the important social qualities like patience, respect for others' opinions, kindness and sympathy, cooperation, courtesy and politeness, cheerfulness, self-confidence, self-control, sentiment of self-regard, respect for fair sex, religions and culture, etc.

6. The area of his social interests and participation is very wide. He possesses refined tastes and adequate social etiquettes.
7. His social behaviour conforms to the norms, mores, social codes and ethics. He never engages himself in any sort of activities or behaviour which is anti-social and looked down upon by the society.
8. He possesses a strong desire to serve the cause of the society. He feels for evils and malpractices in the society and tries to bring desirable reforms.
9. He possesses a greater degree of adaptability and adjustability. He can make himself adjusted easily to the varying needs of the society and social circumstances.

Affecting Factors: How to help the child in the task of his social development is a relevant question at this stage. In this task, the individual in addition to his own physical, mental and emotional development is helped by various social agencies. All these factors — personal and environmental — work together in influencing the social development of the child. What are these factors and how they influence the pattern of social development can be seen through the following discussion:

1. *Bodily Structure and Health:* Development of social behaviour is influenced by the physique and health which one possesses. A healthy child with a normal physique develops self-confidence and a sense of self-respect. He has the strength and ability to make himself adjusted in the challenging social situations. He is always cheerful and cooperative. He is able to mix with the people and maintains proper social relationships. The child suffering from illness or having poor health or any physical deformities and defects develops the feeling of inferiority and feels difficulty in social adjustment. Therefore proper care should be taken for the balanced physical development of the children.
2. *Intelligence:* Intelligence is defined as the ability to make and take the right decision at a right time and the ability to adapt

or adjust to new situations. These qualities are very essential for effective social behaviour. The more intelligent a person is, the more adjustable and social he will prove.

3. *Emotional Development:* Emotional development of the child bears a positive correlation with the social development. Emotional adjustability and maturity is one of the very important elements of social maturity. The persons who can express their emotions in a proper degree at a proper time are found to possess a healthy social personality. Emotionally maladjusted personalities possess poor social qualities. Therefore due care should be taken for the training of the emotions of the child so that he may not feel any obstacles in the path of his social development.

4. *Family Atmosphere:* Family is named as the most important primary agency for socialisation of the child. The home atmosphere and the family relationships exercise much influence upon the social development of the child. The child learns the first lesson of social qualities from his parents. Consciously or unconsciously he imitates the behaviour of his parents and members of the family and thus picks up so many good or bad social characteristics which go with him even up to the end of his life. The size of the family, the relationships within the family, attitude of the parents and family members socio-economic status and position of the family in the society, the traditions, culture, values and the ideals of the family – all influence the social development of the child.

   The family which provides healthy social atmosphere and where basic needs of children are satisfied produces socially balanced personalities whereas in the homes when the family relationships are under strain and the elders possess negative social characteristics, the child is not brought up properly and consequently the socially undesirable and negative behaviour is produced among children. Therefore it is essential to seek the active cooperation of the parents in providing suitable atmosphere at home for the proper social development of children.

5. *The School and its Atmosphere:* Social development in children is greatly influenced by the social environment and functioning of the schools. The human relationships maintained by the school, the kinds of programmes and activities performed, its traditions, values and principles, the social qualities and behaviour of the teachers and school mates – all influence the social development of the child. The school, having a healthy social and democratic atmosphere inculcates so many social virtues among the students while a poor and unhealthy atmosphere of the school and the negative social behavioural characteristics of the teachers and school mates cast a bad influence upon the social behaviour of the child. Therefore the teachers as well as the authorities should try their level best to make the school environment as healthy as possible for the proper social development of the children. They must produce good examples of social virtues and democratic living before children and through curricular and co-curricular activities, proper methods of instruction and personal contact, should help children in their proper social development.
6. *Peer-group Relationship and Gang Influence:* The play mates, school or class mates also influence the social development of the child. He picks up the habits and social qualities of his companions. A good company helps him to learn good qualities while a bad company provides all opportunities to spoil him and turn him into anti-social personalities. On the credit side, through peer group relationships and gang influence he learns to cooperate, to lead and follow, to think for a common cause and to adjust in the challenging social situations. It inculcates the sense of loyalty, sympathetic attitude and the willingness to obey the social rules and regulations. Parents, teachers and other responsible members of the society should remain very careful to see that the child gets a healthy company. The negative influence of the peer group and the gang in the form of an unsocial behaviour for development of evil social characteristics should be checked. The child should be accepted by his peer group. He should get proper environment and opportunities to mix with his peers.

7. *Community and Neighbourhood:* As the child grows older he comes in contact with the social circle of his neighbourhood and the community to which he belongs. The social interests; habits and characteristics of the neighbours unconsciously and consciously, influence the social behaviour of the child. Every community and the society is characterised by its unique cultural pattern, social mores, traditions and social characteristics. The child as a member of the community and the society picks up these things which go on shaping his social behaviour and influence his social development.
8. *Religious Institutions and Clubs:* The social agencies like temple, church, social clubs, etc. also influence the social development of the child. These places serve as a meeting ground for the members of the society and help in developing social contacts and relationships The social behaviour of an individual is greatly influenced by the traditions, values, ideals and social characteristics maintained by these institutions.
9. *Information and Entertainment Agencies:* Agencies like Newspapers, magazines, Radio, Cinema, Television, etc., also exercise their influence upon the social development of children. Sources of information constantly inform the readers, listeners and others about the changes in the social structure, customs, traditions and values and thus bring desirable changes in the social behaviour of individuals. The mass entertainment agencies like radio, cinema, television, etc., play a vital role in moulding and shaping the behaviour of the members of the society. The impact of these agencies in social life can very well be recognised. What a hero or heroine does on the screen is at once imitated. The values of the life, the style of living, the traditions and cultural pattern of the society all undergo a drastic change by the impact of these modern mass agencies.

These agencies should not be allowed to functions unchecked. Society or Government should exercise a desirable control and check upon the functioning of these agencies so that no undesirable and anti-social influence is left over the masses. Directly or indirectly these agencies should be made an important means for the assimilation of the social and democratic virtues among the citizens.

Development of Mind

Emotional development is one of the major aspects of the human growth and development. Emotions like love, anger, fear, etc. play a great role in the development of a child's personality. Not only his physical growth and development is linked with his emotional makeup but his intellectual, social, moral and aesthetic development are also controlled by his emotional behaviour and experiences. The overall importance of emotional experiences in the life of a human being makes it quite essential to know about the emotions. What are these? What is their origin? How do they develop and influence the personality of the organism? What are the factors which are responsible for their proper or improper development and how can they be made more serviceable to the individuals and society? Let us try to think about these problems.

The Definition

1. Etymologically the word 'emotion' is derived from the Latin word 'Emovere' which means 'to stir up', 'to agitate' or 'to excite'. Woodworth by making use of this explanation has defined emotion in the following way:

   "Emotion is a 'moved' or 'stirred-up' state of an organism. It is a stirred-up state of feeling that is the way it appears to the indiuidual himself. It is a disturbed muscular and glandular activity — that is the way it appears to an external observer." (1945, p. 410)

2. Crow and Crow have defined emotion in the following way :

   An emotion "is an effective experience that accompanies generalised inner adjustment and mental and psychological stirred-up states in the indiuidual, and that shows itself in his overt behaviour". (1973, p. 83)

3. McDougall considering instincts as an innate tendency maintains that all the specific human emotions are derived from instincts. According to him an intinctive behaviour has three aspects:

(i) Cognition (knowing)

(ii) Affection (feeling or experiencing an emotion)

(iii) Conation (doing or striving)

When a child sees a bull coming towards him, he experiences an instinctive behaviour and undergoes the above three processes. Firstly, he perceives the bull, secondly he experiences an emotion of fear and thirdly he tries to run away. Therefore he concludes that an emotion is an affective experience that one undergoes during an instinctive excitement. He discovered 14 basic instincts. Each and every emotion, whatever it may be is the product of some instinctive behaviour. These instincts with their associated emotions can be listed as:

S.No.	*Instinct*	*Emotion accompanying it*
1.	Flight or Escape	Fear
2.	Pugnacity or combat	Anger
3.	Repulsion	Disgust
4.	Curiosity	Wonder
5.	Parental	Tender emotion, Love
6.	Appeal Distress	Feeling of creativeness
7.	Construction	Feeling of ownership
8.	Acquisition	
9.	Gregariousness	Feeling of loneliness
10.	Sex, Mating	Lust
11.	Self-assertion	Positive self-feeling or Elation
12.	Food-seeking	Appetite
13.	Laughter	Amusement

From the above definitions and derivation of emotion we can conclude the following important information about emotion:

1. The emotional experiences are associated with some instincts or biological drives. When the basic need is satisfied or challenged (the satisfaction is in danger), the emotions play their part.

2. In general, emotions are the product of perception. The perception of a proper stimulus (object or situation) is needed to start an emotional experience. The organic changes within

the body (favourable or unfavourable) may intensify the emotional experiences.

3. The core of an emotion is feeling, which is essentially linked with some sort of impulsive act or urge to do. For the classification let us try to differentiate between feelings and emotions.

   Actually every emotional experience, whatever it may be, involves feelings — things of the heart. Feelings and emotions both are affective experiences. There is only the difference of degrees. After perceiving a thing or situation, feelings like pleasure or displeasure can be aroused. There may be some intensity or degree of strength in these feelings. When the feelings are so strong as enable to disturb the mind and can excite an individual to act immediately — they are turned into emotions. Therefore the urge to do or act (conative aspect) is the most important emotional experience.

4. Every emotional experience involves many physical and physiological changes in the organism. Some of the changes which express themselves in overt behaviour are easily observable. Examples of such changes are the bulge of the eyes, the flush of the face, the flow of tears, the pulse rate, the beating of the heart, the choke in the voice, the fleeing from the situation or the attack on the emotion arousing stimulus. In addition to these easily observable changes there are internal physiological changes. Examples of such changes are changes in the circulation of blood, the impact on digestive system and the changes in the functioning of some glands like adrenal glands, etc.

These changes become so specific and distinguishable in the human being that a simple glimpse can enable us to detect a particular emotional experience in an individual and we can see whether he is in anger or suffers from fear, etc.

In addition to the above characteristics the emotions have some more specific things to be told about. These are:

1. Emotions are prevalent in every living organism.
2. They are present at all stages of development and can be aroused in young as well as in old.

3. Emotions are the most individual and they differ from person to person.
4. Same emotion can be aroused by a number of different stimuli — objects or situations.
5. Emotions rise abruptly but die slowly. An emotion once aroused tends to persist and leaves behind emotional mood.
6. Emotions have the quality of displacement. The anger aroused on account of one stimulus gets transferred to other situation. The anger on account of the rebuking by boss is transferred in beating the children at home.
7. One emotion can give birth to a number of likewise emotions.
8. There is a negative correlation between the upsurge of emotions and intelligence. Reasoning and sharp intellect provides a careful check on the sudden upsurge or emotions and on the other hand under emotional experiences the reasoning and thinking powers are decreased.

Various Kinds: If we try to analyse the impact of various emotional experiences upon the well-being of an individual, we can come to the conclusion that the emotions have both positive as well as negative effects. Whether an emotion will prove to be helpful or harmful to an individual depends upon the following factors:

1. The frequency and intensity of emotional experience.
2. The situation, occasion and the nature of stimulus which arouses the emotion.
3. Kind of emotional experience or emotions.

The last factor — the kind of emotional experience — counts much in this direction. Emotions, in general, can be categorised into two kinds — Positive emotions and Negative emotions.

Unpleasant emotions like fear, anger, jealousy which are harmful to the individual's development are termed as negative emotions while the pleasant emotions like affection (love), amusement, curiosity, joy and happiness which are very helpful and essential to the normal development are termed as positive emotions.

By their nature of positiveness and negativeness it should not be assumed that all the positive emotions are always good and the negative emotions are bad. While weighing their impact, the other factors like the frequency and intensity, situations and the nature of stimuli should also be considered. Excess of everything is bad. Emotions with too much intensity and frequency, whether positive or negative bring harmful effects. On the other hand, the so-called negative emotions are very essential for the human welfare. The emotion of fear prepares and individual to face the danger ahead. The child who has no emotion of fear is sure to get injured because he has not learnt to save himself against a possible danger.

Different Stages: Development, in general, applies to the changes brought about with the passage of time. Emotional development in this respect reflects the following changes:

1. There is a gradual birth of different emotions in an individual since his birth.
2. There are changes in the conditions or nature of stimuli that arouse the child's emotions.
3. There are changes in the manner in which the child expresses his emotions.

In the light of these changes we will try to discuss the process of emotional development during different developmental stages:

1. From his very birth, the infant cries and his bodily movements seems to give evidence of the presence of emotional element in him. What are the specific emotions, if any, which he experiences at this stage is a difficult question to be answered.
2. Truely speaking, as Mrs. Hurlock puts it, "At birth and shortly afterwards the first sign of emotional behaviour is general excitement to strong stimulation. There are no indications of clearcut, definite emotional patterns that can be recognised and identified as specific emotional states. (1959, p. 216)

   Thus, it is the stage of an undifferentiated excitement to any stimulus.

3. The stage of undifferentiated excitement is over in a very short time, when the general excitement becomes differentiated into simple responses that suggest pleasure and displeasure. The stimuli like sudden loud noise, wet, cold or hot objects applied to the baby's skin, feeling hungry and uncomfortable, etc., bring unpleasant responses. The stimuli like sucking, patting, and warmth, etc., bring pleasant responses.
4. The differentiation of general excitement into pleasant and unpleasant responses takes the following pattern according to Spitz:

   "During the first two months pleasure and displeasure come in response to 'physical' stimulation. By the third month, pleasure is aroused by 'psychological' stimulation as shown in the baby's smile in response to human face. Slightly later displeasure can be aroused by psychological as well as physical stimuli as may be seen in the baby's reaction to being left alone" (Hulock, E.B., 1959, p. 217).
5. As said above, before the age of 6 months the emotional behaviour is expressed through pleasant and unpleasant responses, that is, there are only two emotions (distress and delight) up to this stage. When the infant completes his six months, the negative emotions take the lead and gradually in the coming months, fear, disgust, anger, jealousy all are distinguishable. Between the 10th and 12th months the positive emotions like elation, love, sympathy, enjoyment all enter in the field. Up to 2 years, as the study of Bridges conducted in 1931 shows almost all the emotions, positive as well as negative, take their shape and become quite distinguishable.
6. There is continuous variation in the manifestation of emotions during infancy. In the earlier months it is very difficulty to have distinction on the basis of facial expression and bodily positions. Only the mothers can determine the causes of her child's crying and yelling. Later on gradually they become distinguishable. Moreover in the earlier months of infancy the child reacts more violently to emotionally disturbing

situations, but as the infant approaches childhood, his crying, yelling and the vigorous movements of the body parts become less and less violent. Gradually with increasing age there is an increase in linguistic responses and a decrease in motor responses.

As said above, almost all the emotions make themselves distinguishable up to the beginning of childhood. Therefore emotional development after the stage of infancy, concerns itself, only, to the changes in the nature of situations or stimuli arousing emotions and the changes in the expression of emotional experiences. We find the following changes in the child during childhood:

1. In infancy the child is only concerned with his own well-being. Therefore, the emotions are generally aroused by the conditions which are related with his immediate well-being. But as he grows, his world grows larger and he has to respond to a variety of stimuli. During childhood peer group relationship and school atmosphere and other environmental factors influence his emotional behaviour. His emotions get linked with the new experiences and interests and his emotional behaviour gets linked with the new stimuli. At the same time he does' not react to various old stimuli. For example, he does not show anger at being dressed or bathed, neither does he show any fear of strangers.
2. There is a remarkable change in the expression of emotional behaviour. In infancy this behaviour is usually dominated by too much intensity and is usually expressed through motor responses like crying, yelling, etc. But in childhood and specially in later childhood, the child tries to express his behaviour through reasonable means and is the result of many factors. In childhood the child is in a position to express his feelings through language. Secondly, he becomes social and realises that it may not be desirable or proper for him to show his emotions at all times. Thirdly, his intellect begins to play a proper role in exercising check over emotional outbursts.

In this way the child advances towards emotional stability and control and during the later period of his childhood, demonstrates an appreciable degree of control over his emotions.

The emotional balance is once again disturbed in adolescence. The individual once again experiences the violent and intensive current of emotional experiences. With regard to emotional experiences, this is the period of intensive strain and stress. At no stage this emotional energy is so strong and dangerous as in adolescence. It is very difficult for an adolescent to exercise control over his emotions. The sudden functioning of sexual glands and tremendous increase in physical energy makes him restless. Moreover adolescents are not consistent in their emotions.

Emotions during this stage fluctuate very frequently and quickly. It makes them moody. Sometimes they are very happy and at another time they are extremely sad and all this happens in a very short time. So there is too much uncertainty in the nature of their emotional states.

At this stage there is strong need of the training of emotions and proper channelisation of emotional energy. The Hadow report has emphasised this need in the following words:

> "There is a tide which begins to rise in the veins of youth at the age of eleven or twelve. It is called by the name of adolescence. If that tide can be taken at the flood, and a new voyage begun in the strength and along the flow of its current, we think that it will move on to fortune" (Ross J.S, 1951, p. 153).

Emotional development reaches its maximum in adulthood. During this stage, generally, all individuals attain emotional maturity. Let us try to understand what is meant by emotional maturity.

Meaning of emotional maturity. In brief a person can be called emotionally mature if he is able to display his emotions in an appropriate degree with reasonable control. An emotionally mature person will possess the following characteristics:

1. Almost all the emotions can be distinctly seen in him and their pattern of expression can be easily recognised.
2. Manifestation of emotions is very much refined. Usually he expresses his emotions in a socially desirable way.
3. He is able to exercise control over his emotions. Sudden inappropriate emotional outbursts are rarely found in him. He is able to hide his feelings and check his emotional tide.

4. The person no more hangs in mere idealism, but he actually perceives the things in their real perspective. He is not a daydreamer and does not possess the desire to run away from realities.
5. The intellectual powers like thinking, reasoning, etc., are properly exercised by him in making any decision. He is more guided by his intellect than his emotions.
6. He does not possess the habit of raionalisation, *i.e.* he never gives arguments in defence of his undesirable or improper conduct. Also he never puts the responsibility of his own mistakes on others. He is always honest in his behaviour.
7. He possesses an adequate self-concept and self respect. He never likes to do the things or to show such behaviour as can injure his self respect and is adverse to his self-concept.
8. He is not confined to himself. He thinks for others and is keen to maintain social relationships. He never engages himself in such a behaviour which is anti-social and can result in the social conflicts and blockage of social relationships.
9. He has the guts to exercise his emotions at a proper time in a proper place. If there is a danger to his self prestige or if an innocent person is attacked he can rise to the occasion by exercising his emotion of anger. But on the other hand if he commits a mistake and is rebuked by his boss he is equally able to check his emotion of anger. Mature emotionai behaviour is characterised by greater stability. Person having such maturity shows no sudden shift from one emotion to another.

As a conclusion regarding the meaning of emotional maturity is a quote from Arthur T. Jersild. He is of the opinion that emotional maturity should not involve only simple restriction and control. According to him it is a very narrow view of emotional maturity. He writes, "An adequate description of emotional maturity must take account of the full scope of the individual's capacity and powers, and of his ability to use and enjoy them. In its broadest sense emotional maturity means the degree to which the person has realised his potential for richness of living and has developed his capacity to enjoy things, to relate himself to others, to love and to laugh: his capacity for wholehearted sorrow when an occasion for grief arises......and his capacity to show fear when there is occasion to be frightened, without feeling a need to use a false mask of courage" (Skinner C.E. 1968, p. 281).

The emotional experiences during childhood differ markedly from those of the adulthood. This difference can be easily seen through some of the following distinguished characteristics:

1. *Intensity of Emotions:* Children's emotions are characterised by too much intensity. There are sudden outbursts of emotions among children. If a child weeps, he weeps bitterly. In anger, he loses control over himself. But the child's emotional experiences are not so intensive. Volcano-like sudden emotional outbursts are seldom observed in adults.
2. *Briefness of the Emotions:* Children's emotional experiences are very brief. Their emotions last for a short time and these end all of a sudden. Whereas in adults the emotions play their part for a quite long time and in the last make their existence drawn over a period of time in the form of 'mood'.
3. *Transitoriness of the Emotions:* Children's emotions are transitory in character which means there is a rapid shift from one emotion to another. We find a child weeping and shedding tears, a piece of chocolate is enough to shift his emotion of distress to delight. Similarly we find a rapid shift from anger to smile, from laughter to tears, or from jealousy to affection. Contrary to this, emotions of adults do not shift so rapidly. They are marked by greater degree of stability.
4. *Frequency of Emotions:* On the average, the number of emotional experiences experienced by a child during a day is significantly greater than those experienced by a normal adult. The child passes under different currents of emotional streams during a period of time. Sometimes a specific emotion is repeated so many times. But as the child grows older, he learns to make adjustment and tries to meet situation by reactions other than emotional ones. The result is gradual decrease in the frequency of emotional responses;

5. *Detection of Emotionality*: The emotional state of the child is easily detectable. He is very innocent and does not know the art of hiding his feelings and emotions. The behavioural symptoms like speech difficulties, frequent crying, restlessness, nail-biting and thumb sucking, etc. give indications of his emotionality. The adults, on the other hand are, generally, able to hide their feelings and emotions. Therefore, in their case, it is difficult for others to know how they feel and detect their emotionality.
6. *The Differences in the Emotional Expression:* An infant in quite unable to exercise control over his violent emotional outbursts. Emotions at this stage are expressed through motor responses. As the child grows, the way of emotional expression gets modified. This modification goes on till the attainment of maturity in adulthood. A mature adult seldom engages himself in the motor activity during emotional stress. He learns to exercise control over his emotions and expresses them in a refined and socially approved way. The emotional expression either in the form of motor responses or in socially unacceptable way is labelled as 'childish'. The emotional response of an adult is always guided by his intellect while in the child, the intensity of feelings rules over the reasoning and thinking power. The adults are able to keep their emotions reserved for a future expression but in childhood it is a difficult task.

Affecting Factors: The emotional development of the child rests on so many factors. The important ones are given below:

1. *Health and Physical Development:* Physical development and health has a positive correlation with emotional development. Any deficiency in physical side – internal or external – creates emotional problems. The children, weak in somatic structure or suffering from illness, are more emotionally upset and unstable than are children whose health is better. The normal functioning of the glands is very important for the balanced emotional development. Any abnormal increase or decrease in their power of secretion creates obstacles in the proper emotional development.

2. *Intelligence:* Intelligence, as the ability to make adaptation, has a significant correlation with the emotional adjustment and suitability of the child. Meltzer (1937) concluded that: "There is less emotional control, on the average, among those of the lower intellectual levels than among children of the same age who are bright;' (Hurlock, E.B., 1959, p. 254).

   An intelligent person, with his reasoning and thinking powers, exercises control according to the situation and make proper use of his emotions. At every stage the child's intellectual power guides and controls the emotional development of the child.

3. *Family Atmosphere and Relationships:* Emotional development is very much influenced by the family atmosphere and relationships. The emotional behaviour of the parents and elder members and of the cordial atmosphere at home develops positive emotions among the children, while the conflicts, fights and tensions in family relationships give birth to negative emotions. Also the treatment, given to a child by the parents and the members of the family, influences his emotional development. The order of birth (whether the first or the youngest child), the size of the family, the socio-economic status of the family, the parental attitude (neglected, pampered and over protected child) – all are the decisive factors in emotional bringing up of the child.

4. *School Atmosphere and Teachers:* The school life plays an important role in the emotional development of children. The healthy conducive atmosphere of the school always results in the balanced emotional development of children. All such things like the physical facilities provided in the school, the methods of teaching, the organisation of co-curricular activities and social life of the school, the relationship among the staff members and the head of the institution, the attitude of the teachers towards students and the self-example of the teacher's emotional behaviour, influence the emotional development of children.

5. *Social Development and Peer-group Relationship:* Social development of children is closely linked to their emotional

development. The more social is the child, the more emotionally adjustable he will prove. Socially rejected or maladjusted children always face difficult emotional problems. The maintenance of proper social relationships and acquisition of social virtues are the effective means for bringing essential modification in the emotional behaviour of the child. The proper social development can only bring the desirable and socially approved emotional development in children.

6. *Neighbourhood the Community and the Society:* The other social agencies like neighbourhood, the community and society, of which an individual is the member, also exerts significant influence upon his emotional set-up. He picks up so many traits of his emotional behaviour from these surroundings. The brave community is sure to produce fearless and courageous children. The society where the elder members of the society unnecessarily exhibit emotional outburst of anger leads the youngers to such negative development. Similarly so many good or bad things related to emotional behaviour of an individual can be acquired through the impact of neighbourhood and the society.

In this way the factors influencing the emotional development of an individual can be labelled into two categories — In the first category there are personal factors like his physical, physiological, mental and social development. In the second category there are social factors like parents, family, school, neighbourhood, community and the society. Both of these factors exert a significant influence upon the emotional development of the child. While taking care of the proper emotional development of the child, the parents as well as the teachers should keep in view all the factors belonging to both categories.

Training of Emotions: Emotions in their crude form are harmful to the individual and the society. One of the major objectives of any good scheme of education is to train and modify the emotions for the welfare of the individual and that of the society. The various methods employed for this purpose are:

1. Repression or Inhibition.
2. Industriousness or mental occupation.

3. Redirection and sublimation.
4. Catharsis.

a. *Repression or Inhibition:* Here the undesirable emotional behaviour of the child is checked by imposing restriction and giving punishment. No outlet or opportunity is provided to the child for the emotional expression. Rules and regulations are very strictly observed and the child is always required to express his emotions in socially desirable ways. Actually it is a negative method of exercising control over the emotions and in no way helpful for the healthy emotional development.

b. *Industriousness or Mental Occupation:* Another method for exercising desirable control over the emotions is to keep oneself busy in some constructive activities. Empty mind is said to be a devil's workshop. Therefore it is essential to have provision for co-curricular and leisure time activities for the balanced emotional development of the children.

c. *Redirection and Sublimation:* The direction of the flow of emotional energy is changed through the process of redirection and sublimation from an undesirable goal to a socially desirable one. In both these processes there is only a difference of degrees. Whereas, in redirection, there is no change in the nature of the emotion. Only the direction of the flow is changed. In sublimation, there is modification of original instincts or emotions. Sublimation changes the very form of the emotion.

As far as the method of controlling the emotions is concerned, redirection serves the best purpose. Like repression or inhibition it does not have negative effect upon the personality development of children. It does not destroy the emotion, but only brings desirable changes in the mode of its expression. If a child is very aggressive and displays emotion of anger frequently, his emotion of anger can be diverted towards the enemies of the country and the devils of the society. In this way his energy can be utilised in the defence of the country and for the weaker members of the society. Similarly, the sublimation of the love, in the cases of Tulsidas and Kalidas presents clear example of the role of sublimation in changing the emotional set-up of an individual.

d. *Catharsis:* In this method desirable channels are provided for the release of the emotional energy. In some way or the other, the individual is provided with the opportunity of self-expression so that the pent-up emotions get appropriate outlet. Under emotions the tensions are created in the minds of the individuals. By providing a proper outlet for emotional expression, the tensions can be removed and he is made to feel better and lighter. To listen patiently, the verbal expression of an individual under emotion, is the simplest catharsis process. The opportunity for self expression in the form of co-curricular activities, participation in festivals and fairs and rituals of the society – all provide means for the catharsis of emotional energy.

Teacher's Role: Role of Education and specially of teachers in bringing balanced emotional development of children deserves special mention. The emotional development of children are influenced and controlled by so many factors. These factors have been mentioned earlier. Let us analyse the part played by the teachers in bringing balanced emotional development of children in the light of these factors.

1. Emotional development, as said earlier, depends upon physical and physiological development. Therefore every care is to be taken for the proper physical development of children. Children should be made to learn the ways of healthful living. With due cooperation of the parents and the state authorities, children need to be cared for proper nourishment. The parents should be made aware of the physical weakness, deformities and illness of their children and necessary provision for the treatment should be made in the schools or state hospitals.
2. Home atmosphere exercises a good amount of influence over the emotional character of children. Therefore, teachers

should seek active cooperation of the parents in making the atmosphere of the home suitable for proper emotional development. Parents and the elder members of the family should produce better examples of emotional expression before their children. They should try to develop healthy attitude towards their children and in no way spoil them by their own modes of behaviour. The teacher should try to know the causes of emotional maladjustment of children and find out how far home atmosphere and parents are responsible for this. Accordingly he should take suitable steps for the proper emotional development of children.

3. The teacher in the school, with the active cooperation of the authorities, should take care of the following things:
   (i) There should be an adequate provision of various co-curricular activities for the full expression and outlet of emotional energies of children.
   (ii) Instructional methodology and curriculum should be dynamic, progressive and child-centred.
   (iii) The children should get desired love and sympathy from the teachers. Their individuality should be respected and individual differences should be recognised. The teacher should see that the basic emotional needs of children are satisfied in the classroom or school.
   (iv) With the help of positive methods of controlling and training the emotions, the emotional tension present in the minds of children should be removed and the creation of undesirable complexes should be avoided.
   (v) Moral and religious training should form a part of the school programme. High ideas of life and moral principles should be made the guiding factors of the children's life.
   (vi) Emotions are caught, they are not taught.' Therefore, the teacher should refrain himself from any act or behaviour which can bring undesirable influence upon the emotional development of children. He must put his self example before children for the refined emotional expressions and behaviour.

(vii) Proper care should be taken for the balanced social development of children. The child should get due recognition in his group and in no case he should feel isolated or rejected by his peer group and classmates.

(viii) Teachers need to understand when behaviour is normal and when it is a symptom of something wrong. The causes for the emotional deviation should be sought and when behaviour is excessively immature, the service of a skilled guidance personnel should be obtained.

(ix) Teachers should recognise the place of emotion in the learning process. Balanced emotional feelings can serve as a tonic to the body and can make the learning an active and exacting experience. Therefore, the teacher should make the child emotionally involved in his work.

Significance of Wisdom

Cognitive or Mental Development: We have seen how the mechanism of physical growth and development brings desirable changes in the internal as well as external body organs of an individual in order to increase his physical skill and strength. Due to this development he becomes able to do physical work and to play games he could not, when younger. Similarly the child at the time of his birth or in early childhood cannot be expected to perform such tasks that require high mental abilities. As he advances in his age, his mental abilities and capacities gradually get developed and he becomes able to solve the problems he could not when younger. The growth and development of the mental abilities and capacities which helps an individual to adjust his behaviour to the ever changing environmental conditions or to enable him to accomplish a task that needs complex cognitive abilities is referred to as mental or intellectual development.

Actually, the process of the mental growth and development is responsible for the development of an individual's all cognitive, mental or intellectual abilities like – sensation, perception, imagination, memory, reasoning, understanding, intelligence, generalisation, interpretation, language ability, conceptual ability, problem solving ability and decision making ability, etc. These abilities are interrelated and never develop in isolation. Therefore, mental development of an individual at any stage of his development, includes the overall development of these abilities.

Aspects of Mental Development: As mentioned above, mental or intellectual development takes into consideration, the development of various mental abilities and capacities. How these abilities grow and develop from birth onwards is an interesting as well as useful thing to know. Though the development in the areas of various abilities proceeds simultaneously and is continuous yet the studies have revealed possibility of the differences in the rate of overall mental development at various ages. Similarly it has been also noted that there is a possibility of greater growth and development in one aspect or area of mental activity than in other at one or the other stage of life.

Here we will discuss the changes and development in some of the important mental abilities or aspects of mental power of a small child as he grows older and older.

1. *Sensation and Perception:* Both sensation and perception are considered important aspects of one's mental development. Sensations are elementary impressions gathered by sense organs. When these impressions are interpreted and some definite meanings are attached to them, they take the form of perception.

   In the beginning, the child lacks in sensation as well as in perception. His sense organs are not developed. As a result, he cannot discriminate between things and understand their meanings. Focusing of the eye towards the lamp, bright coloured objects, etc., can be said a beginning of an infant's perceptual growth. Later on, he distinguishes people from objects and then familiar people from strangers and in this way his environment, gradually becomes differentiated into perceived objects. These perceived objects become later on associated with a verbal sound that he can recognise when heard.

   When he becomes able to use his sense organs, he becomes increasingly conscious of the things around him and begins, to ask a series of questions such as why, what and who. At this time he has a poor perception of space, time, form, movement and distance. For example, due to lack of perception of the size of distant objects, the train, when viewed from a distance, may appear to him as a toy train. But gradually, his ability of perception gets developed. As the individual passes through the years of his adolescence, the sensory acquity reaches almost to its peak and perceptual pattern become most organised and refined. His perceptions now become more definite, rich and detailed. They are now beginning to be influenced by his beliefs, opinions, ideals, etc., besides his needs, interests and mental sets. They now need not be associated necessarily with concrete objects.

2. *Concept Formation:* Acquisition of concept is another important aspects of the child's mental development. A concept is the generalised meaning that is attached to an object or idea. It is the result of one's perceptual experiences and involves both discrimination and generalisation.

   Discrimination begins early in life. Sometimes after, the child tries to generalise his perceptual experiences and thus begins to acquire concepts. Experience is a great factor in concept formation. In early childhood, the concrete experiences in the form of actual objects help the child in the formation of concepts. He tries to develop various concepts from direct experiences.

   In the later period, vicarious experiences offered by reading, movies, lectures, etc., also provide the base for concept formation. In the later years, it is not such that only new concepts are formed, the old concepts may also get a new shape. They may be broadened, developed or the wrong concepts can be altogether abandoned. Normally, in developing, concepts go from concrete to abstract, from vague to clear and from inaccurate to definite, depending on the type of experiences one receives as one grows older and older.

   In this way the concepts of the child in the beginning are characterised by vagueness, indefiniteness and inadequacy.

For example, the child has very poor time concepts. As Crow and Crow put it, "Time as such means little to the young child. He cannot distinguish among 'today', 'tomorrow' and 'next week' except as they represent words rather than actual duration of time." (1968, p. 73)

Similarly his concepts of spatial relations, distance and depth are very vague and inadequate in the beginning. Gradually, as a result of learning and maturation, they become clear, specific and definite.

3. *Development of Language:* Development of language adds to the mental growth and development of an individual. The growth and development in speech, vocabulary, length of response are some of the important aspects of language development.

   At birth the child can utter some crying sounds. By the age of one and little later he may learn to speak a few words. After that speaking vocabulary increases rapidly. Much of the speech pattern, that the child learns, is the result of imitation of others in the environment. During the course of learning to speak it is possible that certain speech disorders like omissions, stuttering, stammering, etc., may develop. Therefore the parents as well as the teachers of small children must remain very cautious about this.

   The vocabulary of children in the beginning is too limited. There is continuous increase in the size of one's vocabulary during childhood. Later on as the result of environmental needs and opportunities in learning, the vocabulary goes on developing. Maintenance of the past and addition of the new words in one's vocabulary may continue even upto the period of old age depending upon their reading habits and interests.

   In addition to the change in vocabulary and speech, the pattern of giving responses also changes with age. In the early childhood the child's responses are characterised by the one-word response. Also, generally, he uses more nouns than other forms of language. Later, on, gradually, be begins to use descriptive words like adjectives and adverbs and his responses include a large variety of words and almost every form of sentence structure.

4. *Development of Memory:* Memory is also an important aspect of mental development. At birth, there is little memory; but, gradually with maturation and experiences memory increases. The developmental schedule as discussed by Hurlock and Schwartz indicates that "memory of an impressionistic kind appears in the first half of the year and instances of true rememberance appear by the end of the first year. During the first year memory is only aroused by sensory stimuli. With the learning of speech the child is able to remember ideationally by the end of the second year. During the first and second years, the memory is stronger for persons and objects than for situation. During early childhood, from 3 to 6 years, situations become significant factors in the child's memory. Also the emotional quality of the impressions Influence memory. By 3 years the child can recount the story heard a few days ago and he can also give information about past experiences". (Kuppuswamy 1964, p.98)

   Therefore the child shows signs of memory from the early childhood. The memory which the child possesses in his young age, is generally a rote memory. He enjoys repetition and seldom uses logic and insight in memorising a thing. During later childhood and adolescence the memory tends to function more logically and a selection process of remembering and forgetting begins to operate. In the later years of childhood memory tends to decrease. But from which age the downfall begins, it is difficult to say with certainty. It varies from individual to individual and generally besides the age and health, the situation and stimuli which are associated with a particular kind of memory affects significantly, its rememberance or forgetting.

5. *Development of Problem-solving Ability:* Problem-solving ability is an important constituent of mental development. An individual needs this type of ability in discovering the solution of the problems faced by him. Both thinking and reasoning power are used in problem-solving. Therefore problem-solving ability depends upon the development of thinking and reasoning. Thinking and reasoning powers begin to grow

as early as two and a half or three years. However reasoning at this stage is confined to concrete and personal things from the child's immediate environment. The younger child deals more easily with the concrete than with the abstract. We cannot expect from him to solve complicated problems which require abstract thinking and more developed reasoning. But, gradually, he shows an increase in the ability to deal with abstract as he grows in age. He begins to compare and evaluate the ideas and solve the problems through the utilisation of verbal symbols and imaginary concepts.

It follows from this discussion that in the beginning children should be provided with the simple realistic problems depending on concrete situation and related to their own experiences and environment so that they can solve them with insight and understanding. With the increase in the age the more complicated problems requiring abstract thinking and widened experiences may be given to them. In this way, gradually, the children should be made to increase their problem-solving ability.

In addition to these aspects, the other aspects of mental growth and development include attention, imagination, decision making and ability of interpretation, etc. Like other aspects they also change, grow and mature with the increase in age due to maturation and learning.

Affecting Factors: Mental growth and development is controlled by both the hereditary and environmental factors. An individual's mental abilities, at any age of his life, are the products of his heredity and environment. For the child what he gets from his ancestral stock through his immediate parents at the time of conception in terms of mental traits or characteristics and mental apparatus is in fact a valuable asset to his future mental growth and development. But the environment which he gets afterwards for the development of these innate mental abilities is no less significant. The social and cultural experiences, learning opportunities and education which he avails for the developmental process as he advances in age, contribute significantly towards his mental growth and development.

In fact, maturation and learning are responsible for controlling the process of mental growth and development. Maturation helps in achieving physical growth and development which in turn affects the process of mental growth and development. Brain and the nervous system play a significant role in this direction. At birth the brain and the nerves that lead to it, are not fully developed. They grow and develop rapidly after birth and get matured in due course. As the nervous system advances towards maturity, the mental powers of the child also go on developing. Therefore, organic growth of the nervous system is the basic factor in mental development.

Learning in the form of experiences and education helps the developmental process and in fact intensifies it to reach to its optimum level. It is said to play the same part as exercises play in developing physical skills and power as Sorenson puts it — "A child's legs, arms and body are made stronger by healthful play. We can deduce that the mind with its organic counter part, the nervous system, improves and becomes better equipped because of use and exercise in the form of reading, calculating, memorising, speaking imagining and other mental abilities" (1948, p. 32).

At what age does the increase in mental growth cease is a controversial question. Mental growth is a complex process. There is no universal pattern of mental growth for all individuals. Neither is the pattern same for all mental functions or abilities. Therefore it is difficult to tell the age at which mental growth, with all its aspects, will cease to grow. Actually, the age of cessation of mental growth varies with different individuals and with different mental functions or abilities.

Psychologists have tried to give various ages ranging from thirteen to the early twenties or even much later as the age after which there is no further mental growth. The variation in the results is due to the fact they have worked on the different groups and used different tests of mental ability. Despite such differences in opinion, Sorenson has tried to arrive on some conclusion regarding the age of cessation of mental growth. He writes:

> "It is probably safe to conclude that a person reaches his maximum mental level at about the age of twenty or perhaps a little before or a little after twenty — .

> It is true that on the average there is only a little mental growth during the late teens – nevertheless this small amount may be very important" (1948, p. 44).

Therefore the age of cessation of mental growth can be estimated as twenty or little before or a little after twenty. But now the question again arises: Does the development of mental capacity or power also cease with the cessation of mental growth at the age of about twenty?

In this connection latest researches have shown that the development in mental power and capacity does not necessarily stop with the cessation of mental growth. In most of the cases the mental power or capacity reaches its maximum in the mid of their thirties. But whatever changes after the natural mental growth occur in the mental abilities of capacities, are definitely the result of learning, experience and education. After attaining their maximum height, mental capacity declines gradually but can be maintained effectively even in the old age by those who keep their minds alert and active.

Role of Education: The knowledge of the trend of mental growth and the subsequent changes in the various mental abilities is of great use for the teacher. Briefly, we can summarise this utility in the following way:

1. It can help him in the selection of curricular and co-curricular experiences at various age levels.
2. It can also help him to arrange learning situations, the methods and techniques of teaching and the nature of the aid material for the illustration of his teaching.
3. It can also help him to bring appropriate books suiting to the intellectual growth and development of children at different age levels.
4. It makes him conscious that a particular type of work or activity which needs some or the other developed mental abilities, needs to be introduced when the age of acquiring that approaches. We must not be too hasty to give him a particular piece of knowledge or to train him in a particular act if the mental abilities required for that knowledge or act

have not yet been acquired by the child. Definitely, in such cases, we should wait for the ripe stage.

5. If he understands the pattern of mental growth, he can lead his students to acquire their maximum mental capacity and power. He can impart training in problem solving and creative expression. Also he can develop their logical understanding and take them to intelligent learning in place of mechanical fumbling and parrotlike cramming. Their ability of using language, perception and ability to interpret and generalisation can also be developed through the natural course of their mental growth and development pattern.

In this way a teacher can lead his students to acquire their maximum mental capacities and powers and help them to use them intelligently and judiciously for the welfare of their own as well as of the society.

The Opinion

Mostly, these two terms are used interchangeably and taken as synonymous terms. Both relate to the measurement of changes occurred in the individual after conception in the womb of the mother. Change is the law of nature. An individual starting from a fertilized egg, turns into a full-fledged human adult. In this turn-over process he undergoes a cycle of changes brought about by the process of growth and development in various dimensions-physical, mental, social, emotional, etc. Therefore, in the wider sense, both the terms growth and development can be used for any change brought about by maturation and learning (formal as well as informal education), and essentially is the product of both heredity and environment.

However, in the strict sense of terminology, these two terms have different meanings that can be put in the way given ahead.

	Growth		*Development*
(1)	The term growth is used in purely physical sense generally refers to an increase in size, length, height and weight. Changes in the	(1)	Development implies overall changes in shape, form or structure resulting in improved working or functioning. It indicates the changes in the

Growth	Development
quantitative aspects come into the domain of growth.	quality or character rather than in quantitative aspects.
(2) Growth is one of the parts of development process. strict sense, development in its quantitative aspect is termed as growth.	(2) Development is a wider and more comprehensive term. It refers to overall changes in the individual. Growth is one of its parts.
(3) Growth may be referred to describe the changes, which take place in particular aspects of the body and behaviour of an organism.	(3) Development describes the changes in the organism as a whole and does not list the changes in parts.
(4) Growth does not continue throughout life. It stops when maturity has been attained.	(4) Development is a continuous process. It goes from womb to tomb. It does not end with the attainment of maturity. The changes, however, small they may be, continue throughout the life span of an individual.
(5) The changes produced by growth are the subject of measurement. They may be quantified and are observable in nature.	(5) Development, as said earlier, implies improvement in functioning and behaviour and hence brings qualitative changes, which are difficult to be measured directly. They are assessed through keen observation in behavioural situations.
(6) Growth may or may not bring development. A child may grow (in terms in weight) by becoming fat but this growth may not bring any functional improvement (qualitative change) or development.	(6) Development is also possible without growth as we see in the cases of some children that they do not gain in terms of height, weight or size but they do experience functional improvement or development in physical social, emotional or intellectual aspects.

Hence, observed in minute details, both growth and development show differentiation. But in wider and practical sense both terms are used to denote the changes in the organism's physical as well as functional behaviour. These changes which cover physical, emotional, intellectual and social aspects of a human life are roughly divided into four major classes by Mrs. Hurlock (1959, pp. 2-3).

(i) Change in size.

(ii) Changes in proportion.

(iii) Disappearance of old features.

(iv) Acquisition of new features.

All these types of changes have qualitative as well as quantitative aspects and hence generally, growth and development go hand in hand. And it is in this sense, that the two terms are to be used collectively. Both, taken together, explaining the total changes functional as well as constitutional change-in the body and behaviour of the individual with the lapse of time after the conception. In this text, in the following pages, these terms will be used in synonymous sense for convenience.

Different Paths

For human organism, life starts from a fertilized ovum in the womb of the mother. Not only before birth, but also after birth to many years the child is a helpless organism until or unless he is helped by the continuous process of growth and development and attains maturity. When one attains maturity, one is ceased to be called an adolescent and labelled as an adult member of the society. He is supposed to play a responsible role in the society. Before being called as adolescent, he is named as child or infant, etc. All of these names-infant, child, adolescent and adult, etc., are linked with various stages of growth and development through which the child passes from birth to death.

There are certain common development or practical characteristics belonging to each stage. The human organism shows peculiar quantitative and qualitative changes in his body and behaviour with the help of which we can say at what particular age an individual belongs to which definite stage of his life.

If we also include the pre-birth period, the life span of a human organism can be divided, conveniently, into the following stages:

Name of the Stage	*Period and approximate age*
1. Pre-natal stage	From conception to birth.
2. Stage of Infancy	From birth to two years.

3. Childhood stage	From 3 to 12 years or in strict sense up to the onset of puberty.
(a) Early childhood	From 3 to 5 years
(b) Later childhood	From 6 to 12 years.
4. Adolescent stage	From the onset of puberty to the age of maturity (generally from 13 to 19 years).
5. Adulthood	From 20 years and beyond or in strict sense from the age of attaining maturity till death.

There is no claim of the absolute rigidity in the above classification in terms of either the division of life span into above mentioned stages or the duration of period mentioned against them. There are certainly great individual differences and so we should not imagine that every child will necessarily have each stage according to the period indicted above.

From the angle of school education, the first and the last stage serves no useful purpose. Therefore, in this text we will confine our attention to the remaining three stages of development. For discussing these stages of development, let us first think of the various aspects of growth and development at each stage.

Aspects or Dimensions of Growth and Development: If we use the term growth and development synonymously, the major aspects or dimensions in which a human child goes ahead for his complete development, can be named as follows:

1. Physical development
2. Cognitive or Mental development
3. Emotional development
4. Moral or Character development
5. Social development.

Let us see what we understand by these different aspects of development:

1. *Physical Development:* The physical development of the individual includes the development of his internal as well as external organs.

2. *Intellectual or Mental Development:* It includes the development of intellectual powers like the powers of reasoning and thinking, imagination, concentration, creativity, sensation, perception, memory, association, discrimination and generalisation, etc.
3. *Emotional Development:* Under this aspect, starting with the basic instinct, the evolution of various emotions takes place and also the emotional behaviour is developed to the point of emotional maturity.
4. *Moral or Character Development:* Moral or Character development includes the evolution of moral sense and development of character. The individual develops his ethical and moral codes.
5. *Social Development:* Initially the child is selfish and anti-social. Gradually he is developed into a social being by learning to behave according to the rules and norms of his society and makes adjustment to it.

Basic Laws

The changes brought about in the individual by the process of growth and development tend to follow some well-defined principles. These are known as principles of growth and development. These principles are being described below:

Principle of Continuity: Development follows continuity. It goes from womb to tomb and never ceases. An individual starting his life from a tiny cell develops his body, mind and other aspects of his personality through a continuous stream of development in these various dimensions.

Rate of Growth and Development is not Uniform: Although development follows continuity, yet the rate of growth and development is not steady and uniform at all times. It proceeds more rapidly in the early years of life but slows down into later years of infancy. Again at the dawn of puberty, there is a sudden rise in the speed of growth and development but it is not maintained for long. Therefore, at no stage the rate of growth and development shows steadiness. It rather takes place by fits and starts.

Principle of Individual Differences: According to this principle there exist wide individual differences among children with respect to their growth and development in various dimensions. Each child grows at his own unique rate.

Uniformity of Pattern: Although development does not proceed at a uniform rate and shows marked individual differences, yet it follows a definite sequence or pattern and somewhat uniform in the offsprings of a species, for example, all offsprings of human beings begin to grow from head downwards. Similarly, the motor development and language development in all children seems to follow a definite sequence.

Development Proceeds from General to Specific Responses: In all phases of child's development, general activity precedes specific activity. His responses are of a general sort before they become specific. For example, the boy waves his arms in general, random movements before he is capable of so specific a response as reaching. Similarly, when a newborn infant cries, the whole of the body is involved with growth, the crying is limited to the vocal cords, eyes, etc. In language development, the child learns general words before specific. He uses the word daddy in greeting many men and it is only afterwards that he uses it for his father.

Principle of Integration: Where it is true that development proceeds from general to specific or from whole to parts, it is also seen that specific responses or part movements are combined in the later process of learning or development. "Development", as Kuppuswamy (1971) observes, "thus involves a movement from the whole to the parts and from the parts to the whole". It is the integration of whole and its part as well as of the specific and general responses that make a child develop satisfactorily in the various dimensions of his growth and development.

Principle of Interrelation: The growth and development in various dimensions like physical, mental, social, etc., are interrelated and interdependent. Growth and development in any one dimension affects the growth and development of the child in other dimensions. For example, children with above average intelligence are generally found to possess above average physical, and social development. The lack of growth in one dimension diminishes the bright possibility in other dimensions. That is why, the child having poor physical development tend to regress in emotional, social and intellectual development.

Development is Predictable: With the help of the rate of growth and development of a child it is possible for us to predict the range within which his mature development is going to fall. For example, X-rays of the bones of the wrist of a child will tell approximately, what his ultimate size will be. Similarly, the knowledge of the present mental ability of a child will help in predicting his ultimate mental development.

Principle of Developmental Direction: Kuppuswamy (1971) throwing light on this principle points out two specific facts concerning the direction of the development. He says that development is "cephalic-caudal as well as proximodistal". By cephalic-caudal development he means that development proceeds in the direction of the longitudinal axis (Head to foot) – First, the child gains control over his head and arms and then on his legs so that he can stand. According to the proximal-distal tendency of the development, it proceeds from the centre to the periphery. In the beginning child exhibits its control over the large fundamental muscles but afterwards due to growth and development of smaller muscles he can exhibit more movements that are refined.

Development is Spiral and not Linear: The child does not proceed straight on the path of development with a constant or steady pace. Actually he makes advancement during a particular period but takes rest in the next following period, to consolidate his development. In advancing further, therefore, he turns back and then moves forward again like a spiral.

Growth and Development as a joint Product of both Heredity and Environment: Child at any stage of his growth and development is a joint product of both heredity and environment. The forces of heredity and environment directly or indirectly influence his growth and development in any dimension at all times.

Body Development

Definition and Meaning: Physical growth and development refers to a process which brings bodily and physiological changes – internal as well as external – in an organism from the conception till his death. Generally these changes take place in the following dimensions:

1. *In his Gross Physical Structure or Physique:* It involves changes in terms of height, weight, body proportions' and general physical appearance.
2. *In his Internal Organs:* It involves changes in the functioning of glands, nervous system and other body systems — circulatory, respiratory, digestive, muscular, lymphatic and reproductive.

The process of physical growth and development plays a significant role in the proper adjustment and progress of an organism. In the beginning the infant is quite helpless. He depends upon his parents and other members of the family for the satisfaction of his bodily needs. As a result of the changes brought by physical growth and development, his body organs become adaptable to his increasing body needs and gradually he is developed into a mature responsible adult.

General Pattern: Although there are wide individual differences among the human beings and therefore, it is not possible to describe a perfect general pattern of the growth and development, yet physical growth and development seems to follow, to some extent, a general pattern which can help us to think about some definite structural changes in the case of normal children at each stage of their growth and development.

Below we try to summarise this general pattern of growth and development along with definite structural changes.

1. *Increase in Height and Weight:* On the average, at birth a baby is about 19 or 20 inches in height and between 7 and 8 pounds in weight, boys being slightly taller and heavier. During the first two years, there is rapid increase in both height and weight. There is a steady and slower growth from the third year till the onset of puberty. By five years the height of the child, approximately, becomes almost doubled and he acquires almost five times his birth weight. During the period of adolescence we again find a sudden increase in both height and weight. Girls reach puberty about a year or two earlier than boys do. Therefore, between the age 12 to 14 they are found slightly taller and heavier than boys.

But they are again surpassed by the boys. By me end of adolescence, the young men are generally higher and heavier than the young women. Generally both men and women get their maximum height and weight upto the end of adolescence. But there are variations in weight as it is more susceptible to environmental influences. Therefore, it is no surprise to note the sudden increase or decrease in weight in later years after attaining maturity.

Weight of the brain increases rapidly in the early years of life. By the time the child completes the age of four his brain gains almost 80 per cent of its final weight, another 10 per cent being added by the time he completes his eight years. By the 20th year, the brain gains almost all its weight.

Increase in Height and Weight with Age

Age	*Height (in cms)*		*Average Weight (in kg)*	
	Girls	*Boys*	*Girls*	*Boys*
Below 3 months	55.0	56.2	4.2	4.5
03 months	60.9	62.7	5.6	6.7
06 months	64.4	64.9	6.2	6.9
09 months	66.7	69.5	6.6	7.4
01 year	72.5	73.9	7.8	8.4
02 years	80.1	81.6	9.6	10.1
03 years	87.2	88.8	11.2	11.8
04 years	94.5	96.0	12.9	13.5
05 years	101.4	102.1	14.5	14.8
06 years	107.4	108.5	16.0	16.3
07 years	112.8	113.9	17.6	18.0
08 years	118.2	119.8	19.4	19.7
09 years	122.9	123.7	21.3	21.5
10 years	128.4	124.4	23.6	23.5
11 years	133.6	133.4	26.4	25.9
12 years	139.6	138.3	29.8	28.5

13 years	143.9	144.6	33.3	32.1
14 years	147.5	150.1	36.8	35.7
15 years	149.6	155.5	38.8	39.6
16 years	151.0	159.5	41.4	43.2
17 years	151.5	161.4	42.4	45.7
18 years	151.7	163.1	42.4	47.4
19 years	151.7	163.4	42.4	48.1

Source: Growth and Development of Indian Infants and Children, Technical Report Series No. 18, Indian Council of Medical Research, 1972.

2. *Changes in Body Proportions:* The child does not only grow in size but also shows a marked change in the proportion of the different parts of the body.

   For example, the head constitutes about one-fourth the height of the body at birth, its size is relatively much larger than the arms and legs. As the child grows older, the proportion of the head decreases and by the end of adolescence it becomes one size.

11 years	133.6	133.4	26.4	25.9
12 years	139.6	138.3	29.8	28.5
13 years	143.9	144.6	33.3	32.1
14 years	147.5	150.1	36.8	35.7
15 years	149.6	155.5	38.8	39.6
16 years	151.0	159.5	41.4	43.2
17 years	151.5	161.4	42.4	45.7
18 years	151.7	163.1	42.4	47.4
19 years	151.7	163.4	42.4	48.1

Source – Growth and Development of Indian Infants and Children, Technical Report Series No. 18, Indian Council of Medical Research, 1972.

3. *Anatomical Growth and Development:* The bones of a child are not smaller in size than the bones of an adult, but they differ

also in composition. The child's bones contain, relatively, a great amount of water and smaller quantity of mineral matter than do those of the adult. They are more soft and more blood flows through them than through the bones of an adult. This accounts for their greater reliability. But it also increases the chances of bones deformities and infection.

As regards the eruption of teeth, it has been found that most of the children acquire their milk teeth by the time they are two years of age. Near the end of the fifth year, the permanent teeth begin to appear the growth of which acquires a long time. The last four of the permanent teeth, the wisdom teeth, erupt between the age of seventeen and twenty five years, if they appear at all. Girls usually show more advanced teeth growth than the boys except in the case of wisdom teeth, where boys are usually ahead of the girls.

4. *Growth and Development of Internal Organs:* From birth onward, the internal organs of the child's body undergo constant development. As a result the child's body systems show desirable change in order to satisfy the growing needs. Below we consider the growth and development of these internal organs.

   (i) *Nervous System:* It show a rapid growth during the prenatal period and the first four years after birth. Before birth the development consists primarily of increase in the number and size of nerve cells. Because no new cells are formed after birth, therefore the development in the first four years consists of the development of immature cells present at birth. After the age of 4 years the growth of the nervous system proceeds at a relatively slow rate.

   (ii) *Muscular System:* Muscular system also shows a remarkable development, although no new muscle fibres develop after birth. The muscles of the child are more delicate and less firmly attached to the bones than are adult muscles. But gradually the muscles get themselves changed in shape, size and composition and become firmer and stronger.

(iii) *Circulatory and Respiratory Systems:* Lungs as well as heart are very small in early childhood but gradually they grow in volume as well as in weight and reach to the maximum upto the end of adolescence. They also show desirable improvement in their functioning. The veins and arteries do not follow the same growth pattern as that of the heart and lungs. Prior to adolescence, they grow rapidly, whereas they show little growth during adolescence.

(iv) *Digestive System:* The young child has a small tubular shaped stomach in comparison with the bag like shape stomach of the adults which not only holds a large amount of food but which also empties more slowly. Therefore they require more feeding in the earlier years of their life than they will need later. In addition to the greater quantity of food, they need food with essential energy value for their rapid growth and development.

(v) *Lymphatic System:* It is involved in the elimination of waste and the destruction of bacteria in the body. From birth onward this system shows the sign of rapid development until it reaches to its maximum between the age of 11 and 12 years, when the death rate is about the lowest. After 12 years it decreases rapidly.

(vi) *Reproductive System:* The development of sex organs shows a peculiar trend in contrast with the overall growth and developmental pattern. Their rate of development is very slow during early childhood but picks up its speed as the child advances towards adolescence and becomes almost developed upto the end of adolescence.

The minute observation of the above mentioned pattern can reveal the following important facts regarding the general trend of physical growth and development:

1. It is very rapid from birth to the age of two or three years.
2. Then, it continues at a diminished rate till the beginning of adolescence.
3. The first three years of adolescence are marked as the years of rapid growth and development.

4. This is followed by a period of slow growth and development to the time of maturity.

Affecting Factors: The physical growth and development of an individual is conditioned by both heredity and environment. Some of the important hereditary and environmental factors which influence the process of physical growth and development are:

1. The traits and characteristics inherited at the time of conception.
2. Single birth or multiple births.
3. The physical as well as mental health of the mother during pregnancy.
4. Nutrition received by the embryo within the womb of the mother.
5. Normal or abnormal delivery.
6. Conditions and care at the time of delivery.
7. Care of the baby and its mother.
8. Nutrition received by the child after birth.
9. Presence or absence of physical defects.
10. The living conditions – physical, social and cultural.
11. The opportunities of recreation, self expression, play and exercise.
12. Presence or absence of illness and diseases.
13. Emotional and social adjustment of the child.
14. Adequate or inadequate rest and sleep.
15. Proper or improper medical care.

Importance of Physical Growth and Development and its Educational Significance.

All the aspects of the growth and development – physical, intellectual, emotional, social, moral, etc. are closely interlinked. The growth and development of any one of these aspects affects the growth and development of the other. Physical growth and development is not an exception. Certainly, it influences the development in other directions. For example, growth and development of the nervous system influences the growth and development of intellectual powers. Emotional and social adjustment is also linked with physical growth and development.

While the children having normal physical growth and development are accepted by their age group, the physical deviates — who are very small, very large, too fat or too thin, etc., remain isolated. They are often nicknamed, ridiculed and denied participation in the play and recreational activities enjoyed by their age associates. It brings serious maladjustment and personality problems. The young child is intelligent enough to become aware of the fact that he differs in appearance and physical abilities from other children. His attitude towards self is injured and self confidence is shaken. In this case either he becomes shy and timid or becomes aggressive in order to compensate for his inferiority feelings.

Moreover upon the balanced growth and development of the internal as well as external organs depends the balanced functioning of the body systems. The functioning of the body systems decides the interest, attitude and the total behaviour of an individual. For example glands and their functioning affect his emotional behaviour to a great extent. Similarly his anatomical development, the development of circulatory, respiratory systems, etc., give the person the required abilities for participating in various motor activities.

In this way physical development influences the total make-up of an individual and thus needs a very careful attention. It can help the teachers to achieve one of the most important aims of the educational process — to bring an all round balanced development in the personality of the child. Therefore the knowledge of the process of physical growth and development is very essential for a teacher. Specifically it can serve him in the following ways:

1. He can be aware of the physical deviates, their psychology and problem of adjustment. Consequently he can help them in their social and emotional adjustment as well as in school learning.
2. The children are the back bone of a nation's strength. Their health and proper physical development is an asset to the

progress of the country. Our schools have to play decisive role in the task of physical welfare of children. The teacher with the knowledge of physical growth and developmental process can render valuable help in this-direction.

3. Needs, desires, interests, attitudes and in a way the overall behaviour of an individual is controlled, to a great extent, by his physical growth and development. Therefore at a particular age level what would be the expected behaviour of the child of that age group can be estimated through the physical growth and developmental pattern. For example, with the study of the trend of the physical development in adolescence, one can be aware of their growing physical, emotional and social needs. Accordingly, adolescents can be helped by the teacher in the adjustment to their rapid development and changes.
4. Study of the pattern of physical growth and development helps us in knowing what can be expected normally from the children at a particular age level. In turn it can help us to arrange school programmes like curricular and co-curricular experiences, methods and techniques of teaching, time-table, textbooks, aid material, seating arrangement and learning environment, etc.

In this way we can see that the knowledge of the process of the physical growth and development helps the teacher in the realisation of his objectives. By its knowledge, he does not only become equipped for setting his programmes according to the needed requirements of his students, but can also help them in improving their health and attaining proper physical strength and abilities.

Bibliography

Aggarwal, J.C.: *Development and Planning of Modern Education,* Vikas Publishing House, New Delhi, 1982.

——————: *National Policy on Education,* Arya Book Depot, New Delhi, 1979.

Alva, Myrdal: *The Power of Education,* Lancer Books, New York, 1965.

Andrew W. Halping: *Administrative Theory in Education,* The MacMillan Company, New York, 1967,

Ashok, Kumar: *Women in Contemporary Indian Society,* Anmol Pub., New Delhi, 1993.

Basu, A.: *Education and Political Development in India 1898-1920,* Oxford University Press, Delhi, 1970.

Basu, Aparna: *Growth of Education and School Management in India 1898-1920,* Oxford University Press, Delhi, 1970.

Beteille, Andre: *Position of Women in Indian Society,* Publication Division, Government of India, 1975.

Bhatia, S.C.: *Education and Socio-Cultural Disadvantage,* Xerxes Publications, Delhi, 1982.

——————: *Education: Theory and Practice Disadvantage,* Xerxes Publications, Delhi, 1982.

Bhatnagar, Sudha: *Scheduled Caste Women,* Rawat Pub., Jaipur, 1997.

Boserup, Esther: *Women's Role in Economic Development,* Chicago University Press, Chicago 1970.

Bowman, M.J.: *Education and Economic Development,* Frank Cass, London, 1971.

Carlton, B.: *Foundations of School Management,* Englewood Cliffs, Prentice Hall, New Jersey, 1964.

Carroll, M. H.: *Foundations of Guidance,* Harper and Brothers, New York, 1961.

Cattell, B.B.: *Educational Growth,* Houghton Mifflin Co., Boston, 1971.

Chauhan, S.S.: *Principles and Techniques of Education,* Vikas Publishing House, New Delhi, 1982.

Chourasia, G.: *Challenges and Innovations in Education,* Sterling Publishers, New Delhi, 1977.

Churn, L. Bimla: *Women in Buddhist Literature,* N.E. Bastian, Ceylone, 1927.

Cole, S. Brem: *Education and the Development of Nations,* Holt, Rinehart and Winston, New York, 1966.

Dash, Geetanjali: *Status of Women Workers in Industrial Area in India,* Delhi University, Delhi, 1988.

De'Souza Alfred: *Women in Contemporary India and South Asia,* Manohar Pub., Delhi, 1980.

Desai, A.R.: *Social Change and Educational Policy,* NCERT, New Delhi, 2000.

Devaki, Jain: *Indian Women,* Publication Division, Govt. of India, 1975.

Devasia, L. and Devasia, V.V: *Empowering Women for Sustainable Development,* Ashish Publising House, New Delhi, 1994.

Don, Adams: *Education and Modernisation in Asia,* Addison Wesley Publishing Company, London, 1970.

Dube, S.C.: *Educational Planning in India,* Allied Publishers, Bombay, 1965.

————————: *Some Perspectives on Non-Formal Education,* Allied Publishers, New Delhi, 1977.

Eckerson, L.O.: *Guidance Services in Elementary Schools,* Government Printing Press, Washington, 1966.

Ehsanul, H.: *Education and Political Culture in India,* Sterling Publishers, New Delhi, 1981.

Frank, W.: *Education – Principles and Services,* Charles E. Merrill Books, New York, 1961.

Freire, Paulo: *Education: The Practice of Freedom,* Writers and Readers Publishing Co-operative, London, 1976.

Geeta, Chaturvedi: *Women Administration in India: A Study of the Socio-economic Background,* RBSA Publication, Jaipur, 1985.

Ghosh, S.C.: *Educational Strategies in Developing Countries,* Sterling Publishers, New Delhi, 1976.

Goel, S.C.: *Education and Economic Growth in India,* The MacMillan Company of India Ltd., Delhi, 1975.

————————: *Education in India,* The MacMillan Company of India Ltd., Delhi, 1975.

Gore, M.S.: *Papers in the Sociology of Education in India,* NCERT, New Delhi, 1967.

Gunam, S.: *Education and Social Change: A Study of Some Rural Communities in India,* The Minarva Associates, Calcutta, 1972.

Harshad, Trivedi, R: *Scheduled Caste Women Studies in Exploitation, with Reference to Superstition, Ignorance and Poverty,* Concept Pub. Co., Delhi, 1976.

Hate, C.A.: *Changing Status of Women in Post-Independence India,* Allied Publications, Bombay, 1969.

Henry, W.: *Practice of Education,* McGraw Hill, New York, 1964.

Indra Prof.: *The Status of Women in Ancient India,* The Minerva Book Shop, Lahore, 1940.

Indu, Prakash S.: *Women, Law and Social Change in India,* Radiant Pub., New Delhi, 1989.

Iqbal, Narain and K.C. Pande: *Panchayati Raj and Educational Administration,* Aalakli Publishers, Jaipur, 1976.

Jagannath, Mohanty: *Education for All,* Deep and Deep Pub., New Delhi, 1994.

Joanna, Bunker R.: *Women: Psychology's Puzzle,* Basic Books, New York, 1979.

Jogdand, P.G.: *Dalit Women, Issues and Perspectives,* Gyan Publishing House, New Delhi, 1995.

Joshi, R.N.: *Education – Elsewhere and Here,* Bharatiya Vidya Bhavan, Bombay, 1979.

Kalarani: *Role Coriflict in Working Women,* Chitra Pub., New Delhi, 1976.

Kamat, A.R.: *The Educational Situation and other Essays on Education,* People's Publishing House, New Delhi, 1973.

Kamladevi, Chattapadhya: *The Awakening of Indian Women,* Everyman's Press, Madras, 1939.

Kapur, Promila: *The Changing Status of the Working Women in India,* Ajanta Publication, Delhi, 1985.

Kidwai, Shaikh M.H.: *Women under Different Social and Religious Law,* Seema Pub., New Delhi, 1976.

Kiran, Devendra: *Status and Position of Women in India,* Vikas Publishing House, 1985.

Kochhar, S.K.: *Pivotal Issues in Indian Education,* Sterling, New Delhi, 1981.

Kripal, Prem: *A Decade of Education in India,* Indian Book Company, Delhi, 1968.

Lawton, Denis: *Education and School Management,* Sage Publications, London, 1977.

——————: *Education and Social Justice,* Sage Publications, London, 1977.

Lederer, Wolfgang: *The Fear of Women,* Arun and Strattan, New York, 1968.

Mahan, Rajan and Jain, Pratibha: *Women Images,* Rawat Pub., Jaipur, 1996.

Malassis, L.: *The Rural World: Education and Development,* Croom Helm, London, 1976.

Mathur, R.N.: *Quality of Working Life of Women Construction Workers,* Commonwealth Publishers, New Delhi, 1987.

Mies, M.: *Indian Women and Patriarchy: Conflicts and Dilemmas of Students and Working Women,* Concept Publishers, New Delhi, 1980.

Minault, Gail: *Secluded Scholars, Women's Education and Muslim Social Reform in Cobaial India*, Oxford University Press, Delhi, 1998.

Misra, R.S.: *Women Education and the Upanishadic System of Education*, Chugh Publication, Allahabad, 1993.

Moni, Mohan Bose : *Female Education in India*, B. B. Gupta Publication, Kanpur, 1921.

Mukherji, S.N.: *Administration of Education in India*, Acharya Book Depot, Baroda, 1962.

Myrdal, Gunnar: *School Management in India*, Abridged, Allen Lane, London, 1972.

Nair, Gopinathan: *Education: Population Growth and Socio-Economic Change*, Allied Publishers, New Delhi, 1981.

Narain, Iqbal and Mohan Lal Sarma: *Panchayati Raj and Educational Administration*, Aalakli Publishers, Jaipur, 1976.

Narayan, G. Brij Raj Chauhan and T.R. Singh: *Scheduled Castes and Education*, Anu Publications, Meerat, 1975.

Neera, Desai and Patel Vibbuti: *Indian Women*, Popular Prakashan, Bombay, 1975.

Neera, Desai: *Women and Society in India*, Ajanta Publication, Delhi, 1987.

Niblett, W.R.: *Essential Education*, University of London, London, 1955.

Nural, Hasan S.: *Challenges in Education: Culture and Social Welfare*, Allied Publishers, Bombay, 1977.

Oldhan, J.N.: *Village Education in India*, Oxford University Press, London, 2000.

Padmint, Sengupta: *The Story of Women of India*, Indian Book Co., New Delhi, 1974.

Pal, B.K.: *Problems and Concerns of Indian Women*, ABC Pub., House, New Delhi, 1989.

Pamela, Roby: *Women in the Work Place*, MA. Schenkrnan, Cambridge, 1981.

Pande, K.C.: *Panchayati Raj and Educational Administration*, Aalakli Publishers, Jaipur, 1976.

Prem Kripal: *A Decade of Education in India,* Indian Book Company, Delhi, 1968.

Premi, M.K.: *Educational Planning in India,* Sterling Publishers, New Delhi, 1972.

Pritam, Das: *Problems of Rural Women,* Ace Publishing House, Goa, 2001.

Raghunath, Safaya: *Innovations and Latest Trends in Education,* The Associated Publishers, Ambala Cantt., 1976.

————————: *Latest Trends in Education,* The Associated Publishers, Ambala Cantt., 1976.

Rajagopal, M.V.: *Kothari Commission on School Education,* Telugu Vidyardhi Prachuranalu, Machilipatnam, 1967.

Ram, Mohan Das: *Women in Manu's Philosophy,* ASB Pub., Jalandhar, 1993.

Ram, Sharma: *Women's Education in Ancient and Muslim Period,* Discovery Publishing House, New Delhi, 1996.

Rama, Mehta: *Socio Legal Status of Women in India,* Metropolitan Book Co., Delhi, 1982.

Raman, Lal Mehta: *Legal Rights of Women under Different Communal Laws in Vogue in India,* The Advocate of Indian Press, Bombay, 1933.

Rao, M.S.: *Sociology of Education in India,* NCERT, New Delhi, 1977.

Rao, V.K.R.V.: *Education and Human Resource Development,* Allied Publishers, Bombay, 1966.

Rehana, Ghadially: *Women in Indian Society,* Sage Pub., New Delhi, 1988.

Robert, H.: *Educational Policy and Practice,* Harper and Row, New York, 1962.

Roeber, E. C. and Smith, G. E.: *Organisation and Administration of Guidance Services,* McGraw Hill, New York, 1955.

Rudolph and Rudolph: *Administration and Management in Schools,* Harvard University Press, Cambridge, 1972.

Russell, Bertrand: *Education and the Social Order,* Unwin, London, 1977.

Saini, S.K.: *Development of Education in India: Socio-Economic and Political Perspective,* Cosmo Publications, New Delhi, 1980.

Saxena, Sateswari: *Education Planning in India: A Study in Approach and Methodology,* Sterling Publishers, New Delhi, 1974.

Shah, A.B. and Sundaram P.S.: *Education or Catastrophe?* Vikas Publishing House, New Delhi, 1976.

Shakambari, J.: *The Status of Women in Epics,* Motilal Banarsidas, Delhi, 1966.

Sharma, G.S.: *Educational and Cultural Development of the Minorities,* ICSSR, New Delhi, 1973.

————————: *Educational and Cultural Development of the Minorities – A Study in Social Effects of the Judicial Trends in India,* ICSSR, New Delhi, 1973.

Shri, Prakash: *Educational System of India: An Econometric Study,* Concept Publishing Company, Delhi, 1977.

Shrimali, K.L.: *A Search for Values in Indian Education,* Vikas Publishers, Delhi, 1974.

Shukla, P.D.: *Towards the New Pattern of Education in India,* Sterling Publishers, New Delhi,1976.

Singhal, R.P. and Biswas Dutt Sunnittee: *The New Educational Pattern in India,* Vikas Publishing House, Delhi, 1916.

Singla, M.M.: *Management of School,* The World Press, Calcutta, 1975.

Sinha, Dharni P.: *Descriptive-cum-Critical Study of Education System in Andhra Pradesh,* Administrative Staff College of India, Hyderabad, 1976.

Siqueira, T.N.: *The Education of India: History and Problems,* Oxford University Press, London, 1952.

Suguna, B.: *Working Women and Religion,* Discovery Publishing House, New Delhi, 1994.

Swamy, Lakshmana: *Education in India,* Asia Publishing House, Bombay, 1960.

Tandon, R.K.: *Women, Nature, Education, Teaching and Rights,* Commonwealth Pub., 1996.

Thomas, F.: *School Management and Administration*, MacMillan Co., New York, 1953.

Tiwari, D.D.: *Education at the Cross Roads*, Chugh Publications, Allahabad, 1975.

——————: *Thoughts on Education*, Chugh Publications, Allahabad, 1972.

Ulrich, B.: *Development and Planning of Modern Education*, Vikas Publishing House, New Delhi, 1982.

Uma, Joshi: *Improving the Status of Rural Women*, Sage Publications, New Delhi, 1989.

Upadhya, Bhagvrat Saran: *Women in Rigveda*, S. Chand and Co., Delhi, 1983.

Urmila Patel: *Problems of Working Women in India*, Commonwealth Publishers, New Delhi, 1987.

Uttam, Kumar S. and Nayak, A.R.: *Women Education*, Commonwealth Pub., New Delhi, 1996.

Vashishta, B.K.: *Encyclopardia of Women in India*, Parveen Encyclopaedia, New Delhi, 1976.

Veena, Das: *Indian Women: Work, Power and Status*, Sage Publication, New Delhi, 1990.

Vernon, P.E.: *School Administration in India*, Methuen, London, 1969.

Zaheer, S.M.: *Rural India: The Women Force*, Swan Publications, Kochi, 2001.

Zurich, D.: *Development of Education*, Allied Publishers, Bombay, 1978.

Index

P

R

S

T

U

W

❑❑❑